Navigating Artificial Intelligence for Cultural Heritage Organisations

Navigating Artificial Intelligence for Cultural Heritage Organisations

Edited by
Lise Jaillant, Claire Warwick, Paul Gooding,
Katherine Aske, Glen Layne-Worthey
and J. Stephen Downie

UCLPRESS

First published in 2025 by
UCL Press
University College London
Gower Street
London WC1E 6BT

Available to download free: www.uclpress.co.uk

A CIP catalogue record for this book is available from The British Library.

ISBN: 978-1-80008-835-1 (Hbk)
ISBN: 978-1-80008-836-8 (Pbk)
ISBN: 978-1-80008-837-5 (PDF)
ISBN: 978-1-80008-838-2 (epub)
DOI: https://doi.org/10.14324/111.9781800088375

Contents

List of figures

List of tables

List of abbreviations

AI	Artificial intelligence
CNN	Convolutional neural network
HTR	Handwritten text recognition
HTRC	HathiTrust Research Center
IIIF	International Image Interoperability Framework
ML	Machine learning
NLS	National Library of Scotland
OCR	Optical character recognition
TNA	The National Archives (UK)

List of contributors

Taylor Arnold is Professor of Data Science and Statistics and affiliated faculty in linguistics and cognitive science at the University of Richmond (USA). He is also the co-director of the Distant Viewing Lab. His research in corpus-based techniques for the study of visual and multimodal communication has appeared in dozens of research articles and has received funding from the National Endowment for the Humanities, the Mellon Foundation, American Council of Learned Societies, and the Réseau français des instituts d'études avancées.

Katherine Aske is Lecturer in English at Edinburgh Napier University. A scholar of eighteenth-century literature and cultural history, her research focuses on female beauty, skincare and proto-dermatology in the period. She has been part of several projects on AI use within cultural heritage and the broader digital humanities, and published several articles with *Archival Science*, *Journal of Computing and Cultural Heritage*, and *Digital Humanities Quarterly*. She continues to explore the potentials of AI in her humanities research.

Annalina Caputo is Assistant Professor in the School of Computing at Dublin City University. She is a funded investigator in the ADAPT 2 and I-Form centres, where she conducts research on artificial intelligence and personalisation applied to information access and recommender systems. Her research includes machine learning and artificial intelligence, natural language processing, and information access and retrieval. She was general co-chair for ECIR 2023 and the Irish principal investigator for the UK/Irish network AURA (www.aura-network.net).

Catherine Nicole Coleman is Digital Research Architect for the Stanford University Libraries and Research Director for Humanities + Design, a research lab at the Center for Spatial and Textual Analysis, and a lecturer at Stanford. Her work in system design is strategic and applied, with the goal of putting technology to use for people, to aid and inspire knowledge creation.

Javier de la Rosa is a senior research scientist at the Artificial Intelligence Lab at the National Library of Norway. A former Postdoctoral Fellow at UNED Digital Humanities Innovation Lab, he holds a PhD in Hispanic studies with a specialisation in digital humanities from the University of Western Ontario, and a Masters in artificial intelligence by the University of Seville. Javier has previously worked as a research engineer at the Stanford University Center for Interdisciplinary Digital Research, and as the Technical Lead at the University of Western Ontario CulturePlex Lab for Cultural Complexity. He is interested in natural language processing applied to historical and literary text, with a special focus on large language models.

J. Stephen Downie is Professor and Associate Dean for Research at the School of Information Sciences, University of Western Ontario. He is also the Illinois Co-Director of the HathiTrust Research Center. Professor Downie conducts work in digital libraries, digital humanities and music information retrieval. He holds degrees from the University of Western Ontario, including BA (music theory and composition), Masters of Library and Information Science (MLIS) and a PhD in library and information science.

Ryan Dubnicek is a digital humanities specialist with the HathiTrust Research Center, based out of the University of Illinois School of Information Sciences, where he conducts and supports research in cultural analytics and aids outreach and education efforts of HTRC. Ryan has degrees in English literature and library and information science from University of Illinois.

Paul Gooding is Professor of Library Studies and Digital Scholarship at the University of Glasgow. His research focuses on the relationship between digital library collections, communities of usage and practice, and legal/institutional frameworks for collection development. In recent years, he has published on topics including the impact of handwritten text recognition, and responsible AI principles as applied within libraries. His most recent project (iREAL: Inclusive Requirements Elicitation for AI in Libraries) sought to develop a model for responsible AI systems development in libraries that aim to utilise knowledge from Indigenous communities.

Christopher E. Haley is Director of Research for the Study of the Legacy of Slavery at the Maryland State Archives and Director of the Utopia Film Festival. He serves and/or has served on the following boards: Annapolis Film Festival, Annapolis Pride, Maryland Lynching Commission for Truth and Reconciliation, Kunta Kinte–Alex Haley Foundation, Historic London Town Foundation, Jake Savage Foundation and the Annapolis Arts Alliance Foundation. The Legacy of Slavery Study Haley oversees has conducted research that has produced a web-accessible database containing over 400,000 pieces of information to help recognise and identify thousands of heretofore unknown African American citizens of Maryland.

Lise Jaillant is Professor of digital cultural heritage at Loughborough University. She has a background in publishing history and digital humanities. In recent years, her research has focused on born-digital archives and the issues of preservation and access to these archives. Since 2020, she has been UK Principal Investigator for four AHRC-funded projects on archives and artificial intelligence. These international projects aim to make digitised and born-digital archives more accessible to researchers, and to use innovative research methods such as AI to analyse archival data. Her publications in these topics include the edited collection *Archives, Access and AI* and many articles (see www.lisejaillant.com).

Rajesh Kumar Gnanasekaran is Assistant Director of AI Solutions at the Division of IT, a research fellow at the Advanced Information Collaboratory and a PhD candidate at the University of Maryland iSchool. Rajesh's research interests are to work with culturally rich dataset collections, digitally archived or born digital. Rajesh's focus is to explore, analyse and apply computational treatments on these dataset collections using advanced data-science-based approaches such as machine learning, artificial intelligence, natural language processing and graph database networks to visualise the raw data that unravel narratives of the several entities involved, especially those that are not represented well in the literature. To achieve this, Rajesh collaborates with experts from interdisciplinary backgrounds to incorporate their feedback.

Glen Layne-Worthey is Associate Director for Research Support Services in the HathiTrust Research Center, based in the University of Illinois at Urbana-Champaign School of Information Sciences, and was the US Principal Investigator of the AEOLIAN project on which this volume is based. Formerly, he was Digital Humanities Librarian at Stanford, and was founding head of Stanford's Center for Interdisciplinary Digital Research. He's held many roles in the international digital humanities community, recently serving as Chair of the Alliance of Digital Humanities Organizations Executive Board. His graduate work was in Russian children's literature at the University of California, Berkeley.

Richard Marciano is the founding director of the Advanced Information Collaboratory (AIC) and a professor at the University of Maryland iSchool. The AIC focuses on exploring the opportunities and challenges of 'disruptive technologies' for archives and records management (digital curation, machine learning, AI, etc.), and leveraging the latest technologies to unlock the hidden information in massive stores of records. The AIC explores advances in computational archival science through the mapping of computational thinking to archival science using AI, machine learning and digital curation.

Jill Naiman is a teaching assistant professor in the School of Information Sciences and a faculty affiliate at the National Center for Supercomputing Applications (University of Illinois Urbana-Champaign). After receiving her PhD in astronomy and astrophysics from the University of California, Santa Cruz, she was a National Science Foundation and Institute of Theory and Computation Postdoctoral Fellow at the Harvard-Smithsonian Center for Astrophysics, where her work focused on computational hydrodynamics and data visualisation. Her current work includes automated methods for the digitisation of historical scientific documents and the development of metrics for assessing the accuracy of machine learning digitisation methods on downstream scientific tasks.

Joe Nockels is Research Associate for the University of Sheffield's Digital Humanities Institute (DHI), in the School of History, Philosophy and Digital Humanities. He is responsible for developing and supporting the DHI's strategic research theme, Digital Representation of Cultural Artefacts, which sets out to advance the state of the art in the digital capture, interpretation and representation of physical culture. Joe completed a PhD from the University of Edinburgh assessing the impact of automated text recognition on libraries, and holds an MA from Leiden University in archival studies.

Julia Noordegraaf is Professor of Digital Heritage in the Faculty of Humanities, University of Amsterdam. She leads the research program and lab CREATE that studies the history of urban creativity using digital data and methods. Noordegraaf's research focuses on the reuse of digital cultural heritage for media historical research. She acts as Board Member in CLARIAH, the national infrastructure for digital humanities research. In the context of the European Time Machine project Noordegraaf coordinates the realisation of the Amsterdam Time Machine: a 'Digital Twin' for location-based, personalised access to historical information on the city.

Peter Organisciak is Associate Professor of Library and Information Science at the University of Denver. His work focuses on text mining methods and applications in large-scale digital libraries, as well as artificial intelligence applications in educational measurement. His recent projects have included the IES-funded Measure of Original Thinking in Elementary Students (MOTES) project, which developed new tests of creativity for children, and the IMLS-funded Similarities and Duplicates in Digital Libraries (SaDDL) project, which improved the scholarly value of scanned books in the HathiTrust Digital Library through complex relationship identification.

Thomas Padilla is the founder of Bristlecone Strategy, a consultancy that works with organisations at the intersection of community and technology to realise a more just society. Thomas has held a range of technology-focused roles at the Internet Archive, OCLC Research and the Library of Congress. Thomas is an internationally recognised expert in computational use of collections as data, responsible AI, digital strategy and data curation. Thomas is Advisory Board Member, Roy Rosenzweig Center for History and New Media; Board Member, Recovering the US Hispanic Literary Heritage Program; and National Advisory Board Member, Opioid Industry Documents Archive.

Nikolaus Parulian is a researcher at the HathiTrust Research Center (HTRC) and holds a PhD in information sciences from the School of Information Sciences at the University of Illinois, Urbana-Champaign. During his PhD, he contributed to various information sciences research, including digital libraries, data curation and natural language processing. At HTRC, Nikolaus has published multiple works applying machine learning to the HathiTrust collections. His contributions include developing models for front matter detection and analysis, network analysis of text to explore character relationships in fiction, genre classification and leveraging language models for entity extraction contributing to the digital library and digital humanities fields.

Anna Schjøtt is a technological anthropologist and PhD candidate in the Media Studies Department at the University of Amsterdam. In her PhD research, she ethnographically explores different epistemic spaces across the media sector where AI systems are discussed, presented, developed and evaluated to critically examine the politics of AI design processes and their implications. Anna is affiliated with the Critical Data and AI research group at the Media Studies Department, the Cultural AI Lab, and the AI Media and Democracy Lab. The project is funded by the AI4Media project and the Amsterdam Institute for Humanities Research.

Benjamin Schmidt is Vice President of Information Design at Nomic.ai, where he works on new interfaces for interpreting and visualising embedding models. For several years before that, he was a professor in the history departments at Northeastern University and NYU, where he worked with and led digital humanities groups deploying new approaches to thinking about the past through data analysis and data visualisation. He has also written publicly about higher education (teaching evaluations and humanities policy), narrative anachronism and plot structure, and political history.

Janet Swatscheno is the Digital Scholarship Librarian at HathiTrust and Associate Director for Outreach and Education at the HathiTrust Research Center. In this role she engages with scholars, faculty and students on scholarly computational analysis of the HathiTrust collection. Prior to joining HathiTrust, Janet was the Digital Publishing Librarian at the University of Illinois Chicago and Co-Director of the UIC Digital Humanities Initiative. She is actively involved in the digital scholarship community, recently serving as President of the Library Publishing Coalition Board.

Melissa Terras is Professor of Digital Cultural Heritage at Edinburgh College of Art, University of Edinburgh, UK, and a leading researcher in digital humanities. She is Director of Creative Informatics at the Edinburgh-based AHRC Creative Cluster (2018–2024) supporting innovation in creative and cultural contexts, and a founding director of Transkribus, the AI-powered platform for text recognition of historical documents.

Lauren Tilton is the E. Claiborne Robins Professor of Liberal Arts and Professor of Digital Humanities in the Department of Rhetoric and Communications at the University of Richmond (USA). She is also the co-director of the Distant Viewing Lab and the director of the Center for the Liberal Arts and Artificial Intelligence. Tilton is the author of several texts, including *Distant Viewing* (MIT Press, 2023) and *Layered Lives* (Stanford University Press, 2022).

Ted Underwood teaches in the School of Information Sciences and in the English Department at the University of Illinois, Urbana-Champaign. Trained as a romanticist, his current research is as much about information science as literary criticism. He is especially interested in applying machine learning to large digital collections. Because 'large digital collections' don't quite exist yet in the form we would need for interesting literary research, a lot of his work involves correcting and enriching them. He recently published a book about the new perspectives opened by large digital libraries called *Distant Horizons: Digital Evidence and Literary Change* (University of Chicago Press, Spring 2019).

Claire Warwick is Professor of Digital Humanities in the Department of English at Durham University. Her research is concerned with the way that digital resources, including artificial intelligence techniques, are used in the humanities and cultural heritage, and in reading behaviour in physical and digital spaces. Her monograph on the history of cyberspace – *Digital Humanities and the Cyberspace Decade: A World Elsewhere* – was published in 2024.

Introduction

Lise Jaillant, Claire Warwick, Paul Gooding, Katherine Aske, Glen Layne-Worthey and J. Stephen Downie

This edited collection explores some of the innovative technologies and approaches to digitised and born-digital records within libraries and archives across the United States, United Kingdom and Europe. Thanks to mass digitisation initiatives across the cultural sector, the number of digitised records continues to grow. The increase of born-digital records is also exponential. The issues of digital preservation and of access to these digital records have been central since the 2000s. Simultaneous with this tremendous growth in volume of cultural information, there have been numerous developments in automated processing and artificial intelligence (AI) tools over the past two decades, which continue to adapt to an ever-increasing need to preserve the digital records of our recent histories. To make this possible, archival practice is increasingly turning to the use of automated technologies.

AI is playing a crucial role in many kinds of data management systems within the cultural heritage sector, and information professionals are relying on the creators of digital tools to help them make appraisals and manage workloads in the processing of their collections. Beyond mere data management, though, sector professionals and scholars are also seeking to benefit from the many new affordances and innovative research tools offered by large-scale digital collections. Such collections inspire new questions and areas for research – such as using these collections as data.

However, many born-digital collections are currently inaccessible to users for several reasons, ranging from copyright restrictions and data protections to more practical issues such as staff workload, time, expertise and financial cost. But providing users with access to cultural heritage records is crucial. As highlighted by Jason R. Baron's work on the US Presidential records, the sheer quantity and potentially sensitive nature of many born-digital materials cannot possibly be addressed by manual appraisal processes (Baron et al 2022). This presents a significant problem in terms of public records being openly accessible. Similar issues are being seen across the UK, Europe and elsewhere, and the balance of public interest and individual rights is becoming increasingly critical, as records of our current history exist mostly in born-digital formats.

Questions of how AI and machine learning (ML) should be applied to data in libraries and other cultural institutions are currently preoccupying heritage professionals, computer scientists and digital humanities scholars alike. The debates that sit at the nexus of these fields have been the impetus behind the international network established by the AEOLIAN (**A**rtificial Int**e**lligence f**o**r Cu**l**tural Her**i**tage Organis**a**tio**n**s) project[1] jointly funded by the Arts and Humanities Research Council (AHRC)[2] in the UK and the National Endowment for the Humanities (NEH)[3] in the United States. AEOLIAN's main intention was to facilitate communications among various actors in the development, employment and critique of AI within cultural heritage organisations. This included researchers, computer scientists, digital humanists, data management and information specialists, as well as other professionals across the cultural heritage and archival sector. While the AEOLIAN project began with a focus on UK and US archival institutions, it was soon clear that many of the challenges these institutions faced regarding digital and born-digital records are a concern around the world. In this volume, we have reflected this shared challenge with the inclusion of chapters addressing the National Library of Norway and the Netherlands Institute of Sound and Vision.

Further challenges have manifested in the lack of awareness of technologies and their potential uses within cultural heritage. The chapters included in this volume have therefore been selected to demonstrate the wide range of technological approaches being employed, often in silo, to address the varied and broad span of digital and born-digital records held within cultural organisations. This includes the purposes of and need for AI tools more broadly, as well as specific tools, such as ML, computer vision, handwritten text recognition (HTR) and optical character recognition, as well as more specific projects for certain types of records, including emails, books, visual media and newspapers. However, the collection also considers the impact of these technologies at an institutional level as well as their usability and the challenges inherent in their use for the facilitation of research across the spectrum.

Other significant challenges that the AEOLIAN project has brought to light are not only the accessibility of digital records, but also the accessibility of the tools, skills and technologies required to process these records in the digital age. This volume has been designed to reflect current and state-of-the-art technologies and innovations for the preservation and accessibility of digitised and born-digital records across cultural heritage sectors in the United States, UK, Norway and the Netherlands.[4] Building on key elements identified through the AEOLIAN project's six international workshops and two journal special issues,[5] the authors explore crossovers and collaborative approaches to applying AI tools to digitised and born-digital cultural heritage records. The collection considers a wide range of themes including AI and ML, computer vision, text and data mining, record management, accessibility and sensitivity review, as well as important issues in the sector such as risk, trust and transparency in the uses of AI algorithms and automated systems.

The volume features nine main chapters, grouped together in three thematic parts. Part I looks at current AI technologies for preservation and access within national libraries and cultural heritage institutions. Part II focuses on machine learning, computer vision and other computational methods to aid access and usability. Part III examines digitised collections and the technologies being used to make them more accessible, exploring the current issues, challenges and innovative methodologies.

The volume's overarching focus on the uses of AI in cultural organisations is developed across these chapters, which move from a broader overview of AI tools and their purposes to more specific applications and challenges. The volume closes with a reflection on the state of the art, and a call to pause for reflection and come together to face the future of the digital age.

Part I concerns the role of AI in the preservation and accessibility of digitised and born-digital records – a main aim of the AEOLIAN project and this edited collection.

This part begins with a case-study chapter written by Lise Jaillant, Annalina Caputo and Katherine Aske. This chapter explores the AI technologies being developed and employed within The National Archives UK (TNA), a partner with the AEOLIAN project, and includes interviews with members of staff responsible for the digital archives at TNA. The chapter outlines current approaches from, and issues faced by, TNA and other comparable archives, and makes recommendations of existing technologies for processing digital archives using AI.

TNA's projects have been developed in response to key challenges brought about by born-digital and digitised records. They range from testing existing AI-powered tools to developing new approaches, such as using topic modelling to discover the latent or underlying topics of texts across a corpus. The authors examine a selection of TNA's AI projects and others from across the globe that are addressing similar challenges.

The case study is intended to raise greater awareness of current work on AI applied to archives and to encourage further collaborations with other institutions on both sides of the Atlantic. It brings a critical perspective, from the viewpoint of digital humanities and computer science, to demonstrate the importance of collaborative approaches to making digital records more accessible.

Building on the explorations of AI tools in the TNA, Chapter 2, written by Catherine Nicole Coleman, presents a case study of the employment of innovative computer vision technologies in cultural heritage. This chapter concentrates on discoveries and outcomes of Stanford Global Currents, a project that applied computer vision techniques to mediaeval manuscripts. These are compared to related work with computer vision applied to cultural heritage that has influenced how we think about search and discovery in libraries, archives and museums. Some key terminology is defined and core concepts of computer vision that are essential to understanding the project are explained, but this is not a study of how computer vision works, nor does it address in any detail the methods or techniques applied in the Stanford Global Currents project. Instead, the case study is focused on what can be learned from computational approaches to archival research that rely in some way on computer vision for information retrieval. The reason Stanford Global Currents remains an important case study today is not the technology itself that they use, but rather what emerged from the researcher's and curator's engagement with the technology.

Drawing Part I to a close, Chapter 3, by Javier de la Rosa, moves beyond UK and US archives and libraries to examine current AI initiatives and image classification systems being developed to improve the discoverability and accessibility of collections at The National Library of Norway (Nasjonalbiblioteket). The library, which has recently become a member of the Digital Preservation Coalition, established its own Artificial Intelligence Laboratory in 2018. Ever since, the independent unit has fostered the use of ML solutions in the Norwegian cultural sector, both internally, to assist in their processes, and externally, to contribute to society.

This chapter examines how the Nasjonalbiblioteket (NB) AI-Lab came to be, how it is organised and funded, and what kind of infrastructure allows it to run effectively. It also addresses the different modalities that the Nasjonalbiblioteket has worked with regarding ML models, including the use of computer vision to support new user experiences and to improve the discoverability of its own collection. The chapter details Maken,[6] a similarity search system that benefits from Nasjonalbiblioteket's massive digital library. By running all images and books through semantic embedding models, it provides similarity matches for the final user for each of the records in the catalogue.

Chapter 3 also explores the way in which the NB AI-Lab operationalised the digital catalogue to build the largest Norwegian text corpus to date, which was then used to pretrain and release very performant language models, later adjusted for many different purposes, from sentiment analysis or named entity recognition to bias detection or sentence similarity. Considering the text modality, the chapter describes two approaches for book-length text classification on the work carried out by the Sámi bibliographers and the caveats and lessons learned in the process. Finally, as the NB AI-Lab enters the audio domain, this chapter presents their efforts in collecting a massive speech corpus and the subsequent pretraining of baseline language models for Norwegian speech, later used for the automatic speech recognition and the subtitling of the entire catalogue.

Part II, 'Text and beyond: AI applied to images and audiovisual archives', continues to explore the possibilities of AI technologies, and focuses on the application of AI to images and audiovisual archives. Where Chapters 4 and 5 focus on accessibility in non-textual archives, using computer vision and other computational tools, Chapter 6 explores computational research methods designed specifically for large digital collections at HathiTrust.

In the fourth chapter, Julia Noordegraaf and Anna Schjøtt consider the significance of computational tools for preservation and address the shifting focus towards AI for accessibility in audiovisual archives at the Netherlands Institute of Sound & Vision, which preserves and maintains one of the largest audiovisual archival collections in Europe. They argue that advances in the development of digital technology over the past two decades have significantly impacted the workflow of cultural institutions. Digitisation has greatly expanded the scope of digital information and created the expectation that collections of cultural heritage are generally accessible online. Archives that have the (legal) responsibility to acquire, store, preserve and make accessible the documentary heritage of societies have therefore experimented with new AI technologies to process this vastly expanding body of documentation. One of the consequences of digitisation is that the archival process extends beyond the walls of the archive itself: preserving born-digital information requires the collection of objects and metadata at the moment of production and the involvement of users to meaningfully interpret them. Consequently, the emphasis in the archival workflow has shifted from preservation to access.

This chapter from Noordegraaf and Schjøtt thus critically engages with the growing shift from preservation of heritage to the prioritisation of access, and the role AI plays in that shift. Developments at the Netherlands Institute of Sound & Vision provide an exemplary background that helps to unfold this shift and its implications. Its Media Museum reopened in February 2023 with a brand-new exhibition based on Mark Deuze's notion of 'living in media'. It is one of the first museums in the world to directly incorporate AI into the user experience by utilising facial recognition to personally greet visitors as they walk up to sections of the exhibition and by personalising the experience for each visitor. This provides a unique case to study the adoption and implementation of AI in the workflow of cultural institutions. The chapter asks whether this focus on AI-enabled access induces standardisations of heritage and whether it might potentially contribute to reducing rather than increasing the complexity of the understandings of heritage. To guide this discussion, the authors draw on the work of Johanna Drucker and Melanie Feinberg, who both challenge the notion of data as given, arguing that it should be seen instead as a designed object and where the processes of designing data highly influence the final outcomes. Through this work, the authors highlight how the processes of making the archive accessible via AI contributes to 'formatting' culture in a certain way, which we must consider as AI becomes a more integral part of archival practices.

Chapter 5 continues the discussion regarding accessibility, user experience and the employment of AI in archival institutions in a case study on digital mapping and cultural heritage. Written by two AEOLIAN team members, Co-Investigator Claire Warwick and the project's Research Associate, Katherine Aske, the chapter explores the interdisciplinary research enabled by digital and computer-generated mapping within cultural heritage organisations, and beyond. Examining recent examples from the National Libraries of the UK and Ireland, it focuses on the work of the National Library of Wales through interviews with library staff. The chapter also looks more broadly at the ways a range of archival records could be presented through digital mapping technologies and examines the advances in and potentials of such technologies to make archival collections more accessible to users. Where the authors discuss the impact of state-of-the-art technologies and interactive maps, offering guidance for research methodologies for both researchers and other users, they also address approaches to preservation, digitisation and the creation of linked data and enriched metadata for cultural heritage sites and archives.

The case study has three main focuses. The first is to explore the current national institutions within the UK and Ireland responsible for preserving historical maps as part of cultural heritage. The second is to consider the digitisation process of maps and their born-digital creation, and to examine the information that is made accessible, and the digital tools that are used, within those processes. The third is to consider the potential of digital mapping within cultural heritage institutions, not only as a means of access and preservation, but as a platform for catalogued information and linked data, with potential opportunities for wider collaborations between archival sectors. The study addresses the use of Wikidata, Wikimedia Commons and the International Image Interoperability Framework, as well as current projects using AI tools to create and read digital maps.

The authors also examine the role that information professionals can play in supporting users' understanding of the nature of AI technologies and ensuring that such technologies are suitable for their needs. As a final consideration, the chapter addresses the ethical aspects of the use of AI and the role of information professionals in ensuring that it is used responsibly, both in cultural heritage and more widely in society.

Furthering the discussion of AI to improve access and usability and drawing Part II to a close, Chapter 6 explores the employment of several in-house-developed computational research methods designed specifically for use with large digital library collections (including those with copyright-restricted content). In a collaborative case study centred on the HathiTrust Research Center, a partner of the AEOLIAN project, Glen Layne-Worthey (AEOLIAN US PI), J. Stephen Downie (AEOLIAN US Co-Investigator) and seven of their researcher colleagues discuss the use of a wide variety of AI tools and approaches to improve the access to, discoverability and research uses of these important cultural heritage materials in one of the world's biggest digital libraries.

The HathiTrust Digital Library holds texts in a staggering variety of subjects, including the humanities, arts, natural and social sciences, and government information. Its immense scope (18.2 million volumes and growing) and its broad diversity (of languages, writing systems, topics, genres, legal accessibility, etc.) represent fundamental challenges for traditional research methods, but are ideal for the highly scalable computational research approaches created and enabled by the HathiTrust Research Center (HTRC) and its affiliated researchers. This chapter documents some of the tools and methods that HTRC has created to enable exploration and research in the HathiTrust collection, as well as more experimental approaches that research collaborators outside the HTRC have developed for it.

In all this work there is a particular focus on the special challenges associated with the massive scale, scope, quality and variability of the book-length documents that make up the HathiTrust Digital Library. The authors describe the historical, organisational and legal underpinnings of the HTRC's tools, services and data access regimes, as well as its suite of computational methods (united under the concept of copyright-compliant 'non-consumptive research' for in-copyright works). They also include a series of more focused case studies documenting the variety of AI-enabled research activities undertaken by our research community, including: automatic detection of book front-matter; machine detection of non-textual objects in digitised scientific literature; bit-oriented feature representations; identifying relationships among books using neural network classifiers; large language models to make sense of long-form fiction; and making sense of long runs of serial volumes (typically united under a single catalogue record) as highly complex bibliographic objects.

Part III continues to address specific applications of AI within heritage organisations, and focuses more specifically on digitised historical collections, images and handwritten text, examining challenges and new methods. The final three chapters in this collection are concerned with the development of innovative methodologies to make complex digitised materials, including newspapers and moving-image records, more accessible, particularly for institutions without the budget or staffing level of larger-scale organisations. Chapter 7 explores distant viewing and other approaches to make sense of masses of digital data, while Chapters 8 and 9 work in conjunction to explore significant issues concerning the use of AI for text recognition in archives, and shift the focus to the future of computational research methods and tools for access, discoverability and rediscovery.

Previous chapters have moved from AI-enabled research into predominantly text-based records, and now Chapter 7, by statistician Taylor Arnold and digital humanist Lauren Tilton, looks to more visual cultural heritage materials and the uses of computer vision to make visual objects more accessible through the semi-automated production of metadata. The authors argue that ways of seeing have long shaped how (moving) images are described and catalogued. New practices of looking, specifically computer vision through distant viewing, are facilitating access and discovery of collections through the (semi-)automated production of metadata. This chapter explores how this area of AI is creating metadata for collections of art, photography and television held by national and local archives in the United States, an area of research that is key to both exploration and information retrieval (i.e., searching, recommender systems, etc.). The chapter also addresses challenges associated with computer vision, and potential future directions for development. Finally, the chapter discusses ways in which the legal landscape in the United States, particularly recent copyright decisions, has made the generation of metadata of holdings a crucial activity of research and in support of researchers. This chapter therefore builds on the discussions of current technologies explored in previous chapters to consider the legal landscape regarding copyright, the current challenges in computer vision technology that need to be addressed and the future directions of this technology within an archival context.

Having explored the AI technologies being applied to visual records, Chapter 8, written by Paul Gooding, Joseph Nockels and Melissa Terras, considers the potentials of HTR and the advances in ML tools being developed at the National Library of Scotland (NLS). Stepping back from the technological focus that has driven many of the previous chapters, this chapter explores how the NLS, along with other institutions, are preparing to employ AI and ML to help process large numbers of digitised historical records. The chapter considers the impact of such technologies at an institutional level, as well as looking to the future of computational analysis of collections.

The chapter by Gooding, Nockels and Terras focuses specifically on how institutions are planning for the adoption and integration of AI and ML tools, including the scoping exercises which the NLS is currently undertaking, to understand the impact and potential of HTR across the entire institution. HTR has the potential to affect curatorial practice, digitisation workflows, transcription practices by staff and users, and discoverability at scale of handwritten historical texts. The case study discusses how the NLS is seeking to understand how these potential uses might interact with, and affect, the work of both staff and users. The authors address the issue via two approaches. Firstly, they present the results of qualitative interviews across the institution, which aimed to investigate how NLS staff perceive the potential impact of HTR. Secondly, they present an in-depth analysis from the Digital Scholarship team at the NLS, exploring the potential applications of HTR in supporting computational analysis of its collections. In doing so, the authors aim to provide insights into how institutions understand and normalise new technologies within their existing workflows.

Closing the final part, Chapter 9 continues to address the use of digital technologies to make collections available for computational research. Written by Rajesh Kumar Gnanasekaran, Richard Marciano and Christopher E. Hayley, the chapter looks at the potential of AI and ML for advancing research into slavery and reasserting the legacies lost to it.

Decolonisation and records of slavery in archives are major subjects of concern for many institutions, and this chapter explores a current project using computational research tools to recover memories erased from the archive. With this goal, the chapter explores the use of AI and ML to facilitate the analysis and visualisation of newspaper advertisements from the Maryland State Archives related to the trading of enslaved people. The study focuses on the Domestic Traffic Ads collection of the State of Maryland between 1824 and 1864, which exposes chattel slavery practices where buyers and sellers would interact to exchange and share human beings, often for social and domestic benefit. This case study is part of a larger project to explore computational treatments to remember the legacy of slavery, towards reasserting erased memory. Previous studies have included computational treatments for manumissions, certificates of freedom and runaway slave advertisements. The work has several objectives, including the promotion of technology-based pedagogies in library and information science (part of the so-called TALENT – **T**raining of **A**rchival & **L**ibrary **E**ducators with i**N**novative **T**echnologies – Network), developing new curriculum based on computational Jupyter Notebooks, and addressing the social and ethical concerns that arise from computational and algorithmic thinking.

The chapter also looks at how these technologies can be more broadly employed within archives and libraries through in-service staff training. A lack of skills training at an institutional level is another major issue that has emerged throughout the AEOLIAN project, and this chapter is key to exploring the uses of AI to address these timely and widespread concerns.

Finally, having explored a broad range of AI technologies, their applications and development, their practical uses and the way these tools are enabling not just research but also support in individual institutions, the Afterword, written by Thomas Padilla, offers a summation of this collection, and considers the future of AI for the cultural heritage sector broadly understood. The Afterword reflects on the volume and contributed chapters, placing them within a sense of change, and closing with a call for more critical work to come. Padilla argues that the lure of linear progress is strong, and perhaps few experiences appear more glamorous than individual and collective experiences of technological impact, with AI being a prime example.

Yet, Padilla, like the AEOLIAN team, insists that we must strive for a cyclical rather than linear sense of progress, lest we get lost in the tide of the always already new. Like any good ship, we working in and with the cultural heritage sector have anchors that can hold us steady in the rising technological tide – anchors that should ground us to analogous past experiences while navigating uncertainty in the face of change.

Notes

1. The AEOLIAN Network and its research outputs are hosted on the project website, www.aeolian-network.net/.
2. Arts and Humanities Research Council Award AH/V009443/1.
3. National Endowment for the Humanities Award HC-278124-21. The opinions, findings and recommendations expressed in this book do not necessarily represent those of the National Endowment for the Humanities.
4. We recognise that such issues are not confined to these areas, and that they may pose particular problems in the Global South. The geographical coverage of the book simply reflects the nature of the AEOLIAN network and the location of its participants.
5. *Journal of Computing and Cultural Heritage*, 16(4) (2023); and *Journal of Documentation*, 80(5) (2024).
6. www.nb.no/maken/.

Reference

Baron, J.R., Sayed, M.F. and Oard, D.W. 2022. 'Providing more efficient access to government records: A use case involving application of machine learning to improve FOIA Review for the deliberative process privilege', *Journal on Computing and Cultural Heritage*, 15(1):1–19.

Part I
The role of AI in preserving and making accessible digitised and born-digital records

1
The National Archives (UK)

Lise Jaillant, Katherine Aske and Annalina Caputo

With this chapter on The National Archives UK (TNA), we have two main objectives. First, to raise greater awareness of current work on artificial intelligence (AI) applied to archives and to encourage further collaborations with other institutions on both sides of the Atlantic. TNA's projects have been developed in response to key challenges brought about by born-digital and digitised records. They range from testing existing AI-powered tools to developing new approaches, such as using topic modelling to discover the latent or underlying topics of texts across a corpus. Here we examine a selection of TNA's AI projects and others from across the globe that are addressing similar challenges. Our second objective is to bring a critical perspective, from the viewpoint of digital humanities and computer science. The chapter is written by a team composed of two digital humanists (Lise Jaillant and Katherine Aske) and one computer scientist (Annalina Caputo). Building on this cross-disciplinary expertise, we reviewed TNA's projects and, when appropriate, formed comparisons with projects conducted by other cultural institutions.

Drawing on interviews with TNA staff as well as published materials such as reports, conference presentations and research papers, this chapter is organised into three sections:

- The first section on 'Rethinking the record' examines the transition from print to digital, which has led to an explosion of born-digital and digitised records in central government departments. Established processes to deal with paper records were disrupted, leading to a need for new methods to appraise, select and screen digital records before transfer to TNA. In this section, we focus particularly on AI for digital selection, sensitivity review and discovery of relevant records.

- The second section is on 'Openness, access and use'. We start with the need to strike a balance between risk and access, before turning to the development of tools to make collections more accessible, and finally the need to prevent harmful use of collections through risk management.
- The third section deals with 'Risk, uncertainty and trust'. We look at blockchain to establish the authenticity of records; at the need to balance risk and access; and at explainable AI to build trust.
- The conclusion focuses on ethical uses of AI in the context of large archival collections, at TNA and elsewhere.

In the past decade, TNA has led several AI-driven projects, which have resulted in a substantial portfolio of work that forms the basis for this chapter. As a non-ministerial government department, TNA is the official archive for the UK government and for England and Wales. There are separate national archives for Scotland (National Records of Scotland) and Northern Ireland (the Public Record Office of Northern Ireland). TNA's collections include records of the central government from the Middle Ages onwards, documents such as wills, naturalisation certificates and criminal records, and many others. Since 2003, TNA has also actively curated the UK Government Web Archive, which captures, preserves and makes accessible UK central government information published on the web. The web archive collects born-digital records such as websites, but also videos, images and tweets.

Rethinking the record

The transition from print to digital has led TNA, like other cultural institutions, to rethink the record. As part of this priority research theme, a core challenge is to focus on 'digital recordkeeping at scale'.[1] To deal with the boom in digital records, old approaches – such as manually reviewing collections to identify sensitive documents – can no longer be applied. Digital recordkeeping at scale has led TNA to rethink their practices and explore computational methods and other advanced techniques, requiring close collaboration with central government departments.

Following an amendment of the Public Records Act, the UK government is now required to transfer records of historical value to TNA after 20 years for permanent preservation. Before that, records stay within government departments, first as living records (until Year 7) and then as archival records kept in internal archives (from Years 7 to 20). Good record management is essential both before and after transfer to TNA. As Sir Alex Allan explained in his 2015 review of government digital records:

> Records are needed to support policy development; to help assess the impact of policies; to provide accountability for decisions; to share knowledge across government; to enable departments to provide accurate and comprehensive evidence to inquiries or in legal actions; to answer Freedom of Information requests; and eventually to provide the historical background to government. (Allan 2015)

The key challenge is that digital records are seldom well-organised. The 2017 'Better Information for Better Government' (BI4BG) report – authored by the Cabinet Office, in partnership with TNA – declares: 'much of what has accumulated over the past fifteen to twenty years is poorly organised, scattered across different systems and almost impossible to search effectively' (Cabinet Office 2017). It attributes this digital disorganisation to the lack of incentives for civil servants to sort out their mass of digital data – a time-consuming task that has no or few rewards. As the Allan report had done before, the BI4BG report recommends enlisting the help of senior decision-makers to improve the management of digital records.

Since born-digital records are often scattered across different systems (for example, email accounts, records management systems and shared drives), duplicates or near-duplicates are frequent. The volume of data makes the task of searching for specific information extremely difficult. As Andrew Prescott and Jane Winters have shown, keyword search is not effective with very large datasets (Winters and Prescott 2019). When a search query produces hundreds of thousands of results, potentially ranked only by date, it is difficult to know where to start. While this is an issue that can be approached by the semantic web (a technological effort to make web content more meaningful and readable to machines), it is limited by its inability to identify how knowledge content can change depending on context and use (Fesharaki et al 2020). Moreover, the semantic web presents drawbacks because it can be directly applicable to metadata – provided that an appropriate knowledge base is provided (such as Dbpedia[2]) and that the metadata can be linked to it. However, its application to the textual content of emails, for example, is not so naive, since it requires techniques of natural language processing (NLP) for the extraction of concepts and entities from the text, disambiguation, and then for the linking of such entities to the relevant knowledge base. That said, if methods to search and retrieve information are not effective across the broad range of formats of born-digital records, there will be implications not only for usability and access, but also for archives responding to Freedom of Information (FOI) requests and inquiries, which could present further issues as time goes on.

The BI4BG report mourns the golden age of paper records that were neatly filed according to established processes: 'Files and filing were at the centre of how work got done: they were intrinsic to the flow of work, not an overhead on it' (Cabinet Office 2017). But is it really the case that the lifecycle of paper records, from creation to preservation, was much more robust? In a 2021 interview, Anthea Seles, the former Secretary General of the International Council on Archives, said: 'There's this notion that exists out there, it's like, Norman Rockwell's lovely paintings of the United States at a particular golden era and people have this notion about paper ... [yet] we didn't get it right with paper ... it's less discoverable to some degree.'[3] Seles recommends adjusting expectations to make it clear that no system of appraisal and selection is ever going to be perfect. Accepting a certain level of risk and imperfection is essential to move forward in the digital age.

AI for digital selection

How can government departments receive the help they need to select digital files of long-lasting value? TNA recently conducted a project called 'AI for Digital Selection' to evaluate existing AI tools that could be used for the appraisal and selection of digital records (including emails and datasets) held across government sectors (Venkata et al 2021). After choosing a few relevant tools, TNA tested them on a set of their own corporate records – rather than records from the Cabinet Office or other central government departments. TNA's corporate files had already been sensitivity reviewed and had also been assigned to retention schedules which indicated how long they should be kept, in some cases this being permanently. The tasks assigned to the AI tools were to review the content of test documents and to predict whether they should be preserved or not.

Regarding preservation, many libraries apply a faceted classification system to organise their materials into categories based on multiple characteristics, such as subject, form, place, and so on. However, when archives are dealing with a diverse range of materials, these types of classification systems can present limitations when it comes to preservation selection (Hoffman 2019; Mas et al 2011). Through the 'AI for Digital Selection' project, TNA learned what metadata should be captured about the AI tools and processes to help end users understand and use government records selected via these methods. Moreover, TNA is now in a better position to assist government departments in automating the selection of born-digital documents ahead of transfer for permanent preservation and presentation. However, as Santhilata Venkata (Digital Archiving Researcher at TNA) points out, while the project concluded that AI tools can assist record managers, the machine cannot replace human input.[4]

AI for sensitivity review

Identifying sensitive materials in large digital collections requires technology-assisted review with human oversight. In its 2016 report on electronic discovery (eDiscovery) tools, TNA discussed the issue of born-digital records often containing sensitive information, such as contact details of individuals or financial details (TNA 2016). In the case of FOI requests, this kind of information falls under the category of 'exemptions' and cannot be disclosed. Around three-quarters of exemptions to release relate to personal information, so this is clearly a priority area for government departments. After transfer to TNA, it is also essential that no personally identifiable information is released to the public.

AI-powered tools can sort documents according to their sensitivity level: when no sensitive information is identified, documents can be released – although human input is often necessary to prevent any false negatives (in the case of a personal name spelled in various ways, for example). As the report points out, 'technology-assisted review is never going to be 100% accurate – departments will need to define and accept their risk appetite' (TNA 2016). When sensitive information is identified, documents can be closed for a specific period. Another approach is to redact sensitive/personal information using digital forensics tools (Woods and Lee 2015). The open-source tool BitCurator[5] offers bulk extractor functionality that lexically analyses text looking for sensitive features, such as email addresses, phone numbers and other personally identifiable information.

So how does automatic sensitivity review work in practice? As Graham McDonald et al (2020a, 2020b) note, keywords are not enough to identify sensitive information. However, the relationships between terms and entities in the discourse, in addition to single keywords, can help disclose sensitivities. In other words, the context is as important as the text itself when evaluating the sensitivity of a document. To capture contextual information, and at the same time overcome the ambiguity of language, word embedding features can replace or be juxtaposed with simple keywords. In NLP, *word embedding* is a representation type that links a word with other words with similar meanings. For example, 'terrorism' and 'radicalism' should be closer than 'terrorism' and 'agriculture'. In their study, categorising a collection of c. 3,800 government documents as either sensitive or not sensitive, McDonald et al (2020a) showed that the inclusion of word embeddings significantly increased the accuracy of the classifier.

AI for discovery

AI can be used by creators of data and archivists for selection and sensitivity review, but also by researchers to discover relevant information. To complement or replace keyword searches, topic modelling can group words into clusters based on similarity. Drawing on unsupervised and supervised machine learning techniques, this text mining method can be used to highlight underlying topics across a dataset – for example, on catalogue metadata describing a large collection.

While metadata is often seen as a way to enhance the human findability of archival material, detailed item descriptions also offer vast corpora of machine-readable data to analyse. Christopher Day (Head of Modern Domestic Records at TNA) has undertaken research on the catalogue data of the General Board of Health records, a collection comprising c. 89,000 items of correspondence, individually described. In the mid-nineteenth century, the rapid development of capitalism led to overcrowded, poorly drained cities, creating an environment ripe for diseases. The 1848–1849 cholera epidemic in England and Wales claimed around 52,000 lives. In response, the government passed the Public Health Act of 1848, creating a General Board of Health to oversee sanitary measures throughout the country (Day 2021). Drawing on a test corpus of the 1,967 descriptions dated 1848, Day used an algorithm called 'latent Dirichlet allocation', in which the machine applies probabilistic statistics to discover topics across a corpus and sorts them into a number of groups defined by the user. Topics were then visualised using the Python library pyLDAvis. The results revealed topics such as sanitary inspections, which were central to the activities of the General Board of Health during its first year (Day 2020).

Cholera may no longer be a major risk in Britain, but the COVID-19 pandemic has reminded us of the centrality of government in designing and implementing public health measures. AI-powered approaches such as topic modelling will be invaluable to analyse the other large-scale collections that TNA continues to collect. During the pandemic, TNA set out to capture a detailed record of the government's response to COVID-19 on the web, using high-intensity and in-depth web archiving. Other web archiving initiatives (such as the Internet Archive or UK Web Archive) risked missing this content, which could have been lost to posterity in a rapidly changing context. TNA's COVID-19 collection contains over 50 TB of born-digital material, which could be used as evidence for a future Public Inquiry into the pandemic. As John Sheridan (Digital Director at TNA) puts it, 'How does a Public Inquiry begin to grapple with a collection of this size and scale? What role do AI tools have as we provide the mediation layer between the evidence on one side and the big questions that the Inquiry will be exploring on the other?'[6]

Other large-scale collections are regularly transferred to TNA. In June 2020, the Lord Chancellor and Secretary of State for Justice announced that TNA will be the institutional home for Court Judgments and Tribunal Decisions for England and Wales from April 2022. TNA will inherit a large existing digital collection of judgments and decisions, which will then expand rapidly. For Sheridan, it is essential to think of the contribution that AI can make to improve TNA's intellectual control over this material.[7] Indeed, letting the public access this material (previously not available for reuse) is not without risk. TNA needs to enable that access while protecting against potential harms to the justice system. For example, an unscrupulous user could design an algorithm to game the justice system,[8] which would impact public trust in legal decision-making processes.

Openness, access and use

TNA are committed to making their collections as accessible as possible to their users, from scholars conducting research to the public searching for their family histories. They are finding innovative ways to present their collections in consideration of the rapidly increasing volume of digital records, and how the expectations of users are changing (TNA 2019). The usability of archival records is, therefore, central to their digital strategy: 'Archives need to develop extraordinary capabilities to ensure digital records can be kept' (TNA 2017a). However, opening archival materials up to the public, or providing controlled access to closed records, comes with numerous challenges. Aside from complying with data protection laws and FOI requests, providing access to large-scale digital collections requires user-focused solutions, collaboration and additional ethical considerations.

According to Mark Bell (Senior Digital Researcher at TNA), the transition for TNA from paper to digital since the 1990s has seen a 'phenomenal increase' in the number of records (Bell 2018). It is estimated that 1.7 MB of data was created every second in 2020, approximately 2.5 quintillion bytes a day (DOMO 2018). Collecting and preserving an accurate record of our recent history is a challenging task, and that is without considering how archives can sort and present this information to researchers in a useful way. As archives 'need to be used in order to be useful', developing and using AI to support archival preservation and accessibility is crucial, but the development of these technologies is often siloed (TNA 2017a, 3). Many archives and other sectors develop systems in-house, meaning the possibility of transference to another system, or integrating records developed with different models, will be increasingly problematic as our digital cultural assets grow and alter with new technologies.

However, first and foremost, archives need to know what to archive. The judgement of what should be online and accessible, what needs reviewing and what requires limited or case-by-case access is currently still employing the same methodologies as paper archiving. TNA's digital strategy explains that, as a first-generation digital archive, digital records are currently 'appraised and selected like physical records' (TNA 2017a, 5). But these processes were never designed to deal with the sheer volume and multiple formats of born-digital records, and the same can be said of TNA's online catalogue, Discovery. Primarily designed for users to search descriptions of physical records and services, it is not an adequate system to present born-digital records (TNA 2017a, 3–5). In other words, practices for paper archiving cannot deal with the unprecedented number of born-digital records that archival institutions now hold, or present records in an accessible way. As TNA have observed, the preservation of and access to digital records 'requires nothing less than a revolution' (TNA 2017a, 1). But on the brink of revolution, while we must remember that born-digital records are historical records, not everything can or should be kept.

Releasing records responsibly

Users may find it strange to think that archives want to dispose of documents, but this is part of the curation process and is done through rigorous criteria to avoid the accidental disposal of important documents. But even for those documents that are preserved, archivists, as well as researchers, must accept that not everything can or should be released to the public. While archives may hold and preserve relevant records of our collective history, they also have a responsibility to present those records, not only for user access, but also with the consideration of legal and ethical factors. In this way, digital technologies have transformed how archives are used by the public as online catalogues, and their search boxes give users instant results for millions of digital and digitised records (TNA 2017a, 3). For TNA, their catalogue search results indicate whether a record is available online, must be viewed onsite or if the record is closed access. However, while making more born-digital materials accessible to users may be the goal, offering access to, or even keeping all digital materials, is unrealistic.

To ensure data protection laws are met for archival records, many archives set a high, overly cautious bar on sensitivity review. As John Sheridan points out, it is not a case of 'transparency above everything', as 'archives are not Wikileaks, and we're not in the Wikileak business. … It's not responsible to data subjects; it's not responsible to other people's intellectual property rights; it's not lawful. So, we then need to build the techniques to provide access responsibly.'[9] That said, with continuing advances in AI, the potential to offer more, albeit limited, access to born-digital records is possible. Discussing the balance between risk management and providing access to potentially sensitive materials, Sheridan notes that publishing materials online 'is fundamentally a very different act from providing reasonable facilities for someone to inspect a record'.[10] So how can archive services design and present online access systems to meet the needs and expectations of their users, while also managing risk levels?

Developing tools for access

Discussing the development of tools to access digital records, TNA's research priorities emphasise the necessity of understanding their researchers – and preparing for how research needs and skills will develop in the future. Providing access to users must not only accommodate records in multiple formats, but also the researcher's and the archive's capabilities. Acknowledging these elements to design new approaches to delivery and research with aggregated data, TNA are investing in new tools for quantitative analysis and the manipulation of data at scale.[11] The following sections discuss current issues and solutions to increasing usability and providing safe access to closed materials.

Discovery and access

Accessing physical materials was inevitably made harder by the COVID-19 pandemic, but archives have also had to face the reality of digital accessibility sooner than they might have expected. With a growing demand for remote access to records, archives have focused on numerous ways to provide digital content to users. Providing an online catalogue is a vital part of an archive's usability in today's modern world, and while not everything can be listed, the catalogue is often the first step for the user (Dunley and Pugh 2021). With no or limited access onsite, TNA offered free downloads to registered users from April 2020, allowing access to almost nine million of their digital records from the Discovery online catalogue. But while TNA have digitised over 80 million records, there are just over 24 million records available to search via Discovery, because some of the catalogue entries are closed (TNA 2020).

At the other end of the scale, the UK Government Web Archive, curated by TNA, has over 500 million digital records, dating from 1996 to 2023. However, with only four filters available to users at this time (keyword, website, file type, year), the searchability functions are insufficient for such a huge number of records; there are over 238 million results for 'COVID-19' alone. With the sheer volume of born-digital records in various formats passing on to TNA, as well as other cultural institutions, the development of new tools and methodologies needs to ensure digital records are not only made accessible (or at the very least discoverable), but that their searchability is adequate enough to allow users to sort through records and find what they need.

Providing physical access

At the time of writing, TNA's Discovery catalogue has approximately 756,000 of its closed documents listed.[12] These sensitive materials, much like those held by other archives, must be requested through an FOI request. Traditionally, if a request is granted, these types of records need to be viewed within the specific archive. However, as in-person research returned following the pandemic, TNA signed up to SafePod. Developed by Professor Chris Dibben (University of Edinburgh) and Darren Lightfoot (University of St Andrews), the SafePod Network provides access to sensitive datasets through a series of secure pods located throughout the UK (Lightfoot 2021). According to Mark Bell, the TNA's SafePod is mainly for 'sensitive administrative data' and will allow a researcher to remotely access different datasets without being able to take anything away with them.[13] The data centres that can currently be accessed from a SafePod include the Secure Anonymised Information Linkage Databank, UK Data

Service and Office for National Statistics.[14] While a physical space that allows multiple de-identified or anonymised datasets to be examined securely in the same location is one answer to providing greater accessibility, there are still practical issues.

SafePods are and will be primarily based at universities and aimed at researchers, but they require users to be onsite, and this could potentially cause issues for public users. They also require users to register, and complete a short training questionnaire, to book.[15] Additionally, there is a capacity issue. While a single SafePod may be adequate for a university library, is one SafePod enough for TNA? Until the demand is assessed, it is difficult to predict users' needs in the long term. But the number of records a researcher might need to consult adds time restraints, potentially meaning multiple visits to a SafePod. Looking ahead, the secure technology behind SafePod, providing users with remote access to its partnered data centres, could be adapted to remove the necessity of the 'pod'. Registered users could potentially be provided with temporary access to the required resources through a remote desktop, with the session recorded via webcam and screen capture to prevent issues of photography, copying or misuse. If such steps could be realised, the technology could be used by far more archives, libraries and universities across the UK, and beyond. But for now, SafePods are offering a timely and necessary solution – a first step on a long road to making closed records more accessible.

Providing remote access

Providing physical access can placate user demand but it is not a practical solution in the long term. Content contained in digital records could be made remotely accessible if the sensitive information was efficiently redacted. Personal emails, for example, can contain large amounts of sensitive information, scattered across a potentially huge number of records. Email preservation and review can be a laborious process but can provide evidence of prominent individuals' lives and information that could interest researchers and the public alike (Schneider et al 2019).

AI tools can make the process of sensitivity review more efficient and less time-consuming. Stanford University Library's email archive, a system developed through their open-source software programme ePADD, was designed to address this mammoth task. Started in 2010, ePADD uses machine learning and NLP to meet the multiple challenges of email archiving (Stanford Libraries Projects 2021). The program screens emails for confidential and legally protected information, offering a lexicon-based search for sensitive topics and image browsing. These tools allow ePADD's users to prepare records for preservation, while making them accessible and discoverable for researchers.

While providing access to preserved emails is a pressing issue, it must also be addressed with future users in mind. How will these sources be engaged with once issues of access have been navigated (Decker et al 2022)? While content may be preserved, processes of sensitivity review increase the risk of decontextualisation, presenting challenges for historical researchers and general users. To this end, the TNA has been involved in the project eConDist, a context-based search tool developed using NLP and deep learning. This advanced search tool helps to incorporate human intuition into user queries. It has been developed as part of the AHRC-NEH-funded project 'Contextualisation of Email Archives', where TNA partnered with the University of Bristol (UK), De Montfort University (UK) and the University of Maryland (US) (Decker et al 2022).

AI and other technologies are being applied effectively to address issues of preservation and access. However, the employment of such technologies in archives requires skilled training, and without a dedicated digital department or external assistance, archival staff would be required to learn digital skillsets on top of their existing archival expertise. In this way, and at a policy level, the infrastructure for digital archiving is severely lacking, and changes need to be implemented across the sector.

Addressing this issue, a recent multinational project has paved the way for a more collaborative approach to digital strategy. The European Archival Records and Knowledge Preservation (E-ARK) project has focused on ensuring digital archives and technologies remain usable and consistent over time, and internationally.[16] Running from 2014 to 2017, the project brought together national archives across Europe, Chile and the United States to research consistency in digital archiving with support from the University of Brighton (UK) and the Digital Preservation Coalition (DPC). The collaborative project shared pioneering digital tools and expertise, which in turn improved skills and lowered costs for archives.

With a similar intention, TNA are taking the lead in the UK digital archival sector with the projects Archives for Everyone in 2015, Archives Unlocked in 2017 and Plugged In, Powered Up in 2020.[17] Through these initiatives, they have set up and continue to provide training for AHRC Collaborative Doctoral students and seminars, and launched Bridging the Digital Gap, a National Lottery Heritage Fund training programme for 24 technical apprentices in UK archives (TNA 2021a). They have also worked with the DPC on the online learning pathway Novice to

Know-How (TNA 2021b). TNA, like many across the sector, have recognised the importance of collaborative action to secure future access to and use of digital records. Through collaborative partnerships built on feedback, justification and the exchange of knowledge, those with fewer resources can benefit from those with more (Gurciullo 2017). Although AI methods and technologies may continue to develop in-house to meet the specific needs of individual archives, the experience and advice gained through the employment of these technologies can not only help to address issues of access but inform ethical considerations and highlight potential dangers across the sector.

Managing risk

While AI continues to offer solutions for providing user access to digital records, there is also a danger of making records more vulnerable to abuse, misuse or corruption. The dangers of digital corruption and the potential solutions are more formally addressed in the next section, but here we discuss how archives must address these issues through a risk management approach. TNA's current risk assessment for digital continuity addresses several considerations, from types of risks and timely reaction to learning from past issues. For digital records they complete a risk assessment at least every two years, or when there is a significant change within the technical environment (TNA 2017b).

However, according to Sheridan, the hardest element in anticipating risk is knowing how people will use digital collections. Although there are interventions within the data, are these enough to prevent a user from piecing together potentially sensitive information? TNA have experience using named entity recognition and statistical models to decipher sensitive information (names, addresses, contact information, account numbers, etc.), but unfortunately an adequate digital risk model has not yet been built. As Sheridan has discussed, TNA's current approach, like many other archives, is to manage risk 'through expert knowledge' rather than systems.[18]

Until systematic risk models are an inherent part of archives' digital practice, adaptive approaches can be employed; one of those is gradation. A notion that 'maximises use but manages the risks of publication', gradating access can allow for a more flexible system of publishing potentially sensitive records (but not in breach of data protection laws) by identifying varying levels of risk and determining necessary exemptions.[19] Publishing born-digital materials with an exemption from search engine indexing is one way to make the record less discoverable, but still accessible to those who want to use it. For example, the court jurisdiction database, British and Irish Legal Information Institute,[20] prohibits the 'external indexing of documents' or the publishing of any materials on external websites as a form of risk management.[21] But while imposing publishing and use exemptions may work for certain categories of documents, working at scale requires varying and intuitive approaches.

Even when legal requirements for sensitive data are met, determining the level of risk from an ethical point of view is still at the archives' discretion. In a recent interview, a director of Special Collections at a prestigious American library discussed the ethical nature of the archive.[22] They recalled an occasion with the collection of Susan Sontag's emails held by UCLA, where a student published an essay on a personal relationship detailed in the emails. The legally protected information had been redacted, but some personal information had remained, revealing the additional ethical concerns archives must consider when presenting an individual's intimate correspondence.

AI technology can help to bring archival material to light, but it cannot replicate (at least not yet) the human processing that goes into ethical decision-making, or anticipate the connections users may potentially make from redacted materials. While placing prohibitions for external indexing and unauthorised use on sensitive documents may help to moderate risk, it is not sufficient to prevent harmful use. In this sense, finding a balance between usability and limiting the potential misuse of archive materials must be addressed by adequate risk management. As the number of born-digital records continues to increase, and the capacity of expert assessment becomes overstretched, there are AI technologies that are enabling risks to be managed and reduced.

Risk, uncertainty and trust

The scale and growth rate of the digital world have strong implications on digital recordkeepers. Technology provides an opportunity to empower archivists with new capabilities of processing and inference from digital collections otherwise lost in the deluge of information. But in this process, two questions need to be answered: (i) To what extent do we try and use AI to help us? (ii) How can we be mindful of the harmful uses of material that we are trying to prevent through the application and use of AI?[23] To answer these, TNA is investigating technologies and tools to manage risk and uncertainty while reconciling with trust.

One of these is the use of blockchains, or distributed ledger technology (DLT). A blockchain is a series of blocks of digital data stored in a digital ledger (like a database) that multiple organisations can maintain, check, share and add to, but, most importantly, the data in the blockchain cannot be altered. The claim that blockchain is immutable is supported by the decentralised nature of blocks of data. If an attempt is made to change any of the data, this needs to be verified by the other blocks in the chain, making editing nearly impossible. The ARCHANGEL project combined the use of blockchain and AI to guarantee the authenticity of digital records and foster trust while accounting for some of the most important weaknesses of digital archives – including their dependency on ephemeral file formats.[24] Statistical risk management allows risk models to incorporate the uncertainty surrounding the digital collections in terms of the probability of known events and unknown variables. To this purpose, TNA has explored a Bayesian network. A Bayesian network is a graphical model that represents a set of variables and conditions; they are often used for probability analysis. These networks can either be specified by an expert or, for larger models, trained using data, such as that stored in blockchains. In conjunction with the Applied Statistics and Risk Unit at the University of Warwick, TNA have developed the Digital Archiving Graphical Risk Assessment Model (DiAGRAM) to provide a decision support system capable of quantifying risks and benefits of possible interventions and help prioritise investments (Barons et al 2021).

The adoption of AI in many sensitive domains has raised awareness about the implications of this technology for decision-making processes, highlighting the requirements for fair, accountable and transparent tools. A tool that has attempted to answer this need is explainable AI (XAI). Discussed in more detail below, XAI allows its decision-making processes to be understood by humans, unlike AI, and this enables users to ensure that the XAI is making good decisions. However, the focus of the research community has been mostly directed towards the technology, forgetting the role of humans and their environment when engaging with AI.

Blockchain to establish the authenticity of records

It is natural, talking about archive preservation, to think about the physical artefacts and how to protect them from damage and natural deterioration. This concept, although less intuitive, also extends to digital archives. There are many challenges posed by the preservation of digital and born-digital archives, but one crucial aspect is related to integrity and trust. Indeed, while the possibility of copying digital content allows for escaping the natural expiration date of storage supports, it paves the way for digital corruption, tampering and modifications. Some of these are wanted. Redacting sensitive records or removing personal information is essential to open archives to the public. Others conceal malevolent intentions such as rewriting history or generating fake or counterfeit artefacts, or simple faults and corruption of the supporting devices. How do we guarantee that unauthorised manipulations do not take place while still allowing authorised modification to happen? How can this process be carried out in a way that engenders trust towards archival and memory institutions?

Technology may provide the answer through the combination of DLTs and AI. As pointed out by Lemieux (2016), 'the discussion about trusted records or systems boils down to two interlinking concepts: reliability and authenticity, and closely related concepts such as identity, integrity and provenance'. Blockchain, the technology used as the backbone of Bitcoin, can be exploited to ensure trustful digital records: 'In medieval time, pages of court records were stitched together into a patchwork, an obvious hole would be left if anyone removed a page. Today, blockchain uses a similar idea to stitch together blocks of data to detect tampering' (ARCHANGEL Project 2019). In a blockchain, trust is achieved by using a decentralised database to keep a record of transactions, usually packaged in *blocks* along with a hash code pointer (a unique reference code), used to check the integrity of the block. The focus of trust moves from the individual parties to the network of members (called nodes) which are now required to reach a consensus before a block is added to the chain (Open Data Institute 2018). Generally speaking, a consensus of 51% is required to modify data in the blockchain, making the addition of malicious blocks incredibly difficult. Additionally, to remove the risk of malevolent parties taking control over such data, permissioned access can be implemented.

ARCHANGEL, which brought together TNA, the Open Data Institute and the University of Surrey, used permissioned access to provide reader access to the general public. In using a permissioned ledger, it is possible to reach a balance between control and transparency. From one side, the general public can access and view the records and openly verify their integrity. On the other, only authorised individuals are allowed to add to the ledger. The consensus to add a block to the chain is achieved through two practices based on a process called proof-of-work (PoW), that is, proof that the work of a participant 'node' qualifies them to add to the blockchain (this is usually gauged through the completion of a complex computational puzzle). One implementation of the practice allows only private nodes, maintained by multiple archives and memory institutions (AMIs), to generate such PoWs. Another form allows access from the public, but controls write access by using a smart contract (a computer program that acts like a third party) with a user key to verify the identity of the user (Collomoss et al 2018; Porat et al 2017).

In a DLT, 'fingerprints' (i.e., hash codes) are used to uniquely identify a digital object. These fingerprints exist within the content metadata of a file, so even if the system metadata (such as its name or extension) is altered, the hash identifier remains the same. They are deposited in a DLT-based system in order to (i) ensure that there were no unauthorised modifications since the deposit of the fingerprint and (ii) if there were authorised modifications, these leave a transparent auditable trail. In this way, it is possible to ensure the identity, integrity and provenance of digital objects. The verification of authenticity is based on the match between the deposited fingerprint and the one generated by the object.

However, to address integrity and authenticity in archival records, emphasis needs to be placed on new media, like audiovisual streams, as these forms of records are becoming a predominant way of documenting and capturing our society. The wealth of publicly available video, photo and audio, combined with the unscrupulous use of AI to generate new content, is at the basis of phenomena like fake videos ('deepfakes') or simply video/photo editing. To ensure archival integrity and limit the risk of manipulation, the US National Archives incorporated hash codes within the metadata of the John F. Kennedy assassination archive (Bhatia et al 2020).

In addition to being highly subject to distortion and manipulation, video media forms are characterised by their ephemeral nature, often relying on formats that are quickly becoming obsolete. This can present issues, even with the use of hash codes, because although the code will only alter if the content of the file is altered, opening files in different-format applications (like creating a PDF from a Word document) changes the embedded content, and therefore the hash. The changing of file format in this way is known as transcoding. The need to create a copy due to transcoding can easily result in errors and corrupted files, hence requiring methods capable of detecting accidental or malicious alteration of content while being invariant to format. It is important, then, to decouple the object from its format, which may change over time. While this can be easily done for textual data, it is more complex for formats like videos.

To solve this issue, the ARCHANGEL project created digital 'fingerprints' that were 'sensitive to tampering, but invariant to the format' (Bui et al 2019, n. p.). Using blockchain technology, the content-based hash, the file identifier and a unique identifier of the process used to extract the hash were stored with other metadata to ensure the file's and format's integrity as technologies change (Collomosse et al 2018). In addition to an integrity check, smart contracts, which are essentially programmable contracts that sit on the blockchain and are run when predetermined conditions are met, could be used to access the metadata associated with the object fingerprint, providing support to implement indexing and search capabilities over these digital objects.

The need to provide mechanisms to check for authenticity and integrity by detecting attempts at tampering and forgery is also the motivation behind a research and development project conducted at the National Archives of Korea (Wang and Yang 2021, 90), which led to two case studies to inform the adoption of this technology using Hyperledger Fabric (Hyperledger Fabric 2020), an open-source blockchain platform designed for use in enterprise. The first study was inspired by ARCHANGEL and aimed at using blockchain to verify the authenticity of audiovisual content and provide an audit trail of transactions. The second focused on datasets generated by government agencies and aimed at ensuring the integrity of datasets from tampering and forgery when they are self-managed and stored in multiple institutions.

Balancing risk and access

Two main concerns of digital archives are inevitably connected with the risks associated with preservation, from faulty devices and file corruption to missing metadata and loss of integrity, and access. Risk management's 'ultimate goal is to define prevention and control mechanisms to address the risk attached to specific activities and valuable assets, where risk is defined as the combination of the probability of an event and its consequence' (Barateiro et al 2010). It is natural to think of pairing archive preservation and access with risk management processes, since these help to identify the limitations of the context, to assess the risks and plan for treatments. Barateiro et al (2009) propose an approach to risk management specific for digital preservation consisting of three steps: (i) identification of requirements; (ii) classification of threats and vulnerabilities; and (iii) treatment of the risks deriving. However, one limitation with these types of approach comes from the impossibility of quantifying outcomes and probability, hence resulting in qualitative evaluation rather than quantitative indication for decision-makers. In an environment often constrained by high volume of data and low available resources, how to select what to preserve and prioritise accordingly?

This is the concept behind the 'Safeguarding the Nation's Digital Memory' project: to approach preservation risk by employing statistical methods for decision support based on data and evidence (Merwood 2020). The outcome, DiAGRAM, combines the knowledge of domain experts and statisticians into a Bayesian network used to infer the risks associated with four key areas:

1. *preservation* – caused by the fluidity and fragility of digital artefacts;
2. *context and provenance* – due to the facility with which these records can be moved around, lost or hidden;
3. *transparency, trust and inclusion* – imputable to the greater complexity faced by digital archivists when creating a digital story; and
4. *policy* – when idealistic benchmarks, processes, standards and models collide with the lack of resources for local and small archives, and their necessity to prioritise.

The risk here is that standards and processes hinder the archival preservation process. Hence, the project aims to provide practical decision support tools that guide archivists through the quantitative assessment of risks and threats. Through these quantifications, decision-makers can examine different risks and benefits associated with threats and make informed decisions and plans. Additionally, the use of statistical risk models provides the flexibility to adapt through time and navigate risks when it is hard to predict all possible outcomes and uses of a digital collection.

The power of the model resides in its capability to tackle uncertainty, that is, to provide estimates even in the presence of limited or imperfect data. This is a characteristic of Bayesian networks, which provide a framework to model expert knowledge necessary to compensate for the lack of information and provide a robust tool for reasoning under uncertainty. However, even when risk management practices are employed, there are challenges due to the lack of shared details around the experience of system failures, as pointed out by Dearborn and Meister (2017, 83–93). To this end, the authors discuss the past experience of failures within the MetaArchive Cooperative as a way to plan for success in the future. Openness and transparency can thus be interpreted in terms of shared experience and practices.

Explainable AI to build trust

As AI is creeping into many aspects of our life, it raises questions regarding the reliability of these systems and, consequently, the risks deriving from AI-based decision-making. While the black-box model fuelled by big data and complex deep architectures has determined the popularity of AI solutions in many domains in the past decade, now we are faced with the requirements of interpretable and explainable models as the top prerequisites to establish fairness, accountability and trust in this technology. Although often used interchangeably, explainability and interpretability refer to two separate aspects of AI algorithms. Interpretability looks at how an AI works, focusing on what the algorithm does. Explainability is concerned with how the AI behaves, and aims at creating a trust link between the AI and its users, producing insights into their decision-making (Bunn 2020).

But how can an AI explain itself? In 'Explaining explanations: An overview of interpretability of machine learning' Gilpin et al survey current work on XAI, trying to identify challenges and foundational concepts used to create a taxonomy of XAI approaches. There are three categories for XAI (Gilpin et al 2018, 86):

1. *Processing*, that is, methods that try to rebuild the internal decision process of the algorithm, trying to identify connections between input and output. This category of XAI is mainly concerned with the impact of AI on users, and how to create transparency, and eventually trust, in their use.
2. *Representation* looks at the internal model of the AI, trying to understand how data are represented. This is particularly important to help understand the role of bias in data and how this propagates in the algorithm.
3. The last category looks at ways of *producing explanation*, that is, the capability of AI to engage in a conversation around its own decisions.

It is interesting to note how concepts of transparency and accountability are shared between AI and digital archives. In this way, the next step is to direct efforts towards a shared definition that benefits people.

As Abdul et al have pointed out, while the AI community is working towards explainable algorithms, 'their focus is not on usable, practical and effective transparency that works for and benefits people' (2018, 10). Building towards a shared view, the workshop on 'Human-Centred Explainable AI' (HeXAI) organised by University College London (UCL) and TNA focused on the human-centred multidisciplinary exploration of and engagement with XAI. Working towards XAI there is a 'need to understand a lot more about explanation as a contextual human behaviour with a role in cementing social cohesion and trust' (UCL 2019). Building explainable AI is not just an algorithmic matter, but needs to consider the individuals, and the environment in which it will operate.

Conclusion

Over the past few years, TNA has been at the forefront of the exploration of AI applied to archives and has contributed substantial thought leadership and pragmatic case studies for the wider libraries, archives and museums sector to reflect on and learn from. The work has been driven by the knowledge that how archives select, appraise, manage, preserve and provide access to their collections has changed, and continues to change dramatically as digital technologies develop. From early trials with eDiscovery and computation tools to support selection and appraisal processes, to collaborative projects with emerging technologies like blockchain, TNA has an established appetite for experimentation. However, while the adoption of AI has often been thought to solve problems related to the preservation and access of digital archives, it is also raising concerns regarding bias and ethics.

Indeed, AI can increase the risk of amplifying data and algorithmic bias, reinforcing stereotypes and skewed perceptions of the world, reframing discourse around popular topics statistically more prominent while filtering out niche views, and inducing decisions based on uncertain assumptions, without enough consideration of their confidence. Explainability is seen as a panacea for trust, in turn relying on fairness, accountability and transparency (FACT). However, there is still a gap between the interpretation of trustworthiness and FACT within the AI and the archive community. While sharing a common vocabulary, they prioritise different aspects: algorithmic from one side, and humans and their environment from the other. Convergence among these points of view can inform both sides and lead to greater progress in their disciplines. Jo and Gebru (2020) have already highlighted the exemplary role that archives can play in creating datasets for learning algorithms. Building on the concepts of consent, inclusivity, power, transparency, ethics and privacy in archival and library science, the authors describe how these can be applied in machine learning to limit bias and ethical concerns. However, we also need to be pragmatic about the expectation we set forth and the desired outcomes. Using data 'in the wild' is doomed to raise issues similar to those recently found in Buolamwini and Gebru's study, which outlined the way 'machine learning algorithms can discriminate based on classes like race and gender' (2018, 77). But would library staff have been aware of demographic bias in the datasets before such a study? The answer, as pointed out by Catherine Nicole Coleman, is 'likely not' (2020, 9). This is why an honest discussion needs to take place, where the focus shifts from ways to *remove* bias to ways of *managing* it. In doing this, guiding principles of beneficence, non-maleficence, autonomy, justice and explicability can 'serve as the architecture within which laws, rules, technical standards, and best practices are developed for specific sectors, industries, and jurisdictions' (Floridi and Cowls 2019, 9), in which these principles can have either an enabling or a constraining role.

Acknowledgements

We would like to acknowledge the information provided by interviewees at The National Archives, and their colleagues who reviewed this chapter prior to publication. We are very grateful for their contribution.

Notes

1. TNA. 'Priority research themes'. www.nationalarchives.gov.uk/about/our-research-and-academic-collaboration/our-research-priorities/priority-research-themes/.
2. www.dbpedia.org.
3. Anthea Seles. 2021. Interview with the authors for the AURA project (Archives in the UK/ Republic of Ireland and AI), 28 May.
4. Santhilata Venkata. 2021. Interview with the authors for the AURA project (Archives in the UK/ Republic of Ireland and AI), 21 May.
5. https://bitcurator.net/.
6. John Sheridan. 2021. Correspondence with L. Jaillant.
7. Sheridan. 2021. Correspondence with L. Jaillant.
8. Sheridan. 2021. Interview with authors for the 'Unlocking our Digital Past' project, Loughborough University (29 June).
9. Sheridan. 2021. Interview for the 'Unlocking our Digital Past' project, Loughborough University, 29 June.
10. Sheridan. 2021. Interview.
11. TNA. 'Openness, access and use'. www.nationalarchives.gov.uk/about/our-research-and-academic-collaboration/our-research-priorities/priority-research-themes/openness-access-and-use/.
12. TNA Discovery Catalogue Advanced Search Results from filters: all dates; closed document; The National Archives. Accurate as of 18 October 2023.
13. Bell, M. 2021. Interview.
14. www.nationalarchives.gov.uk/about/visit-us/researching-here/the-national-archives-safepod/.
15. https://safepodnetwork.ac.uk.
16. www.eark-project.com.

17. TNA, All accessed 28 June 2023. 'Archives for everyone', www.nationalarchives.gov.uk/about/our-role/plans-policies-performance-and-projects/our-plans/archives-for-everyone/; 'Archives unlocked', www.nationalarchives.gov.uk/archives-sector/projects-and-programmes/strategic-vision-for-archives/; 'Plugged in, powered up', www.nationalarchives.gov.uk/archives-sector/projects-and-programmes/plugged-in-powered-up/.
18. Sheridan. 2021. Interview.
19. Sheridan. 2021. Interview.
20. British and Irish Legal Information Institute. www.bailii.org.
21. Sheridan. 2021. Interview.
22. Anon. 2021. Interview with L. Jaillant.
23. Sheridan. 2021. Interview.
24. www.archangel.ac.uk/.

References

Abdul, A., Vermeulen, J., Wang, D., Lim, B.Y. and Kankanhalli, M. 2018. 'Trends and trajectories for explainable, accountable and intelligible systems: An HCI research agenda'. In *Proceedings of the 2018 CHI conference on human factors in computing systems*, April 2018, CHI, 1–18.

Allan, A. 2015. 'Review of government digital records'. Accessed 6 December 2023. www.gov.uk/government/uploads/system/uploads/attachment_data/file/486418/Report_-_Digital_Records_Review.pdf.

ARCHANGEL Project. 2019. 'Trusted digital archives'. Accessed 7 September 2023. www.youtube.com/watch?v=xKCdKo6rQXw.

Barateiro, J., Antunes, G., Borbinha, J. and Lisboa, P. 2009. 'Addressing digital preservation: Proposals for new perspectives'. In *Proceedings of InDP-09, 1st International Workshop on Innovation in Digital Preservation*.

Barateiro, J., Antunes, G., Freitas, F. and Borbinha, J. 2010. 'Designing digital preservation solutions: A risk management-based approach', *International Journal of Digital Curation*, 5(1):4–17.

Barons, M., Bhatia, S., Double, J., Fonseca, T., Green, A., Krol, S., Merwood, H., Mulinder, A., Ranade, S., Smith, J.Q. and Thornhill, T. 2021. 'Safeguarding the nation's digital memory: Towards a Bayesian model of digital preservation risk', *Archives and Records*, 42(1): 58–78.

Bell, M., TNA. 2018. 'Machine learning in the Archive'. Accessed 6 December 2023. https://blog.nationalarchives.gov.uk/machine-learning-archives/#note-39468-1.

Bhatia, S., Douglas, E.K. and Most, M. 2020. 'Blockchain and records management: Disruptive force or new approach?', *Records Management Journal*, 30(3):277–86.

Bui, T., Cooper, D., Collomosse, J., Bell, M., Green, A., Sheridan, J., Higgins, J., Das, A., Keller, J., Thereaux, O. and Brown, A. 2019. 'Archangel: Tamper-proofing video archives using temporal content hashes on the blockchain', in *Proceedings of the IEEE/CVF Conference on Computer Vision and Pattern Recognition Workshops*, Long Beach, CA, USA, IEEE. https://arxiv.org/abs/1904.12059.

Bunn, J. 2020. 'Working in contexts for which transparency is important: A recordkeeping view of explainable artificial intelligence (XAI)', *Records Management Journal*, 30(2):143–53.

Buolamwini, J. and Gebru, T. 2018. 'Gender shades: Intersectional accuracy disparities in commercial gender classification', *Proceedings of Machine Language Research*, 81 77–91.

Cabinet Office (UK). 2017. 'Better information for better government'. Accessed 5 February 2024. www.gov.uk/government/publications/better-information-for-better-government.

Coleman, C.N. 2020. 'Managing bias when library collections become data', *International Journal of Librarianship*, 5(1):8–19.

Collomosse, J., Bui, T., Brown, A., Sheridan, J., Green, A., Bell, M., Fawcett, J., Higgins, J. and Thereaux, O. 2018. 'ARCHANGEL: Trusted archives of digital public documents'. In *Proceedings of the ACM Symposium on Document Engineering, August 2018, Halifax, NS, Canada*, ACM DocEng, 1–4.

Day, C. 2020. 'Computing cholera? 'Distant reading' General Board of Health catalogue data'. Accessed 10 December 2023. www.nationalarchives.gov.uk/about/our-research-and-academic-collaboration/our-research-projects/2020-annual-digital-lecture-staff-research-poster-exhibition/#computing-cholera.

Day, C. 2021. 'Cholera! Public health in mid-19th century Britain'. Accessed 10 December 2023. https://media.nationalarchives.gov.uk/index.php/cholera-public-health-in-mid-19th-century-britain/.

Dearborn, C. and Meister, S. 2017. 'Failure as process: Interrogating disaster, loss, and recovery in digital preservation', *Alexandria*, 27(2):83–93.

Decker, S., Kirsch, D., Venkata, S., and Nix, A. 2022. 'Finding light in dark archives: Using AI to connect context and content in email', *AI & Society*, 37:859–72.

DOMO. 2018. 'Data never sleeps 6.0'. Accessed 10 December 2023. www.domo.com/assets/downloads/18_domo_data-never-sleeps-6+verticals.pdf.

Dunley, R. and Pugh, J. 2021. 'Do archive catalogues make history? Exploring interactions between historians and archives', *Twentieth Century British History*, 32(4):581–607.

Fesharaki, M.N., Fetanat, A. and Shooshtari, D.F. 2020. 'A conceptual model for Socio-Pragmatic Web based on activity theory', *Cogent Education*, 7(1).

Floridi, L. and Cowls, J. 2019. 'A unified framework of five principles for AI in society', *Harvard Data Science Review*, 1(1):1–15.

Gilpin, L.H., Bau, D., Yuan, B.Z., Bajwa, A., Specter, M. and Kagal, L. 2018. 'Explaining explanations: An overview of interpretability of machine learning'. In *2018 IEEE 5th International Conference on data science and advanced analytics (DSAA)*, October 2018, IEEE, 80–89.

Gurciullo, S. 2017. 'Keeping born-digital literary and artistic archives in an imperfect world: Theory, best practice and good enoughs', *Comma*,1: 49–65.

Hoffman, G.L. 2019. *Organizing Library Collections: Theory and practice*. London: Rowman & Littlefield.

Hyperledger Fabric. 2020. 'Introduction'. Accessed 10 December 2023. https://hyperledger-fabric.readthedocs.io/en/release-2.2/whatis.html.

Jo, E.S. and Gebru, T. 2020. 'Lessons from archives: Strategies for collecting sociocultural data in machine learning'. In *Proceedings of the 2020 Conference on Fairness, Accountability, and Transparency*, January 2020, 306–16.

Lemieux, V.L. 2016. 'Trusting records: Is blockchain technology the answer?', *Records Management Journal*, 26(2):110–39.

Lightfoot, D. 2021. 'The SafePod Network (SPN)'. Accessed 26 August 2023. https://safepodnetwork.ac.uk.

Mas, S., Maurel, D., and Alberts, I. 2011. 'Applying faceted classification to the personal organization of electronic records: Insights into the user experience', *Archivaria*, 72:29–59.

McDonald, G., Macdonald, C. and Ounis, I. 2020a. 'Active learning stopping strategies for technology-assisted sensitivity review'. In *Proceedings of the 43rd International ACM SIGIR Conference on Research and Development in Information Retrieval*, 2053–6. New York: Association for Computing Machinery.

McDonald, G., Macdonald, C. and Ounis, I. 2020b. 'How the accuracy and confidence of sensitivity classification affects digital sensitivity review', *ACM Transactions on Information Systems*, 39(4):1–34.

Merwood, H. 2020. 'Risk alert: Insufficient technical metadata' [Blog], Digital Preservation Coalition. Accessed 10 December 2023. www.dpconline.org/blog/risk-alert-insufficient-technical-metadata.

Open Data Institute. 2018. 'How can smart contracts be useful for business?'. Accessed 7 September 2023. https://theodi.org/wp-content/uploads/2018/05/378720579-How-can-smart-contracts-be-useful-for-businesses.pdf.

Porat, A., Pratap, A., Shah, P. and Adkar, V. 2017. 'Blockchain consensus: An analysis of proof-of-work and its applications', Stanford Labs Projects. Accessed 10 September 2023. www.scs.stanford.edu/17au-cs244b/labs/projects/porat_pratap_shah_adkar.pdf.

Schneider, J., Adams, C., DeBauche, S., Echols, R., McKean, C., Moran, J. and Waugh, D. 2019. 'Appraising, processing, and providing access to email in contemporary literary archives', *Archives and Manuscripts*, 47(3):305–26.

Stanford Libraries Projects. 2021. 'About ePADD'. Accessed 25 August 2023. https://epadd.stanford.edu/epadd/about.

TNA. 2016. 'The application of technology-assisted review to born-digital records transfer, Inquiries and beyond'. Accessed 7 September 2023. www.nationalarchives.gov.uk/documents/technology-assisted-review-to-born-digital-records-transfer.pdf.

TNA. 2017a. 'Digital strategy'. Accessed 7 September 2023. www.nationalarchives.gov.uk/documents/the-national-archives-digital-strategy-2017-19.pdf.

TNA. 2017b. 'Risk assessment handbook'. Accessed 7 September 2023. www.nationalarchives.gov.uk/documents/information-management/Risk-Assessment-Handbook.pdf.
TNA. 2019. 'Areas of research interest'. Accessed 7 September 2023. www.nationalarchives.gov.uk/documents/areas-of-research-interest.pdf.
TNA. 2020. 'Digitisation and digital archives'. Accessed 7 September 2023. www.nationalarchives.gov.uk/about/our-role/transparency/digitisation-and-digital-archives/.
TNA. 2021a. 'Bridging the digital gap'. Accessed 7 September 2023. www.nationalarchives.gov.uk/archives-sector/projects-and-programmes/bridging-digital-gap-technical-traineeships-archives/.
TNA. 2021b. 'Novice to know-how'. Accessed 7 September 2023. www.nationalarchives.gov.uk/archives-sector/projects-and-programmes/plugged-in-powered-up/novice-to-know-how/.
UCL. 2019. 'From black box to tip of the iceberg: Creative engagement with the emergence of XAI (explainable artificial intelligence)'. Accessed 10 September 2023. https://cpb-eu-w2.wpmucdn.com/blogs.ucl.ac.uk/dist/e/653/files/2019/10/HeXAI-leaflet.pdf.
Venkata, S., Young, P., Bell, M. and Green, A. 2021. 'Alexa, is this a historical record?', *Journal on Computing and Cultural Heritage*, 15(1):7.
Wang, H. and Yang, D. 2021. 'Research and development of blockchain recordkeeping at the National Archives of Korea', *Computers*, 10(8):90.
Winters, J. and Prescott, A. 2019. 'Negotiating the born-digital: A problem of search', *Archives and Manuscripts*, 47:391–403.
Woods, K. and Lee, C.A. 2015. 'Redacting private and sensitive information in born-digital collections'. In *Archiving 2015 Final Program and Proceedings, May 2015*, 2–7. Los Angeles: Society for Imaging Science and Technology.

2
Computer vision and cultural heritage

Catherine Nicole Coleman

This case study for the AEOLIAN project on computer vision applied to cultural heritage looks at critical points of intersection between research questions, the affordances of the technology, and curatorial desires. The primary focus of this case study is 'Stanford Global Currents', a project completed in 2016 that applied computer vision techniques to medieval manuscripts. The discoveries and outcomes of that project are used as a point of departure to touch on related work at other institutions, and independent work with computer vision applied to cultural heritage that has influenced how we think about search and discovery in libraries, archives and museums. The case study is based on interviews, project reports, conference papers and published research. Some key terminology is defined, and core concepts of computer vision that are essential to understanding the project are explained, but this is not a study of how computer vision works, nor does it address in any detail the methods or techniques applied in the 'Stanford Global Currents' project. Nor is the case study about computer vision as a field of study. Rather, it is about what can be learned from computational approaches to archival research that rely in some way on computer vision for information retrieval. The reason 'Stanford Global Currents' remains an important case study today is not the technology they used, but how the researcher's and curator's engagement with the technology changed the research and influenced how technological innovation can be put to practical use in libraries, archives and museums.

The first section gives an overview of the project, its intended outcomes and the approaches used. It also addresses the research questions that drove the project and the unexpected discoveries enabled by the team's technologies. The second section, 'Segmentation of images', delves into the way the technique of segmentation itself transforms the presentation of archival materials. This section looks back to an important project from 2011 that made use of computer vision turned on the archives to create windows into materials that were previously invisible. 'Reconfiguring the collection' considers the tension between what researchers want to see and what our systems of discovery make possible. The systems and services that govern access to collections are grounded in textual description and classification. What happens when we just see the visual instead? The fourth section, 'Classification lessons', looks at computer vision as a prosthetic that allows us to see differently. Computer vision algorithms are human-made, but they enable super-human vision, similar to how binoculars allow us to see clearly things that are far away. This technology has encouraged a critical examination of the assumptions built into classification systems. Finally, the conclusion, 'Democratising access', considers how computer vision is influencing new modes of discovery and delivery of cultural heritage and why it plays an important role in reimagining the possible uses of and engagement with digital collections.

Images of all kinds live particularly complicated lives within the organisational and information retrieval systems of libraries, archives and museums. Discovery in these systems depends upon metadata, part of which includes descriptive text. This forces a visual medium into a textual system. Early work done by John Resig (2014) applying image similarity to anonymous Italian works at the Frick Collection, New York, revealed how existing metadata is incomplete and inaccurate. The implications of this mismatch between the image and its metadata are being explored anew as we adopt computer vision methods to augment description and introduce new modes of discovery.

In the visual studies field this shift is understood as an algorithmic reconfiguration of subject–object relations, specifically an algorithmic intervention between the viewing subject and the object viewed. William Uricchio (2011) writes, 'it is this algorithmic layer that stands between the calculating subject and the object calculated, and that refracts the subject-centered world charted by Descartes, that merits closer inspection' (Uricchio 2011, 27). Though Uricchio is particularly interested in very intentionally algorithmically constructed environments using techniques like Photosynth and augmented reality, his underlying point that algorithmic processing fundamentally changes or realigns subject–object relations is also relevant to the reordering of images within archives. The work documented in this case study demonstrates that a visual (re)organisation of the past not only enables new ways of seeing, but changes, in turn, how we see and understand our archives.

This algorithmic turn for the sake of image exploration and discovery has entered slowly into libraries, archives and museums. Even in the digital humanities, the vanguard of revisiting cultural heritage through computational methods, the analysis of text rather than images has been the norm, despite a call for visual cultural analytics (Manovich 2009). Optical character recognition (OCR) brought about a revolution in research and reading that has not been equalled for images. In the print world, the availability of large, digitised text corpora in libraries soon led to the availability of large, searchable and analysable text corpora. But when 'Stanford Global Currents' began, no such benefit was afforded to researchers working with handwritten materials. Nor has there been a practical and obvious technological intervention in image exploration adopted as widely as OCR. Computer vision, and specifically the development of convolutional neural networks and transformer models, is beginning to change that equation and enable handwritten text transcription to match the OCR of print materials.

Digital humanists have been exploring applications of computer vision to better understand and engage with digitised materials from the past. In *Seeing the Past with Computers*, the editors Kevin Kee and Timothy Compeau (2019) argue that 'seeing technologies' are becoming essential tools for historians. This move is inevitable, in part due to the quantity of material being generated but also because it presents new avenues for investigation of the past. In the early 2010s this work was still considered experimental; now it is becoming essential and, as this case study will demonstrate, cultural heritage institutions are helping to shape the technology in collaboration with researchers. Libraries, archives and museums are often doing the digitisation work. Even in the cases where libraries are acquiring materials that have already been digitised, since they are responsible for storing and preserving those materials, they are also responsible for making them accessible in ways that are aligned with these new modes of inquiry.

Stanford Global Currents

The 'Stanford Global Currents' project began in February 2014 as part of an international, inter-institutional research project with team members in the United States, Canada and the Netherlands. The overarching multi-institutional project was known as 'Global Currents: Literary Networks,

c. 1090–1900' and was spearheaded by Professor Andrew Piper at McGill University. That larger project considered book production over time, across geographies and languages. The Stanford project, which is the focus of this case study, looked at British manuscripts. Expertise in computer science, humanities research, and library technology was brought into conversation to explore image processing and machine learning applied to textual and codicological analysis. The team, led by Professors Elaine Treharne and Mark Algee-Hewitt, and Dr Benjamin Albritton, received funding from the National Endowment for the Humanities' 'Digging into Data' programme.

The Stanford team used an already digitised corpus of manuscripts from the Parker Library of Old-English Manuscripts,[1] a collaborative project between Stanford University and Corpus Christi College, Cambridge, consisting of 210 manuscripts dated between 1060 and 1220 with 63,000 total page images. The manuscripts were digitised, but not transcribed. The Stanford corpus was made up of medieval manuscripts from a range of genres, spanning two centuries, 1080–1220, and including text in three languages: Latin, English and French. Even printed material across a 200-year span varies significantly in letterforms. What makes computational approaches to the transcription of medieval manuscripts particularly difficult is that each object is unique. As Treharne (2021) explains in *Perceptions of medieval manuscripts: The phenomenal book*, the materials upon which the scribes have written will show variations from one square inch to another. In addition, there are idiosyncrasies at the level of the format, which could be sheets or scrolls, and differences between the stylistic patterns and choices of the scribes. Handwriting text recognition (HTR) has improved significantly in recent years and is explored in Case Study 5, but at the time of this project, in 2014, it remained a particularly challenging task.[2] 'Global Currents' set out to experiment with two different approaches of visual language processing. One approach was to identify similarities of lexical formation in handwritten materials. This investigation had, initially, similar goals to OCR for print. The idea was to automatically discover and isolate particular words, which might allow manuscripts to be machine-read.

In order to achieve automation of this kind, it is necessary to collect enough varied examples of the same word, or token, that the lexical recognition software could learn to recognise that token when it encounters an example it has not seen before. This is a fundamental concept of machine learning: given enough examples, it is possible to train a model to identify with some measure of accuracy another example of the same kind of thing. Producing the necessary training data for this effort proved extremely difficult and time-consuming. One issue, as mentioned above, was the material qualities of the folios themselves. A number had to be weeded out of the process because of damage, intentional annotations, marginalia and other marks that interfered with reading the selected words. In addition, the texts contained characters that are not in contemporary use in English or Latin, such as ð, Đ, þ, æ, Þ, Æ, Ƿ and ƿ. And, of course, there was the inherent variability resulting from the fact that the documents are handwritten rather than typeset. The clear frustration with the process is written into the team's report. They wrote, 'the software initially showed few signs of learning: even at the end of processing one of the manuscripts, when nearly 60 examples of the word "thing" had been entered, the software was still not able to reliably recognise the token' (Treharne 2016, 3).[3]

Though the transcription effort was not successful, the process yielded new insights into the kinds of variation in the manuscripts. MONK,[4] the lexical recognition software developed by Lambert Schomaker's team at the University of Groningen, presented the group at Stanford with an analysis of the selected images of words for review and verification. By taking individual images of words from the folio and looking at those visual fragments side by side, the Stanford team discovered that certain scribal characteristics were identifiable across manuscripts. Abbreviations, for example, have distinctive characteristics that make it possible to distinguish between scribes not only within the same codex, but across different codices. This was just the type of cross-textual analysis the project was hoping to discover. This offered clues to many possible investigative paths. To identify a distinct scribal hand, for example, across a corpus that spans two centuries and multiple geographic locations, one can learn a tremendous amount about scribal practices. It was at this point that the team's attention shifted from trying to extract words held within the texts to what could be learned from a computer vision enabled study of the material qualities of the manuscript.

A study of the relationships between elements in the page layout or *mise-en-page* was undertaken in collaboration with Professor Mohammed Cheriet at the Synchromedia Laboratory at École de Technologie Supérieure (ETS) in Montreal. Rather than attempting to recognise words as they did with MONK, with Cheriet the team turned their attention to identifying the information retrieval tools used by medieval scribes and designers. The features considered included running heads, catchwords, writing grid format, *litterae notabiliores*, enlarged initials, minor flourishes and decorative devices, rubrics, intertextual space, ink-filled graphemes and interlexical space. Over the course of the project, these four became their focus: *litterae notabiliores*, notable letters that mark the start of a section; enlarged initials, which, as the name suggests, are large initials usually drawn two or three lines high in red, blue, green, yellow or purple; rubrics, which are titles of new texts or important sections of text, almost always in red in the body of the text; and intertextual space, which is white space within text, often found around rubrics and enlarged letters. Intertextual space is an important component of page design. For example, the amount of space in a manuscript often reflects the resource available to the scribe-compiler.

This shift in attention to *mise-en-page* proved to be a particularly fruitful study of manuscript production in the long twelfth century. Cheriet's team successfully identified the four visual features of interest to the Stanford team. Work with those important page elements revealed trends in their evolution. As recorded in the white paper, 'palaeographical and codicological developments in the second half of the twelfth century are critical and include notable shifts in the complexity of folio design (double- or triple-column from single; introduction of running heads; systematisation of rubrication; introduction of more navigational aids, including capitals, *capitula*; and recognition of the significance of clearly demarcated textual boundaries)' (Treharne 2016, 3). The study of *mise-en-page* also allowed them to make important discoveries about localisation. 'Localisation remains one of the most vexed, but important, aspects of manuscript studies in modern scholarship: fewer than one-third of manuscripts can be assigned to a place of origin' (Treharne 2016, 3).

What really made the work of Cheriet's team valuable was the Stanford team's ability to analyse the results in digital image galleries on a page. The galleries provided a link from the visual feature out to the full codex so they could see that feature in its native context. This was new. Research questions that had emerged from traditional scholarship, which, as their report explains, involves looking through the material folio by folio, quire by quire, codex by codex, could now be tested by seeing all types of a feature together, side by side. This view on the material, which is simply impossible when working with physical objects or even digital surrogates that are arranged only for page-by-page online viewing, became the catalyst of a cascade of questions answered and the formulation of new questions.

Segmentation of images

'Focusing on singular components aligned, often fortuitously, really does show this old material in a new light' (Treharne 2016, 14).

Within the field of computer vision, image segmentation describes partitioning an image into meaningful regions or objects for processing. Images can be segmented, for example at the pixel level or at the level of the bounding box. At the pixel level, you can more precisely capture the shape and contours of a region, whereas the bounding box is, as it sounds, a simple box. The bounding box approach is often used during the process of creating labelled training data. As in the preparation of training data for MONK mentioned above, a person draws a line around the word 'thing' in a manuscript and labels it as 'thing'. Algorithms can be trained to identify objects, regions and faces, and, today, are commonly used in policing and surveillance as well as in the commercial products used by owners of smartphones and people browsing the internet.

The web project 'The real face of White Australia' developed by Tim Sherrat and Kate Bagnall in 2010 applied algorithmic face detection to an archive.[5] The results captivated librarians, archivists and curators, and transformed our engagement with the material. The online project presents the visitor with a page of 100 faces, no text. Scrolling down the page produces more and more faces. The images of faces were selected from thousands of immigration documents held in the National Archives of Australia – the result of the 'White Australia' policies of the nineteenth and twentieth centuries intended to limit and discourage immigration by non-Europeans. A practice that was first instituted in the port city of Sydney in New South Wales to keep track of convicted criminals, which involved taking mug shots accompanied by descriptions of distinctive physical traits, was later applied to people crossing all borders into and out of Australia. The intent of 'The real face of White Australia' was to reveal the people inside systems of historical record-keeping; because the photographs in these archival documents identify race as well as face, this gallery of faces very intentionally confronts Australia's claim of being a white country (Sherratt and Bagnall 2019).

'The real face of White Australia' offered an entirely different and compelling way to see and engage with archival records; a visually striking collage of faces and a document browser. 'We know that the records, the photographs, the handprints, all carried emotive weight,' wrote Sherratt and Bagnall, 'it was the very reason we sought to expose them. What we did not quite realise was the effect of scale. Bringing all those photos together, without interpretation or intermediation, created a different type of experience' (2019, 21). They scraped the document images from the National Archives of Australia and then used an open-source Python computer vision library to detect the faces. The facial detection algorithm returned coordinates to define a bounding box where a face is detected in the image. Based on those coordinates, they could crop the original image, save the selection as a new file, and present a wall of faces – large thumbnail images that link through to the full document image.

The 'Stanford Global Currents' project galleries of *litterae notabiliores*, enlarged initials, rubrics and intertextual space do not carry the immediate social and political power that the faces in Sherrat and Bagnall's work do, but they, too, transformed the research process, leading to unanticipated questions. The outcomes described in the project white paper explain how taking elements out of the page and placing them side by side in gallery view provided an experience that was entirely novel:

> The gallery has had useful consequences in permitting the team to formulate and begin to answer globally significant research questions. For instance, from experience of working with medieval manuscripts, it might be assumed that green is a prevalent color in the embellishment of large capitals. Our results indicate that this is not the case, and that where green does occur, it may have important information to provide about date and place of origin of the manuscript. Our rapid overview of manuscript *mise-en-page*, facilitated by the gallery of images, also intimates that it is possible to offer a chronological typology of features of decoration; of the introduction of running headers; of the uses of rubrics; of the tendencies towards effects, like diminuendo display scripts, by particular scriptoria at particular times. (Treharne 2016)

'Stanford Global Currents' used image segmentation as part of the process of defining regions of interest on manuscript folios that would be used by their partners as training data for the machine learning models. The Stanford team drew bounding boxes around the *litterae notabiliores*, enlarged initials, rubrics and intertextual space. As mentioned above, the bounding box defines coordinate space on an image which makes the selection of part of an image possible. The team used IIIF (International Image Interoperability Framework; Snydman et al. 2015), a set of application programming interface (API) specifications, to support the entire process of viewing the digitised folios, annotating them with area selections, delivering the annotations to the team in Montreal, receiving the results and viewing them in galleries. They explain this process in the white paper:

> A secondary, but significant, research goal was to test the mechanism for large-scale image processing to be done on a corpus of digital resources held by an institutional repository in such a way that all new knowledge produced through analysis of those resources could be re-incorporated into the repository to enhance the digital resources themselves. This 'virtuous circle' of scholarly communication, where a project consumes and then enriches re-usable repository data, has proven to be an ongoing challenge in the information sciences and library communities. Using the protocols specified by the International Image Interoperability Framework (IIIF), the project provided images via API (rather than the more usual exchange of hard-drives through the post) and requested returned data be provided to conform to the IIIF specifications as well, insuring full re-usability of the results outside of the context of this particular project. (Treharne 2016)

By using IIIF protocols, Cheriet's team at ETS had the freedom to determine the size of the image they wanted to use. This is an important control for the computational team to have because the resolution of the image can have a significant effect on the success of the model. Too much information can take too long to process. It can also sometimes add unnecessary noise when considering visual saliency. And removing the long interruption of sending hard drives back and forth through the mail added to the thrill and satisfaction in the collaboration. Even in the very early stages of the collaboration, results could be viewed by the Stanford team almost immediately through simple HTML galleries pulling again from the archived image files. As Albritton described it, they were 'pulling the images on the fly as the processing is happening, as the presentation is happening, and as the re-presentation is happening' (2022).

Reconfiguring the collection

'It's like looking at the world through a kaleidoscope. You know what it looks like and then you put the kaleidoscope up to your eye and it's a whole new world' (Treharne 2022).

Both 'The real face of White Australia' and 'Stanford Global Currents' used the capabilities of computer vision to intentionally fragment the whole of an archive in order to see it in a new way. With the physical archive, cutting images out of documents would be a destructive act and an illegal one. Medieval manuscripts have been particularly susceptible to this kind of damage. But the plasticity of the digital image makes what was a destructive act into a generative one. These transformative engagements with the digital surrogates are, in some ways, opportunistic applications of a technology that was built for another purpose. Segmentation is intended for computational analysis, not human viewing. But these projects break down the barriers imposed by the technological systems of information delivery in our libraries and archives. 'We are deeply in love with the records and the stories they reveal' wrote Sherratt and Bagnall, 'We cannot say the same about the National Archives' collection database, RecordSearch' (2019, 17). Discovery systems reflect the underlying data models and long-standing data management practices within the institution rather than research practices. These systems, built to aid in discovery, can often hinder discovery when their organising principles dictate the questions one is required to ask to find objects.

Since machines trained to 'see' images do not see the way humans see, the results provide opportunities to see differently things we thought we understood well. The algorithmic layer that stands between the subject and the image object relies entirely on an abstraction of the visual object into numbers. Digital or digitised images are processed as a matrix of pixel values, effectively converting a semantically complex whole, as the human being sees it, into a grid of numbers that can be filtered, or broken up into sections, and analysed to identify subtle patterns and collections of patterns. As discussed above, much of the research in computer vision has focused on distinguishing objects represented in an image, known as object detection. Training an algorithm on labelled examples makes it possible to learn the features that make those examples similar to each other and, on that basis, find other visually similar objects. But some of the most important discoveries come from what could be understood as errors. Reflecting on the project years later Treharne noted, 'Working with images the way that we did created contiguities that I would never have otherwise seen, but also strange juxtapositions' (2022). Some of the ways that discoveries led to new research questions are captured in the 'Stanford Global Currents' white paper:

> Inductive research questions leapt off the galleries put together by Dr Albritton from the raw data sent from Professor Cheriet's team. We were surprised to see how dissimilar particular *litterae notabiliores* are from others in the gallery. Dissimilarity might be attributable to national trends in color use; to the 'rusticity' of specific initials in manuscripts not produced at major writing centers;

> or to the idiosyncrasy of scribe-artists, who we might now be able to trace with greater precision. We were delighted to discover that manuscripts never before associated with one another might, in fact, be related in terms of their production methods. We saw this emerge through the serendipitous juxtaposition of initials in the gallery. (Treharne 2016, 9)

The serendipitous juxtapositions were made possible in part because of the segmentation described in the previous section, but also because the collections were presented based on visual features, not based on search terms. The galleries of visual elements created by the 'Stanford Global Currents' team were intentionally separated into the four classes that they were seeking so that they could compare similar items side by side. Since that time, a number of projects have applied computer vision to heterogeneous image collections in order to find visual similarities without predefining classes. There are echoes of the discoveries of the 'Stanford Global Currents' project in these other projects that reveal sometimes unexpected visual patterns in image collections.[6]

In 2017, the National Endowment for the Humanities funded an experimental computer vision collaboration between the Frank-Ratchye STUDIO for Creative Inquiry at Carnegie Mellon University and the Carnegie Art Museum. They worked on the Charles 'Teenie' Harris Photography Archive, a collection of 80,000 exposures by Charles Teenie Harris (1908–98) who photographed Pittsburgh's African American community for about forty years in the mid-twentieth century.[7] 'One of the most detailed and intimate records of the Black urban experience in America' (Luster, Levin and Record 2018). Working with 60,000 digitised images from the archive, they used the InceptionV3 classifier which was pretrained on labelled images from the ImageNet benchmark dataset to generate labels for each image. Then they took the top five labels from each photo and compared them with the top five labels for every other photo as a method of identifying similarity.[8] The experiments with this type of automated classification revealed groupings like women in fur coats and car crashes – image sets that, according to collection archivist Dominique Luster (2018), could never have been discovered via the existing metadata.[9] The results were surprising and intriguing. They also revealed the limits of applying an algorithm trained on twenty-first-century photos to images from the mid-twentieth century. InceptionV3 is one of a set of convolutional neural network architectures developed by Google that was intended to automate captions for images. It is a pretrained supervised model, meaning that it has already learned to how to classify images into many predefined categories. As Peter Leonard explained in his description of the Yale DH Lab's experiments with the Inception algorithm, 'There are likely to be labels such as "cup of coffee", "cat", and "automobile" – but you're unlikely to find "parasol" or "steam engine".'[10]

At the DH 2016 digital humanities conference in Kraków, Benoît Seguin presented an alternative way to use the Inception model, taking the penultimate layer of the convolutional neural network, before text classification labels are assigned (di Lenardo, Seguin, and Kaplan 2016). Convolutional neural networks like Inception are multilayer architectures. The input to the process is the image and the output are the scores indicating how well the image matches the different predefined classifications. Layer by layer, it builds a more and more complex understanding of visual elements like edges, textures and shading, refining and aggregating that information such that, at the penultimate layer, just before the image is rated by its similarity to specific classes, the algorithm has captured a sophisticated understanding of the image based on high-level features that place it into multidimensional vector space. The image's position in vector space makes it possible to relate it to other images that are similar based on those features. The type of similarity that the algorithm produces at that penultimate layer is complex and multidimensional, based on 2,048 features.

Sequin's work was soon adopted by others working with materials from libraries, archives and museums. One of those experiments, again involving the STUDIO for Creative Inquiry, used Seguin's technique to compare the visual distribution of collections in the National Gallery of Art (NGA).[11] The NGA team used the uniform manifold approximation and projection (UMAP; McInnes and Healy 2018), a dimensionality-reduction technique to visually cluster the images in two-dimensional space. They then placed them into a grid layout; 'like pressing a flower into a book to best illustrate its unique botanical features, this reduction helps us do comparative work at a scale that wouldn't be easy to do otherwise' (Lincoln et al 2019b). In an essay describing their findings, they describe unexpected, but explainable, artefacts of clustering based on the neural network's featurisation:

> If you look closely in the portraiture section, you'll glimpse a black and white Robert Motherwell painting amidst the varied portrait heads. Although the Motherwell is an abstract painting, its forms do bear some resemblance to a silhouette, explaining why it ended up in the same visual neighborhood. Inception's fixation on broad geometric qualities can eclipse more important features, though. For example, it is quick to cluster together circular paintings,

> prioritizing the general overall outline shape over the fact that the Holy Family inside one *tondo* might be more appropriately placed next to other images of robed groups of figures. (Lincoln et al 2019a)

At the Yale DH Lab, Peter Leonard and Doug Duhaime decided to fully embrace the twin challenges of dimensionality reduction and featurisation in the development of the dynamic, interactive PixPlot viewer (2018). Pixplot is a tool into which one can load and explore – by panning and zooming – tens of thousands of images. Like the NGA project, Pixplot makes use of UMAP, but Leonard and Duhaime stay with the topological structure that the algorithm produces based on adjustable parameter settings rather than force it into a grid structure. Leonard describes the result as a 'semantic field' of images, which reveals continuities between feature clusters as you traverse it through a web browser. And yet, there is no one embedding result.

> this dimensionality reduction is always contingent and arbitrary and actually stochastic … So when you're doing UMAP, there are some defaults, but there are many levers you can pull. You can pull a lever that says, 'Take account of more neighbours in the high dimensional space when you then compress, or take account of fewer' … instead of having a static visualization of positionality, you could have a world where, with certain parameters for dimensionality reduction, you would get the cups near the saucers and in other parameters, you'd get the cups near the bowls. (Leonard 2023)

Both the dimensionality reduction parameters and the featurisation parameters are potentially mutable and the fact is that outcomes are somewhat arbitrary. This idea that a curator or researcher can intervene or 'pull levers' to see the collection in different ways provides agency and opens opportunities for the kind of shifting kaleidoscope view that Treharne values. Both approaches, in different ways, inspire and facilitate a critical examination of classification in libraries, archives, museums and academic fields of study.

Classification lessons

There are two primary genres of classification problem that the project teams mentioned in this case study have encountered. One appears when, trying to train an algorithm to understand existing classification schemes, it fails because those existing classification schemes are incorrect or inadequate. The other appears when a pretrained model is used that has – built into it – assumptions about how things ought to be classified and organised that are problematic in many ways. A close look at the lessons learned about classification by 'Stanford Global Currents' and those of other projects in libraries, archives and museums that make use of the techniques of segmentation and reconfiguration of collections based on visual features, point to ways that computer vision can contribute to a critical assessment of discovery systems.

Treharne (2022) found that the 'Stanford Global Currents' project revealed to her how unhelpful contemporary classifications of data can be: 'You have to have [the algorithm] distinguish between things that we categorise as the same thing when, in fact, they are not at all the same thing.' An example of this problem arose when determining which examples should define the class *litterae notabiliores*. *Litterae notabiliores* are often decorated with flourishes and are visual cues for the beginning of a new textual item. The team soon discovered that the class *litterae notabiliores* contained at least three different types of visual cues for the start of a new paragraph. And *litterae notabiliores* as a category was difficult to distinguish from the 'enlarged initials' category because both are enlarged initials. *Litterae notabiliores* can be very large initials when at the beginning of a text or they can be smaller, pen-drawn initials indicating a new 'paragraph' or section.

Another class that challenged their assumptions about which information retrieval devices are most important in medieval manuscripts was rubrics. Rubrics are titles of new texts or important sections of text, almost always in red in the body of the text. The algorithm trained on examples of rubrics ended up finding other similar elements, like numeration systems, that were red, but not rubrics. As with the application of the *litterae notabiliores* class, a computer vision algorithm in the hands of a subject expert becomes a versatile instrument that not only speeds up the process of identification of visual elements, making study on a much larger scale possible, but also allows the subject expert to see difference and distinctions with more precision.

Computer vision can, similarly, serve as an instrument in the hands of information professionals who are actively seeking ways to improve cultural awareness in curatorial practices in order to address the legacy problems with textual classification systems and the way they define what can be discovered (see Engseth 2018). It can begin, as in the 'Stanford Global Currents' project, with examining the classification practices of the field. There are striking examples of racial bias in classification made obvious by comparing a search term to the results. Writing about collecting infrastructures, Yanni Loukissas (2019) recounts a presentation in 2015 by Marya McQuirter in which she reveals the way the academic descriptions of artwork that drive the search engine reveal the racism in the curatorial practice. McQuirter demonstrated that searching a Smithsonian online image catalogue for the term *black* would bring up examples of work by African American artists because the curators document racial identity in those descriptions, whereas a search for the term *white* brings up little about race. Dominique Luster (2021) describes this in terms of the dual problems of white normativity, in which whiteness appears neutral/natural/right, and the white gaze in which the descriptive practices assume that the viewer is white. Applying pretrained classifier algorithms produces similar biases, even if, as in the examples above, the classifier is used for its ability to produce a visual representation of similarity. That layer of high-level visual abstraction that considers a Motherwell painting similar to a silhouette is also capable of propagating the bias that McQuirter revealed in a keyword search in the Smithsonian's online catalogue because the similarity of the visual elements is ultimately defined by the label that a human being has given them.

Biases in pretrained commercial models are difficult to trace because the practice of tracking provenance and documenting data collection are not part of the process. Pretrained computer vision models, as described above, are intended to assign labels or categorise images. Not only are the criteria for selection of those categories entirely different than those applied in libraries, archives and museums, the data collection practices are, too.[12] Thomas Smits and Melvin Wevers (2022) looked closely at six of the widely used benchmark datasets to understand how they were collected and how they were used to train computer vision models. What they discovered is that the image collection was not rooted in any theory of visuality. Rather, it was based on matters of economic convenience including the availability of images, perceived practical applications, and a favouring of categories that can be unambiguously described by text.[13] In other words, they did what was expedient. This approach reflects the big data conceit that not only is more data better but that lots of data render theory dead. It is particularly problematic when it drives image search in commercial services like Google that are guided by business interests rather than operating, as libraries, archives and museums more often do, in the interest of the public good.[14] But libraries, archives and museums are also often driven by expediency and expense. And legacy problems with classification systems are expensive to solve. With visual materials, as Benjamin Lee (2021) has argued, biases are also propagated through the long history of digitisation practices even before machine learning enters the process.

Conclusion: democratising access

Computer vision and other applications of AI are understood in the context of computer science in terms of automation and optimisation. But these tools in the hands of librarians, curators, artists, designers and scholars more often drive critical encounters with the systems that organise, classify, restrict and confine access to cultural heritage. In our attempts to train machines to see as we do, our own biases and normative assumptions are revealed. This tension between the stochastic machine and the specialised academic training that we impart to it is, as in the 'Stanford Global Currents' project, encouraging a more pluralistic approach to interpretation with an underlying motivation of liberating the objects of study to better provide access to cultural heritage.

The 'Stanford Global Currents' project challenged assumptions about the interpretation of manuscript materials. The collaborative nature of the project meant that people who had never encountered medieval manuscripts before were seeing them and sharing their experiences with the research team. The Stanford team reflected on this as a design opportunity in the white paper: 'The team at Stanford will determine if these initial audience responses can be employed in the design of better interpretative frameworks for digital repositories that present complex early textual materials, often to interested viewers who have little or no expertise in paleography, codicology, and modern methods of curation and display' (Treharne 2016, 8).

At the Harvard Art Museums, Jeff Steward, the Director of Digital Infrastructure and Emerging Technology, has similar motivations. His institution holds about 250,000 art objects. 'When you run the numbers', says Steward (2022), 'it's less than 1% that is ever physically on view'. Much of the material has been digitised, but the cataloguing remains very thin. This problem of the cataloguing backlog is common at institutions that hold unique objects. At https://ai.harvardartmuseums.org, Steward created a space where the digital images of items in the collection can be searched based on terms applied by pretrained computer algorithms. But rather than attempting to reduce the machine-generated labels to the top three terms, Steward allows the patron to see competing results from four different commercial services, including the confidence levels for each tag. When machine-generated labels are used in existing information retrieval systems, an opportunity to engage with 'seeing' the image is lost. As Steward describes it, the academic descriptions that accompany objects in the museum are very subjective. They reflect the interpretation of the curator, based on their expert training. Exposing the variety of tags assigned by the commercial algorithms, including the confidence level, reveals uncertainty. In Steward's words, this 'exposes people to the idea that it is alright to have an opinion' (2022).

Peter Leonard has taken image discovery in a different direction with something he calls 'evocative search' based on the dual text–image model Contrastive Language–Image Pretraining (CLIP; Radford et al 2021), designed to predict a natural language caption to an image. Whereas ImageNet – the training data behind the Inception model used in projects described earlier – is based on labels and assumes the goal of object identification, the training data for CLIP is descriptive; it is taken from the many caption–image pairs available on the internet. For Leonard, this means image search is open to adjectives and adverbs rather than things.

> [With ImageNet] you could look for big categories like animal, but you can't look for wildness. You can't look for solitude[. T]he examples we've done with Stanford campus photographs are 'together with friends' or 'a formal affair'. What's nice about that is you're not looking for tie. You're not looking for dress. You're not looking for tuxedo. You're not looking for candle at dinner … you're searching a pixel distribution with a linguistic distribution, which is really powerful. And it's what we are thinking about when we talk about evocative search. (Leonard 2023)

Making the wealth of cultural heritage objects accessible, whether to research or public engagement broadly, requires much more than digitising them and presenting them as one-to-one virtual replicas of each piece online. For Peter Leonard and Jeff Steward, albeit in different ways, it also means extracting visual elements, maximising the capabilities of digital display, cutting through the narrowly academic descriptions of the objects in the catalogue, and exposing the subjectivity of human and machine descriptions. While these experiments going on within libraries, archives, museums and galleries to provide access to the full extent of the catalogue may seem worlds away from the interests of a Stanford professor and Welsh medievalist specialising in manuscript studies, they intersect around the possibilities of computer vision to influence interpretation. Since the 'Stanford Global Currents' project concluded, Treharne has continued her work exploring digital interpretative frameworks, the phenomenology of the digital environment and the phenomenology of the book.

Notes

1. https://parker.stanford.edu/parker/.
2. HTR relies on more advanced machine learning techniques than OCR, like recurrent neural networks, convolutional neural networks and, more recently, transformer models. These models are capable of handling sequences and variations, which is necessary for the way we currently approach the task of recognising handwriting.
3. Research in the applications of computer vision to manuscripts continues to make significant strides. See, for example, *In Codice Ratio*, a transcription project focused on the Vatical Secret Archives that was presented at the Fantastic Futures Conference at Stanford University, 2019. www.inf.uniroma3.it/db/icr/index.html.
4. www.ai.rug.nl/~lambert/Monk-collections-english.html.
5. The original project title was 'Invisible Australians'.
6. A recent example, launched in spring 2023, is 'Machines reading maps', a project that enables text search within maps and uses a similar gallery view in the Luna implementation to present the search results as snippets of text in maps that cascade down the page as they load.
7. https://cmoa.org/teenie.
8. This process was confirmed in conversation with Zaria Howard (2019), a student at the time, who worked with Kyle McDonald in 2017 at the Studio for Creative Inquiry on the Teenie Harris Photography Archive at the Carnegie Museum of Art.
9. See an example image cluster. Accessed 5 January 2024. www.flickr.com/photos/creativeinquiry/34456612652/in/album-72157681593431871/.
10. See Leonard (2016).
11. The project team included Sarah Reiff Conell (University of Pittsburgh, Department of History of Art and Architecture), Lingdong Huang (Carnegie Mellon University, STUDIO for Creative Inquiry), Golan Levin (Carnegie Mellon University, STUDIO for Creative Inquiry) and Matthew Lincoln (Carnegie Mellon University Libraries). You can see the results at https://nga-neighbors.library.cmu.edu/essay.
12. As noted in Chapter 1, The National Archives (UK), Eun Seo Jo and Timit Gebru have highlighted the potential advantages of bringing archival data collection practices into conversation with the machine learning community.
13. The Smits and Wevers (2022) study also addresses the temporal bias in the image datasets. A critical and damning point they make is that the way these benchmark datasets and the technology they are enabling are presented in the literature obscures the power and subjective choices of its creators.
14. For an examination of the racialisation of classifying people both in commercial and public information systems, see Safiya Noble's *Algorithms of Oppression* (2018).

References

Albritton, B. 2022. 'Interview for the "Stanford Global Currents" project'. Interview by Catherine Nicole Coleman, 10 March.

di Lenardo, I., Seguin, B.L.A. and Kaplan, F. 2016. 'Visual patterns discovery in large databases of paintings'. Digital Humanities 2016, Kraków, Poland, July 11–16, 2016. https://infoscience.epfl.ch/record/220638.

Duhaime, D. and Leonard, P. 2018. 'PixPlot' Yale Digital Humanities Lab. Accessed January, 2023. https://github.com/YaleDHLab/pix-plot.

Engseth, E. 2018. 'Cultural competency: A framework for equity, diversity, and inclusion in the archival profession in the United States', *The American Archivist*, 81(2):460–82.
Howard, Z. 2019. 'Experiments with the Teenie Harris archive'. Phone interview by Nicole Coleman, 2 February.
Kee, K. and Compeau, T., eds. 2019. *Seeing the Past with Computers: Experiments with augmented reality and computer vision for history*. Ann Arbor, MI: University of Michigan Press.
Lee, B. 2021. 'Compounded mediation: A data archaeology of the *Newspaper Navigator* dataset', *Digital Humanities Quarterly*, 15(4):1–44.
Leonard, P. 2016. 'Semantic image clustering with neural networks'. Accessed 9 February 2022. www.pleonard.net/semantic-image-clustering-with-neural-networks/.
Leonard, P. 2023. 'PixPlot', Interview by Catherine Nicole Coleman, 27 June.
Lincoln, M. et al 2019a. 'National neighbors: Distant viewing the National Gallery of Art's collection of collections'. Available at: https://nga-neighbors.library.cmu.edu.
Lincoln, M. et al 2019b. 'About'. https://nga-neighbors.library.cmu.edu/about.
Loukissas, Y.A. 2019. *All Data Are Local: Thinking critically in a data-driven society*. Cambridge, MA: MIT Press.
Luster, D. 2021. 'AI, metadata creation and historic bias'. Lecture, NISO Plus 2021, 23 February. Available at: https://nisoplus2021.cadmore.media.
Luster, D., Levin, G. and Record, C. 2018. Library AI conversations speaker series, Stanford Libraries, 21 August.
Manovich, L. 2009. 'Cultural analytics: Visualising cultural patterns in the era of "more media"'. Available at: http://manovich.net/index.php/projects/cultural-analytics-visualizing-cultural-patterns.
McInnes, L. and Healy, J. 2018. 'UMAP: Uniform manifold approximation and projection for dimension reduction'. arXiv:1802.03426.
Noble, S.U. 2018. *Algorithms of Oppression*. New York: New York University Press.
Radford, A., et al. 2021. 'Learning transferable visual models from natural language supervision'. Available at: https://doi.org/10.48550/arXiv.2103.00020.
Resig, J. 2014. 'Using computer vision to increase the research potential of photo archives', *Journal of Digital Humanities*, 3(2).
Sherratt, T. and Bagnall, K. 2019. 'The people inside'. In *Seeing the Past: Experiments with computer vision and augmented reality in history*, edited by K. Kee and T. Compeau,11–31. Ann Arbor, MI: University of Michigan Press.
Smits, T. and Wevers, M. 2022. 'The agency of computer vision models as optical instruments', *Visual Communication*, 21(2):329–49.
Snydman, S., Sanderson, R. and Cramer, T. 2015. 'The International Image Interoperability Framework (IIIF): A community and technology approach for web-based images'. In *Proceedings of the IS&T Archiving Conference 2015*, 16–21. https://doi.org/10.2352/issn.2168-3204.2015.12.1.art00005.
Steward, J. 2022. 'Interview for Aeolian Case Study 2'. Zoom interview by Catherine Nicole Coleman, 2 March.
Treharne, E. 2021. *Perceptions of Medieval Manuscripts: The phenomenal book*. Oxford: Oxford University Press.
Treharne, E. 2016. 'Global Currents: Cultures of literary networks, 1050–1900'. White paper. Accessed 1 February 2022. https://securegrants.neh.gov/publicquery/main.aspx?f=1&gn=HJ-50187-14.
Treharne, E. 2022. 'Interview for the "Stanford Global Currents" project'. Interview by Catherine Nicole Coleman, 10 March.
Uricchio, W. 2011. 'The algorithmic turn: Photosynth, augmented reality and the changing implications of the image', *Visual Studies*, 26(1):25–35.

3

Machine learning at the National Library of Norway

Javier de la Rosa

The National Library of Norway (Nasjonalbiblioteket) stands as a beacon of cultural heritage and intellectual pursuit within the Norwegian landscape. As technology continues to reshape the world, the library has recognised the transformative potential of machine learning in redefining its operations, services and accessibility. In this context, the Nasjonalbiblioteket has embarked on a journey to leverage machine learning to revolutionise its role in preserving Norway's rich literary and cultural heritage, while enhancing user experiences and expanding the reach of its collections.

The Nasjonalbiblioteket has long been a custodian of Norway's intellectual wealth, amassing an extensive collection of books, manuscripts, maps, photographs and other valuable resources. However, as the digital age ushers in a new era of information dissemination and consumption, the library recognises the need to adapt and embrace cutting-edge technologies to meet the evolving needs of Norwegian society. Machine learning, with its capacity for data analysis and algorithmic learning, presents a plethora of opportunities. By harnessing the power of machine learning, the Nasjonalbiblioteket can automate labour-intensive processes, optimise resource allocation, improve information discovery and strengthen accessibility to its collections. This integration of machine learning technology holds the potential to transform the library's operations, ensuring its continued relevance and impact in the digital age. As a result, the Nasjonalbiblioteket Artificial Intelligence Lab (NB AI-Lab)[1] was formally founded as an independent unit in 2018. It was tasked with investigating and providing solutions based on the latest advances in the field of AI while leveraging the extensive library collections and collaborating with other units within the library, such as the Language Bank (Språkbanken). We understood the assignment and elevated the NB AI-Lab and the Nasjonalbiblioteket to the top of the world in terms of research and application of AI in libraries.

Today, the Nasjonalbiblioteket counts over 500 employees distributed physically between Oslo in the south of the country and Mo i Rana at the edge of the polar circle, and a number of people working mostly remotely. The NB AI-Lab reports directly to the director of the library, employs four people working full time, and a temporary visitor researcher position. In the short time it has been in existence we have utilised our rather limited local infrastructure as well as external cloud computing resources through grants and agreements to train machine learning models and create value for the library and Norwegian society. We have also contributed strongly to the establishment of international networks on AI for archives, libraries and museums. Together with Stanford Libraries we founded AI4LAM,[2] an international, participatory community focused on advancing the use of AI in, for and by libraries, archives and museums. With the Bibliothèque nationale de France, we helped establish the Conference of European National Librarians AI in Libraries Network Group,[3] which aims at enhancing the utilisation of AI by fostering comprehension, utilisation, collaboration and standardisation among institutions in the field of AI, and identifying key areas of relevance for libraries. Our international contributions are significant, also through the series of Fantastic Futures AI conferences, which started in our library in Oslo.

One important aspect in the success of such a unit within the Nasjonalbiblioteket is the freedom and agency that the researchers and engineers possess. There is no formal process for NB AI-Lab members to follow in order to start working on a prototype or to explore a specific research topic. In fact, we share an 'all ideas are welcome' mentality that fosters new developments that ultimately might lead to new services. Brainstorming sessions, prototyping, and trial and error are built in the core of the laboratory. Interestingly, other units might collaborate by exposing their use cases, needs or problems, or by developing the user interfaces or integrations needed for the machine learning proofs of concept to become usable services.

AI-assisted workflows

One way in which machine learning is making a significant impact at Nasjonalbiblioteket is by helping library staff deal with some of their more tedious tasks more efficiently. Cataloguing, metadata extraction and content classification are crucial but time-consuming activities that require meticulous attention to detail. By training machine learning algorithms on vast collections of data, the Nasjonalbiblioteket has streamlined some of these processes, reducing manual effort and allowing staff to focus on more specialised and value-added tasks, such as curating unique collections or engaging with our patrons. Two specific cases in which the NB AI-Lab has provided value is by helping in the identification of front pages after bulk scanning newspapers, and in the cataloguing of resources potentially relevant for the Sámi population.

The Sámi Bibliography

The Sámi Bibliography[4] holds metadata for publications relevant to the Sámi community in Norway, and a special office at the Nasjonalbiblioteket maintains it. Until recently, the workflow involved the physical transportation of publications in Norway to and from this office. Both the transport in itself and the physical handling and reading of the items is labour intensive, and those operations do not by themselves contribute to the bibliography. Most of the items handled by the office also exist as digital versions within the collection at the library. Moreover, only a very small fraction of the total number of publications are relevant to the Sámi Bibliography.

The NB AI-Lab ran an experiment to investigate whether this workflow could benefit from the support of an AI-based system. Building a model on records included and excluded from the existing Sámi Bibliography should make it possible to assist the workflow in the office by suggesting candidates for the Sámi Bibliography based on analysing the content of the digital versions of the items. This process could be carried out both on historical digitised volumes and new publications delivered to the library within the legal deposit agreements. However, makes a publication relevant is not strictly defined and it is usually up to the expert opinion of the bibliographers to determine upon the close examination of the items.

In order to produce a model capable of predicting whether a record in the Nasjonalbiblioteket catalogue could potentially be of relevance for the Sámi Bibliography, we first had to collect a curated dataset with samples of entries already in the bibliography (the positive class), and samples not contained and ideally deemed not relevant for the Sámi Bibliography (the negative class). Next, we developed a series of binary classifiers capable of assigning a probability to any given text, indicating its relevance for inclusion in the Sámi Bibliography.

	author	title	year	lang	urn	label	text	split
0	Oates, Joyce Carol	Enkes fortelling	2012	nob	digibok_20113011408113	0	EN ENKES FORTELLING \nOVERSATT AV TONE FORMO O...	train
1	Søe, Synnøve	Fars	1990	nob	digibok_2009071001020	0	FARS \nFARS \nTrykk og innbinding: Moestue Bøk...	train
2	Miller, Rebecca	Pippa Lees hemmelige liv	2010	nob	digibok_2014110308137	0	OYERSATT AV MERETE ALFSEN \nPAX FORLAG A/S, OS...	train
3	Wilder, Laura Ingalls	Det vesle huset på prærien	1994	nob	digibok_2008020400053	0	Det vesle huset pa prerien\nDet vesle huset på...	train
4	Lindkjølen, Hans	Viddas folk	1991	nob	digibok_2007030502001	1	Heimen min er i hjertet mitt og den flytter me...	train
...	...	...	...	...	...	...	...	...
6595	Hammer, Harald Kaasa	Bibliografi til nordnorsk kirkehistorie	1990	nob	digibok_2017112948079	1	Under arbeidet kom det fram at overraskende ma...	test
6596	Inches, Alison	Storesøster Dora!	2012	nob	digibok_2013071508040	0	Gjenfortalt av Alison Inches illustrert av Dav...	test
6597	Lie, Tove	Jordsang	1977	nob	digibok_2012100106121	0	Tove Lie \nJordsang \nDIKT \nTove Lie \nFORLAG...	test
6598	Applegate, K.A.	Prøven	2003	nob	digibok_2009060904067	0	1. Invasjonen 2. Gjesten \n3. Nærkontakt 4. Bu...	test
6599	Lie, Erik	Ut i media!	2000	nob	digibok_2009022304025	0	Dette heftet tar sikte på å gi en del rå om h...	test

Figure 3.1 View of a few records in the dataset. © Javier de la Rosa.

Using metadata from the catalogue records, we compiled a dataset that contains the plain text data of books and periodicals from 1674 to 2020, although most of the records are from 1925 to 2020 (see Figures 3.1 and 3.2). The 6,600 records are split into two sets, one for training and the other for testing, containing 4,950 (75%) and 1,650 (25%) records, respectively. The dataset is balanced in terms of how many records are assigned the positive and negative classes, although some noise is expected in this labelling. The total number of words in the dataset is over 250 million (257,732,593).

In recent times, artificial neural networks trained using deep learning techniques have achieved the best results in tasks related to the processing of natural language. In 2021, our lab released the first such neural network trained exclusively for the Norwegian language, exhibiting performance

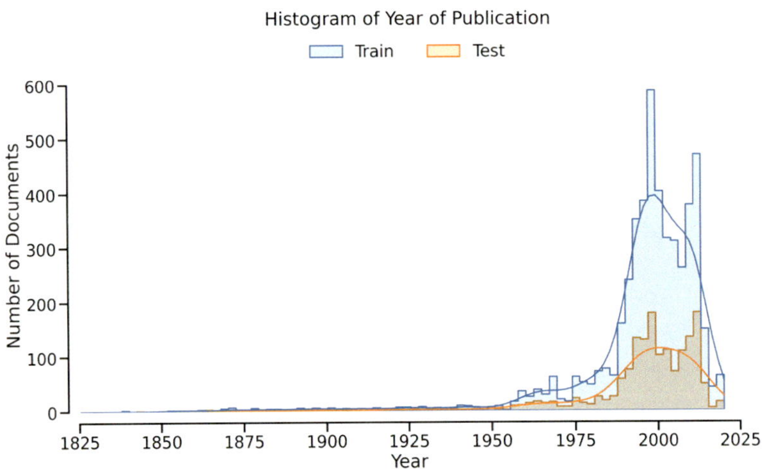

Figure 3.2 Histogram of the years of publication per split in the dataset. © Javier de la Rosa.

that is still unrivalled at the time of writing. NB-BERT (Kummervold et al 2021), as this model was named, surpassed other multilingual models in the classification of sentiments or the identification of named entities in text. Thus, we decided to put NB-BERT to test on the Sámi Bibliography dataset. Unfortunately, this new breed of statistical artefacts for language is usually limited to a handful of words, which is very inconvenient when dealing with entire books. Specifically, the BERT-base architecture upon which NB-BERT is built (Devlin et al 2019) is only able to work with around 500 words at a time. This means that in order to leverage the power of NB-BERT for the classification of records in the Sámi Bibliography, we had to split each text into chunks. Several factors in this chunking affect the performance of the final classifier. We experimented with several of these parameters: the number of words in the chunks, the amount of overlap between any consecutive pair of chunks (defined using a sliding window with an arbitrary width), as well as other internal bits and bolts that need to be adjusted (dropout, learning rate, weight decay, etc.).

In order to assess which set of options performed best, we measured the four rates of any binary classification problem, that is, true and false positive rates, and true and false negative rates, and compared them against a baseline model built using classic text features and logistic regression. As the models trained, we made predictions on the test set to calculate how many times the model was correctly predicting whether a record should or should not belong to the Sámi Bibliography, and how many times the model was mislabelling records as relevant or not. With these rates, we computed a couple of summary metrics that allowed us to compare the different models trained. Specifically, we used the harmonic mean over precision and recall (F1) and Matthew's correlation coefficient (MCC), a couple of metrics that go from zero (for really bad performance) to one (for the best). The evaluation was also done at both the chunk level and the whole record level, depending on the kind of training.

We also evaluated a novel technique that leverages an adjusted version of NB-BERT that learnt to identify passages of text that logically entail each other (Bowman et al 2015). This natural language inference (NLI) approach allowed us to assign a score to every chunk of text based on a list of labels created ad hoc for the task. We then used different threshold values over this score to filter out parts of the training data with the goal of improving the fine-tuning process of the binary classifier. Figure 3.3 shows a summary of the 10 best-performing models after our experiments. While two of the NLI-based methods performed slightly better than the rest, as reported by their F1 score, the MCC score was higher for the models trained normally. Since MCC is, in general, a more

Name (48 visualized)	eval_f1	eval_precisi	eval_recall	eval_mcc ▾	langs	train_on	eval_on	stride	sami_prob
NbAiLab-nb-bert-base	0.9534	0.9259	0.9827	0.921	nob,nno	chunks	records	0.75	0
NbAiLab-nb-bert-base	0.9606	0.9471	0.9746	0.9204	all	records	records	1.	0.7
NbAiLab-nb-bert-base	0.9595	0.9438	0.9758	0.9181	all	chunks	records	0	0
NbAiLab-nb-bert-base	0.9595	0.9438	0.9758	0.9181	all	records	records	1.	0
NbAiLab-nb-bert-base	0.9592	0.9366	0.9831	0.9175	all	chunks	records	1.	0
NbAiLab-nb-bert-base	0.9513	0.9287	0.975	0.9172	nob,nno	chunks	records	1.	0
NbAiLab-nb-bert-base	0.9591	0.9396	0.9794	0.9172	all	chunks	records	0.75	0
NbAiLab-nb-bert-base	0.951	0.9335	0.9693	0.9168	nob,nno	records	records	1.	0.7
NbAiLab-nb-bert-base	0.9507	0.94	0.9616	0.9163	nob,nno	records	records	0.75	0.7
NbAiLab-nb-bert-base	0.9459	0.9372	0.9547	0.916	nob,nno	chunks	chunks	0	0.7

Figure 3.3 Top 10 best-performing models based on the MCC score. © Javier de la Rosa.

reliable metric for binary classification (Chicco and Jurman 2020), and since the NLI approach was a two-step pipeline involving doing inference twice plus a prior non-negligible training, we decided to choose the first model based solely on MCC. Our best model was trained on chunks of approximately 500 words of Bokmål and Nynorsk text with a sliding window of 25%.[5] As shown in Figure 3.4, it is important to note that there was no difference between including or excluding the few texts in the Sámi language in the dataset.

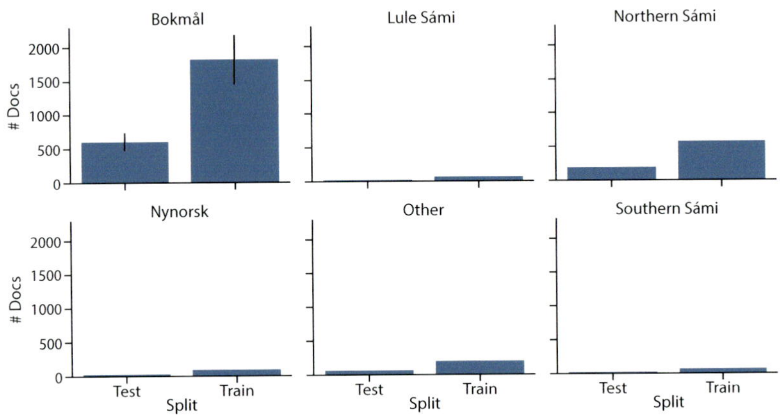

Figure 3.4 Number of records in the training and test splits per language. Language codes in ISO 639-3: 'eng' for English, 'fin' for Finnish, 'fra' for French, 'ger' for German, 'nno' for Norwegian Nynorsk, 'nob' for Norwegian Bokmål, 'swe' for Swedish, 'sma' for South Sámi, 'sme' for North Sámi and 'smj' for Lule Sámi. © Javier de la Rosa.

From the library catalogue, we made a new non-overlapping subset of over 55,000 records containing textual information from 1980 to 1989. With our well-performing classifier model in place, we generated the predictions for all the corresponding ~7.8 million chunks and established which ones could potentially be of relevance to the Sámi Bibliography. It took a week on a very powerful device to do the inference on the 7,791,233 chunks. A whole record was considered to be of relevance if the majority of its chunks were also considered to be of relevance with a probability over 50%.

With a model to do predictions, and with the predictions of a decade's worth of library records, we put the system up for the ultimate test: the Sámi bibliographers. Built on top of the predictions of the models, we designed a web-based application with a specialised database with metadata and inference results, along with a user service that supports office workflow by displaying a sorted list of documents with average probability scores, allowing browsing, flagging, date selection, viewing IIIF presentations and tagging resolved records.

In early 2022, we deployed the experimental solution to our production environment and gathered feedback from the Sámi Bibliography office to evaluate its performance and usefulness. The feedback guided further development, including the addition of an automated asynchronous inference process for newly accessioned documents and updating the web interface's database. Despite the baseline logistic regression model scoring lower than our best neural model (0.84 vs 0.92), we decided to deploy the baseline predictions to strike a balance between record availability and perceived accuracy. This experience highlighted the importance of testing on real users over abstract metrics, and the concept of 'good enough', which we also verified in our newspaper front-page detector.

Newspaper front-page detection

The Nasjonalbiblioteket is well known for its immense digitisation efforts. Millions of newspapers, books, photographs, manuscripts, musical records and many other types of media have been digitised in a streamlined process involving manual labour aided by automatic machinery.

One prevalent task in these digitisation pipelines involves bundling together consecutive newspapers, thus facilitating their collective scanning by a machine to avoid the need for frequent switching. However, this practice presents the challenge of accurately determining the boundaries between individual newspapers within the bundle. Currently, human operators address this issue by manually tagging the endpoints of each newspaper, a time-consuming task that calls for automated alternatives.

In order to minimise this burden on human staff, we decided to conduct an experiment centred on exploring the potential of machine learning by leveraging image recognition techniques. Our aim was to identify and isolate front pages automatically. The initial pages in newspapers are typically very distinct from the rest of the pages and could serve as clear indicators demarcating the end of one newspaper and the commencement of another within each bundle.

For an effective classifier for this task, a high-quality dataset is crucial. Our iterative process involved refining datasets and testing different foundation models for computer vision (Bommasani et al 2021). The final dataset consists of 59,000 newspapers from different publishers and years. It includes front pages, back pages and four randomly selected middle pages from each newspaper, each labelled accordingly: front, middle, back. The best-performing model was Google's Vision Transformer (Dosovitskiy et al 2021), with a final accuracy of almost 95% in the 1:4:1 ratio training set, which we deemed good enough at first. Figures 3.5a, b and c show the performance plots during training for the accuracy, F1 and loss scores.

When evaluated on full newspapers, the accuracy of the model actually increased slightly. It went up to 96% with all labels and 99.6% when just separating between the front page and not the front page. However, although the accuracy is reasonably high, bundles are often very large. That is, even if a single page is misclassified, the whole bundle is considered incorrect. Since the average bundle contains 383 pages, an estimate of bundle-level accuracy is, therefore $0.996^{383} = 22\%$. This is way too low to fully automate the task. Instead of attempting endless incremental improvements to the dataset and the model, we took advantage of some extra information we had about the nature of the data and the process itself.

The model assigns confidence levels (probabilities) to its predictions for each class. Therefore, when the model predicts a back page, it might indicate that the next page would likely be a front page. Moreover, the first page in a bundle is always a front page, allowing for easy comparison with subsequent pages. Front pages also always occur on odd-numbered pages, while back pages are on even-numbered pages. We also trained a separate model solely on front pages, which enhanced prediction robustness as we only used the top part of the page where the logo and masthead of the newspaper are usually shown. The bundle identifier provides extra information on the expected number of newspapers in a bundle, aiding in prediction management. Figure 3.6 shows a diagram of the full process.

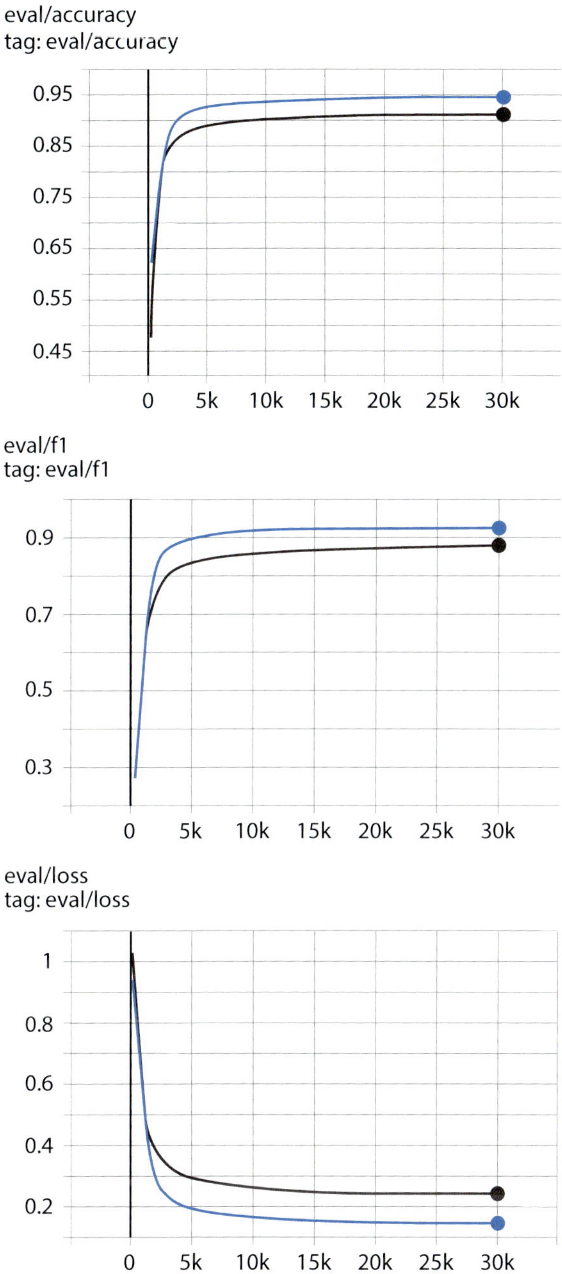

Figures 3.5a, 3.5b, 3.5c Graphs of performance throughout training. Model with images rescaled to 384×384 (https://huggingface.co/google/vit-large-patch32-384) in blue, model with images rescaled to 224 (https://huggingface.co/google/vit-large-patch16-224) in grey. © Javier de la Rosa.

In this scenario, every page is run through each of the two models, generating a set of probabilities of the page being front, middle or back, as well as a vector representing the contents of the page. After all the pages are evaluated, all the information for all the pages is used to rank the pages in the bundle, with all front pages (hopefully) ending up at the top. Using the bundle identifier, we then select the most likely pages and declare those to be front pages. Using this method, the system is able to correctly predict 65,072 out of all the 66,750 bundles ever processed at Nasjonalbiblioteket. That is a bundle-level accuracy of 97.5%.

Through collaboration with another unit at Nasjonalbiblioteket dedicated to all things text and in charge of the manual marking of the front pages during the scanning process, we deployed the system in production. This was the first example of an AI system being used in a production line at the Nasjonalbiblioteket. Unfortunately, despite the system being at least as good as its human counterparts, the integration into their workflow was not as seamless as we had hoped. It caused a bit of disruption in their processes as it apparently took just too long for the users to be waiting on a prediction by the system before they could continue their work. We are still exploring the possibility of a deployment using special hardware to run model inference, but the solution might then not be as cost-effective as planned.

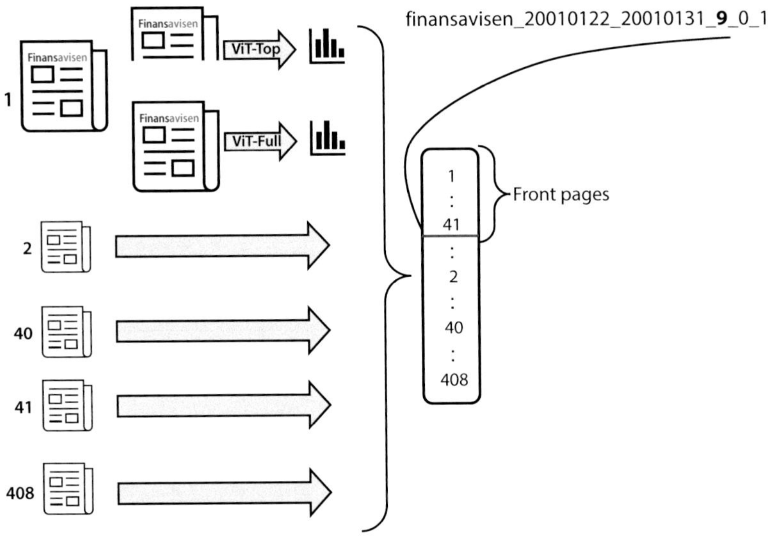

Figure 3.6 Diagram including all prior knowledge we encoded into the system. © Rolv-Arild Braaten.

Collection discovery

While integrating production-level AI-based solutions into the internal workflows of a national library is hardly a breeze, facilitating collection discovery through the main website has proven more successful. Through a decade-long digitisation effort, the Nasjonalbiblioteket has built up a large-scale digital collection of all media in the Norwegian languages. As such collections grow, discoverability becomes a difficult task. Metadata may be missing or insufficient, and the content may be difficult to search within. Machine learning can enhance information discovery and access within the Nasjonalbiblioteket. By analysing user behaviour, preferences and historical data, machine learning algorithms can provide personalised recommendations to library users, guiding them towards relevant resources that align with their interests. This personalised approach fosters a more engaging and enriching user experience, allowing individuals to explore a diverse range of perspectives and discover hidden gems within the library's extensive collections. By leveraging recommendation systems powered by machine learning, the Nasjonalbiblioteket could promote serendipitous learning and facilitate the discovery of knowledge for its users. However, collecting and capitalising user data is a sensitive topic within Europe and is heavily regulated under several data protection directives, such as the General Data Protection Regulation (Intersoft Consulting n.d.).

In this context, and inspired by other efforts in similarity-based services (Duhaime 2023), the Digital Outreach and the AI Lab units at Nasjonalbiblioteket joined forces to conceive Maken, a project for user-oriented continuous discovery via embedding similarity. Maken, an ambiguous Norwegian word that roughly translates to 'the matching other', aims at creating useful services for a variety of user segments and their needs. Informed by previous surveys and usage data collected on the Digital Library services, our core personas were defined as ancestry researchers, authors, journalists and patron-facing librarians. We defined these personas to acquire a better understanding of the context and motivations of our users, and to help us recruit the relevant test users to properly evaluate the performance of a similarity-based discovery service. In parallel with the definition of these roles, we envisioned a brand new AI-driven interface to help users find content within collections, while at the same time evaluating the success of the development efforts in this task. We wanted to create connections between content items, with AI's interpretations of the content as navigation for discovery, radically unlike any metadata-driven or 'text query'-oriented approach. While the user-facing web-based app needed to be responsive and look and feel fast, handling similarity searches for over half a million books and more than a million images was a tremendous technical challenge. For the purpose of the first prototype version of Maken, and with the goal of releasing an early version as soon as possible, we limited ourselves to a subset of the books and image collections that were freely available to the general Norwegian public.

We then extracted vector representations from both the full text of the books and the images in the collections using machine learning models specially designed for feature extraction. For a single item, these models produce a representation of the content in the form of a long vector (embedding) that can later be used to look for similarities in the Euclidean space against the vectors of other items. Specifically, we used a Doc2Vec approach for text (Mikolov et al 2013a; Mikolov et al 2013b), crafting our own model built on a subset of the catalogue using Gensim (Rehurek and Sojka 2011).[6] For the image embeddings, after experimenting with more modern techniques, we settled on a pre-trained Inception v3 and collected the vectors of the next-to-last layer (Szegedy et al 2016). These vector representations were then ingested into an experimental Elasticsearch-based index with vector support to accommodate rich real-time queries. An internal first version of a fully functioning prototype was successfully released in December 2020 and it has been working uninterrupted ever since (see Figures 3.7 and 3.8).

Since interacting with users requires compliance with privacy regulations (GDPR), we formed a working group inside the project to ensure compliance with all regulations and laws. We did interviews and prototyped user testing with people from our user panel to discover possible use cases and the user experiences of the service. We have been demonstrating Maken to various target groups, tracking the use of the service, and have been listening to real-world user feedback since the launch in November 2021.

However, after the successful release to the public, many new books and images were added to the catalogue. This progressively impacted the user experience of the service, which deteriorated as the collection grew, since more and more items were not yet in vector form. In order to accommodate the constant in-flow of new material from library collections into Maken, we had to devise a system to automatically

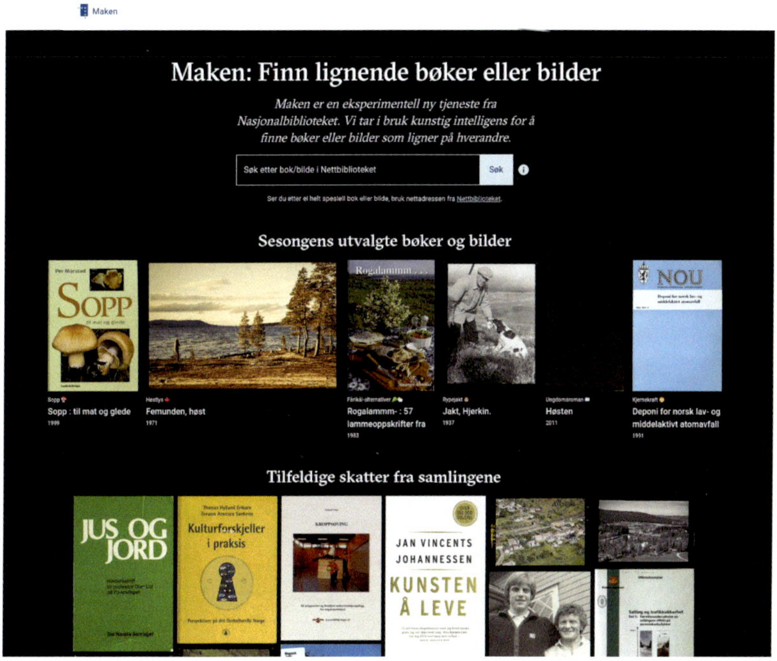

Figure 3.7 Frontpage of Maken at https://nb.no/maken. © Javier de la Rosa.

update the embeddings for both books and images on a weekly basis (see Figure 3.9). Fortunately, the choice of somewhat old but very performant techniques and models to produce the embeddings allowed us to process the contents in-house at sufficient speed and using only CPU cores, which are much cheaper than the specialised hardware on which most modern machine learning models run. The core of this new weekly updates feature is the IIIF server that serves the entire library (Snydman, Sanderson and Cramer 2015), and an internal ALTO XML server that the library uses to serve the visually impaired users of the library (Library of Congress 2022). With IIIF we supply images on demand, and with the ALTO XML server we extract the plain text needed to feed the vectorisers that ingest embeddings into the vector database to keep it up to date. The new system to automatically update the contents is planned for release by the end of 2023. With it, all software will be released to the public in the hope that other institutions can implement their own Maken similarity service.

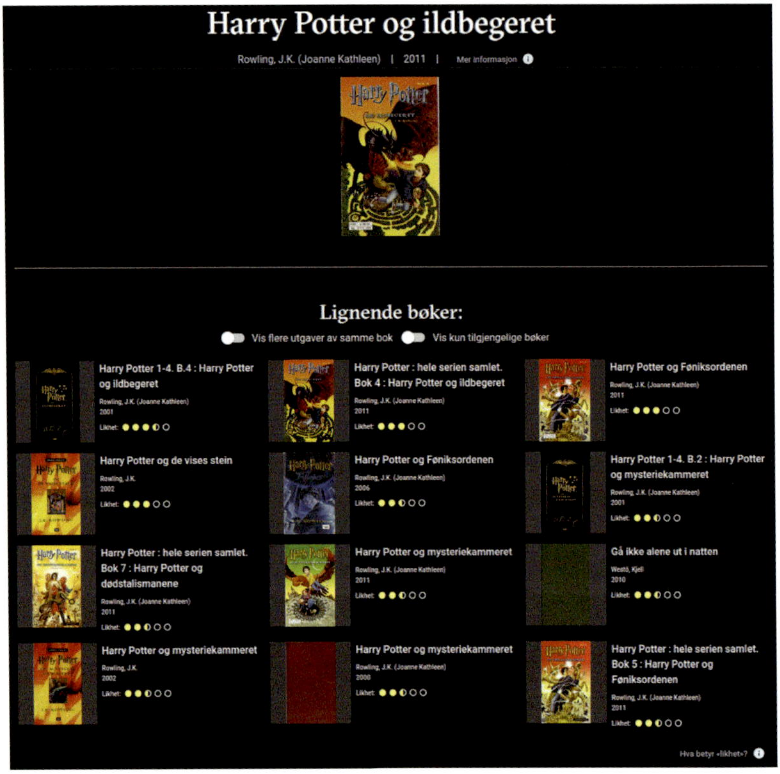

Figure 3.8 Detail of items similar to the Norwegian edition of *Harry Potter and the Goblet of Fire*. © Javier de la Rosa.

Giving back to society

In addition to sharing code, the Nasjonalbiblioteket actively contributes to the open data movement by creating and disseminating valuable datasets. One notable example is the Norwegian Colossal Corpus (NCC; Kummervold, Wetjen and de la Rosa 2022), a comprehensive collection of text data that encompasses a wide range of Norwegian language sources. This dataset serves as a valuable resource for researchers, linguists and language technology enthusiasts, enabling advancements in various natural language processing tasks and fostering a deeper understanding of the Norwegian language.

Moreover, the Nasjonalbiblioteket goes beyond datasets and actively contributes to the development of large language models. Building on top of the NCC, the AI-Lab created and shared NB-BERT (Kummervold

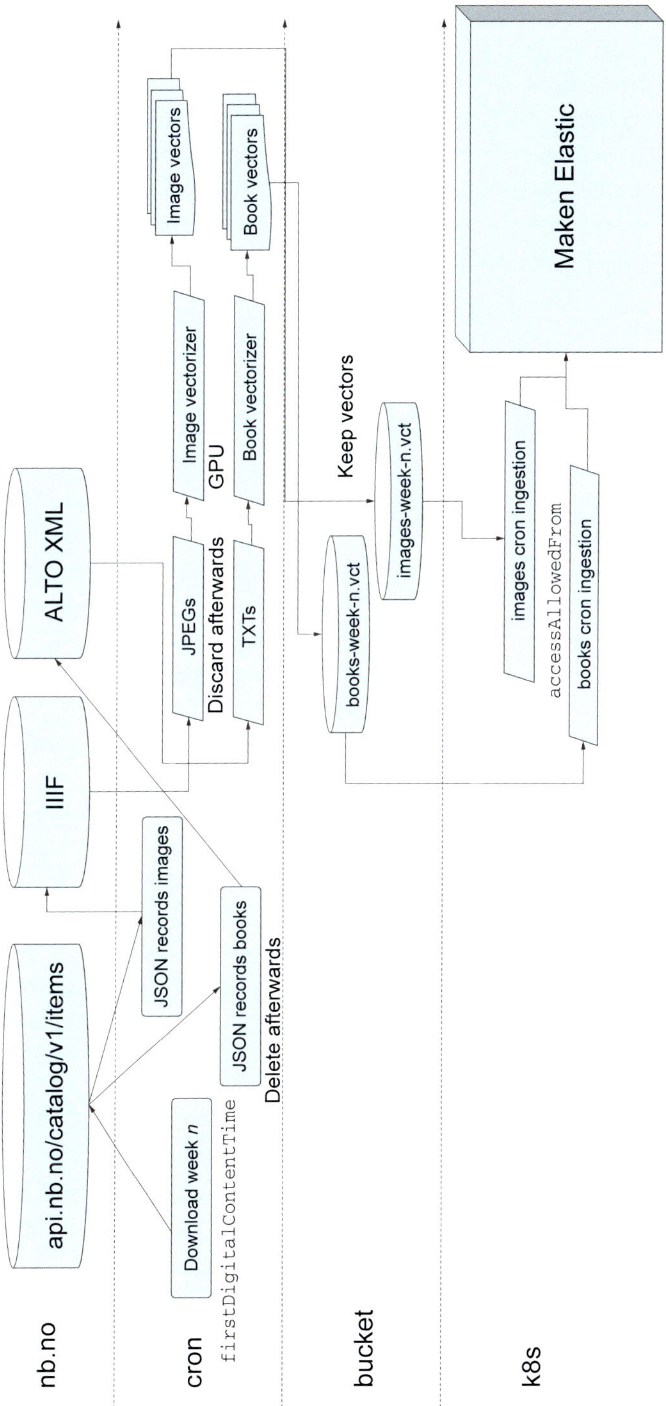

Figure 3.9 Maken weekly updates diagram. © Javier de la Rosa.

et al 2021), a Norwegian version of the BERT (Bidirectional Encoder Representations from Transformers) model. NB-BERT offers pretrained language representations specifically tailored to the nuances and characteristics of the Norwegian language. By providing access to such models, the National Library of Norway empowers researchers, developers and organisations to leverage state-of-the-art language models in their Norwegian language-based applications, thereby fostering innovation and advancing language technology within the Norwegian context.

The Norwegian Colossal Corpus

Large language models like BERT require extensive textual sources to accurately represent language usage (Devlin et al 2019). However, acquiring vast corpora sizes is challenging for lower-resource languages like Norwegian, which has a relatively small population and two official written forms: Bokmål and Nynorsk. Supporting both forms is crucial since the Norwegian Language Act (Lovdata 2022) mandates public entities to produce at least 25% of their publicly available documents in Nynorsk.

Until recently, utilising language models for languages like Norwegian was limited to the use of multilingual models. An example of such a model is the multilingual version of BERT (mBERT), which was trained on Wikipedia dumps containing 104 different languages, including Norwegian Bokmål and Norwegian Nynorsk. Although the specific size of the Norwegian text in the corpus was not explicitly stated, our estimate suggests it ranged between 0.5 GB and 1.0 GB of text, equivalent to approximately 70 million to 140 million words. Notably, around 80% of the Norwegian text was in the Bokmål variant. As the main role of the Nasjonalbiblioteket is to preserve and provide access to all published information in Norway, our collections comprise texts spanning several centuries and reflecting diverse societal uses. A significant portion of these texts has been digitised and made digitally accessible, thanks to a combination of digitisation efforts and the inclusion of born-digital documents through legal deposit agreements. While the collections encompass various types of historical written materials, it has been observed that books, magazines, journals and newspapers (as indicated in Table 3.1) are particularly relevant resources for constructing an appropriate corpus for natural language processing purposes.

As a result, the NCC is a collection of multiple heterogeneous data sources (Kummervold, Wetjen and de la Rosa 2022). All the work in the preparation of the dataset and all the software produced are licensed under the terms of a CC BY-SA 3.0 licence. However, the individual corpora are under different licences. Table 3.1 presents an overview of some of the main characteristics of the sub-corpora and their associated licences. The NCC can be simplified as follows: books and newspapers from the National Library of Norway that are out of copyright; public documents (governmental or otherwise); online newspapers; and Wikipedia. These categories are also reflected in the licences they are published under.

- *Library books and newspapers*. The Nasjonalbiblioteket has had a large and well-established digitisation program in place since 2006. This includes all kinds of printed materials, such as books, newspapers, journals and other small prints. Most of the books included in the NCC are out-of-copyright material, and released under the terms of a CC0 1.0 licence. Newspapers are subject to a special agreement between Nasjonalbiblioteket and the publishers, and are released under the CC BY-NC 2.0 licence. Together, text from these sources account for 6.2 GB and 14.0 GB (860 million and 2 billion words), respectively.
- *Public documents*. The Norwegian Copyright Act (Åndsverkloven; Lovdata 2018) includes an exemption (§14) that allows public entities to freely distribute materials produced as part of their work. This exemption covers a wide range of documents, such as reports, laws, regulations and official translations. Materials made publicly available according to the act were incorporated into the NCC. The government has also introduced the Norwegian License for Open Government Data 2.0 (Norwegian Digitalisation Agency 2023), which facilitates the sharing of public data by providing a licensing framework similar to CC BY-SA. This ensures compliance with copyright regulations while promoting effective dissemination of public materials. Thus, NCC encompasses various sub-corpora that contribute to the richness of the collection. The LovData CD collection offers a comprehensive compilation of legal resources, excluding sensitive material such as court verdicts, with a text volume of 0.4 GB (55 million words). Government reports, propositions and notes from 1995 to 2021 are also included, forming a sub-corpus of 1.1 GB (1.3 billion words). The parliament collections, comprising 8.0 GB of text (1.3 billion words), contain materials that have undergone OCR processing, maintaining a high standard of print quality and accuracy. Additionally, the NCC incorporates public reports from government institutions totalling 3,365 documents and representing 0.5 GB of text (80 million words). Finally, the Målfrid Corpus, obtained through a web crawl, contributes 14.0 GB of text (1.9 billion words) from approximately 9.2 million PDF documents sourced from 311 Norwegian institutions.

Table 3.1 Sub-corpora in the Norwegian Colossal Corpus

Corpus	Licence	Size	Words	Documents	Average words/doc
Government reports	(NLOD 2.0, 2021)	1.1 GB	155,318,754	4,648	33,416
Library books	(CC0 1.0, 2021)	6.2 GB	861,465,907	24,253	35,519
Library newspapers	(CC BY-NC 2.0, 2021)	14.0 GB	2,019,172,625	10,096,424	199
LovData CD	(NLOD 2.0, 2021)	0.4 GB	54,923,432	51,920	1,057
Målfrid collection	(NLOD 2.0, 2021)	14.0 GB	1,905,481,776	6,735,367	282
Newspapers online	(CC BY-NC 2.0, 2021)	3.7 GB	541,481,947	3,695,943	146
Parliament collections	(NLOD 2.0, 2021)	8.0 GB	1,301,766,124	9,528	136,625
Public reports	(NLOD 2.0, 2021)	0.5 GB	80,064,396	3,365	23,793
Wikipedia	(CC BY-SA 3.0, 2021)	1.0 GB	140,992,663	681,973	206
Total		**48.9 GB**	**7,060,667,624**	**21,303,421**	**332**

- *Online newspapers*. The online newspapers section in the NCC is a revised version of the Norwegian Newspaper Corpus, obtained through web crawling by the Norwegian Language Bank (Språkbanken 2022). It includes substantial newspapers from Norway, and its distribution is authorised by publishers under the CC BY-NC 2.0 licence.
- *Wikipedia*. A dump from Wikipedia was downloaded on 20 June 2021. The text contains both Bokmål and Nynorsk, and it was previously distributed by Wikipedia under the CC BY-SA 3.0 licence and accounts for 1 GB of text (141 million words).
- *Excluded sources*. Common Crawl (Common Crawl n.d.) is a non-profit organisation that has been collecting data from the web and providing these archives to the public since 2011. Common Crawl-based datasets are popular for training transformer models and are the basis for the enormous 800 GB The Pile English dataset (Gao et al 2020), the multilingual Open Super-large Crawled Aggregated coRpus (OSCAR; Suárez, Sagot and Romary 2019) and the multilingual Colossal Corpus from Common Crawl (mC4; Raffel et al 2019). OSCAR

contains 4.7 GB (800 million words) of Norwegian Bokmål and 54 MB (9 million words) of Norwegian Nynorsk, while the Norwegian part of the mC4 dataset is roughly 94 GB (14 million words). Unfortunately, their respective licences do not allow for redistribution within the NCC, which we tried to overcome by releasing scripts for the preparation, cleaning, deduplication and formatting of these datasets, so they can be interleaved with the NCC. By combining NCC with OSCAR and mC4, it should be possible to create a deduplicated Norwegian corpus with over 100 GB of text (15 billion words).

The dataset processing involved several steps to prepare the sub-corpora for language model training (see Figure 3.10). First, the source files in various formats, such as XML-based METS/ALTO, HTML, JSON and plain text, were uniformly processed. These files were unpacked if necessary, while maintaining their original formats. For OCR-derived sources, a two-step pipeline was implemented, involving the creation of digital copies in JPEG 2000 format and subsequent OCR and structure analysis using METS/ALTO formats. To improve OCR quality, older documents underwent a second OCR pass using Tesseract version 4.0, and any document or paragraph with OCR confidence below 90% was filtered out.

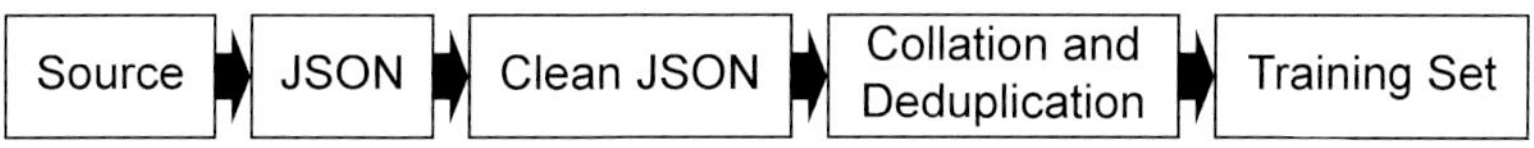

Figure 3.10 Processing pipeline. © Freddy Wytjen.

Next, all sub-corpora were converted to a common JSON Lines format, which facilitated further processing and retained relevant information from the sources. While the JSON Lines objects shared common keys like an identifier and the document type, the specific keys varied depending on the available metadata. The JSON Lines files were then standardised and cleaned using a set of parametric rules specific to each sub-corpus, addressing issues like OCR artefacts, UTF-8 character encoding normalisation, and removing sensitive information. Deduplication was performed based on paragraph-level MD5 hashes, followed by collation and annotation of the main language using FastText.

Finally, the deduplicated and cleaned files were transformed into the distribution JSON Lines format, where merged paragraphs were grouped together with associated metadata. The resulting dataset was distributed as a single large JSON Lines file comprising 21 million documents, as well as compressed 1 GB shards for convenient streaming access.

To encourage alternative uses of the corpus, we did include metadata like language, document type and publishing year. This allows for the creation of, for instance, a Norwegian Nynorsk-only corpus. It also allows for combining several of these metatags for creating even more specialised corpora. While the NCC was created with current transformer models in mind, we hope the corpus will be used for purposes beyond our expectations.

Language models

One of the first uses of the NCC was the training of the first Norwegian pretrained language model, NB-BERT[7] (Kummervold et al 2021). While the NCC was not yet ready for the training of this first model, we did employ an earlier version of the corpus. In order to build our own pretrained language model for Norwegian, we decided to use the original BERT architecture pretrained with the masked-language modelling (MLM) objective. We evaluated the effect of changes in hyperparameters in terms of MLM performance and of the fine-tuning of the pretrained models on various downstream tasks. To get optimal performance out of a pretrained model, the hyperparameters in the fine-tuning should be adapted. However, we were not primarily interested in optimisation but in a comparison of the performance of our model against the mBERT model.

Language models, especially encoder-only models like BERT, are commonly evaluated through fine-tuning on several classification tasks for both tokens (akin to words) and sequences of words (like phrases). For token classification, performance in tasks like named-entity recognition (NER) and part-of-speech tagging are usually reported. We evaluated our model's multilingual abilities using NER datasets in both included and less-represented languages, and excluded automated or semi-automated NER datasets. For sequence classification, we used a well-established sentiment analysis dataset (Øvrelid et al 2020) and a corpus of speeches from the Norwegian Parliament for political affiliation classification. Our NB-BERT model performed significantly better than the mBERT model for both Bokmål and Nynorsk, and on both token and sequence classification. Our model was also able to outperform the English-only and multilingual BERT for both Norwegian Bokmål and Nynorsk, as well as for Swedish and Danish, which are languages with a shared tradition with Norwegian. For English, our results are also marginally better than those obtained using the English-only

BERT model. For Spanish and Finnish, for which there is no close relationship with Norwegian and just anecdotal documented occurrences of text in such languages in the NCC, the mBERT model outperformed both the English-only BERT and our model, suggesting that our model was unlearning some of the languages not included in the corpus.

A major motivation for training our own BERT-based model was to investigate whether the digital collections at Nasjonalbiblioteket could be used to create a suitable corpus to train state-of-the-art transformer language models. The texts available through the library are heterogeneous in nature, including cartoons, novels, news articles, poetry and government documents published over time and in different contexts. As the results suggest, this seems to be a strength rather than a weakness, in that it enables us to build high-performance transformer models for smaller languages, such as Norwegian. Consequently, our Norwegian corpus is not only richer in diversity but also significantly larger in size than any other Norwegian corpus, and it even rivals the size of previous work on a major language such as English. Therefore, collections such as the digital collection at Nasjonalbiblioteket, even if they contain occasional OCR errors, may contribute significantly toward the creation of well-performing language models by providing large training corpora. We did not see any indication that the OCR errors negatively impacted the performance, and we might speculate that the model has learned to distinguish OCR errors from ordinary text.

As part of an effort to democratise the use of technology and digital resources at the Nasjonalbiblioteket, we released NB-BERT as well as other models trained on versions of NCC, such as fine-tuned versions of NB-BERT for NER, or a GPT-style model (NB-GPT-J-6B)[8] that can be adjusted to work like a chatbot.

Speech recognition and low-resource languages

Machine learning also offers the Nasjonalbiblioteket the opportunity to enhance access for individuals with diverse needs. By analysing user data, machine learning algorithms can generate tailored accessibility features, such as providing alternative formats for visually impaired users, offering multilingual interfaces, or creating adaptive recommendation systems. And by leveraging machine learning technologies, the library can strive for inclusivity and ensure that its resources are accessible to all members of Norwegian society, regardless of individual requirements.

In this sense, automatic speech recognition (ASR) is the task of converting speech into text. ASR systems are used in a wide range of applications, such as voice assistants, transcription services and speech-to-text translation. It is also increasingly becoming a tool for research in spoken language as the accuracy of the more recent neural-based models is approaching that of humans for certain metrics. However, despite the high accuracy in resource-rich languages, ASR models are currently unavailable for the vast majority of the world's languages due to the lack of gold-annotated data to train such models.

Besides the two official written standards of Norwegian, Bokmål and Nynorsk, which have somewhat different inflexion, vocabulary and spelling, the Norwegian language has many spoken dialects that differ lexically, grammatically and phonologically. Consequently, high-quality datasets for acoustic modelling of Norwegian require speech data in different dialects and should ideally include transcriptions in both written standards.

Norwegian ASR

Early work on Norwegian speech recognition was mostly focused on very limited vocabularies and numbers, tailored for telephone applications and menu navigation (Svendsen et al 1989; Paliwal 1992; Kvale 1996). Compound words are more frequent in Norwegian than English, but using traditional pronunciation dictionaries seemed sufficient in controlled lexicons. In Norwegian, natural numbers between 20 and 99 can be pronounced differently (e.g. 'twenty-four' and 'four-and-twenty'), which poses a challenge for natural number recognition. By the year 2000, and under the umbrella of a few EU-funded projects, research focused mostly on overcoming these limitations and extending the use cases to dates, times, nouns and the spelling out of words, which yielded several important datasets (e.g., SpeechDat, SpeechDat-II, TABU.0) and technical improvements over a short period of time (Amdal and Ljøen 1995; Hoge et al 1997; Johansen, Amdal and Kvale 1997; Kvale and Amdal 1997; Amdal, Holter and Svendsen 1999; Martens 2000). Most approaches were based on hidden Markov models and some relied on Mel frequency cepstral coefficients, commonly by using the Hidden Markov Model Toolkit (HTK; Young and Young 1993).

Unfortunately, traditional approaches to speech recognition struggled with open-ended recognition and handling out-of-vocabulary words. However, the introduction of newer datasets in the last decade led to the emergence of systems with better performance. Three noteworthy datasets are the Nordisk Språkteknologi (NST; Nordisk Språkteknologi 2020), the Norwegian Parliamentary Speech Corpus (NPSC; Solberg and Ortiz 2022), and the Few-shot Learning Evaluation of Universal Representations of Speech (FLEURS; Conneau et al 2022) benchmark.

NST is a multilingual dataset with speech in Swedish, Danish and Norwegian Bokmål. It includes various conversation types, read-aloud passages and word spellings. Speaker metadata and high-quality audio recordings are provided. NPSC consists of approximately 100 hours of unscripted speech from the Norwegian parliament, along with orthographic transcriptions. It addresses the lack of available speech data for Norwegian ASR and improves recognition performance. FLEURS is a multilingual benchmark dataset supporting various speech tasks. It contains parallel speech data in 102 languages, with around 12 hours per language. FLEURS aims to enable speech technology development in low-resource languages.

In early 2022, we released a series of wav2vec 2.0 (Schneider et al 2019; Baevski et al 2020) models of different sizes.[9] These models were released for Bokmål in sizes of 300 million and 1 billion parameters; for Nynorsk, only the 300 million parameter size was available. They were fine-tuned using the NPSC dataset. The 1 billion parameter models were based on the multilingual XLS-R models (Babu et al 2021), which were trained on over 436,000 hours of publicly available speech recordings from various sources, including parliamentary proceedings and audio books, covering 128 different languages. The 300 million parameter models were based on the Swedish VoxRex model, developed by the National Library of Sweden (KB; Malmsten, Haffenden and Börjeson 2022), and trained on the P4-10k corpus consisting of 10,000 hours of Swedish local public service radio and 1,500 hours of audiobooks and other speech from KB's collections. Choosing a Swedish acoustic model for fine-tuning Norwegian ASR was motivated by the similarities between the two languages as part of the North Germanic language family, originating from Old Norse and sharing common spoken and written features.

After the initial success and good reception of these models by the public, we conducted more thorough and systematic experiments aiming at better performance for ASR (De La Rosa et al 2023). We trained the models on NPSC following roughly the same hyperparameters and ablated on different data-supplementing strategies derived from the NST. FLEURS would allow for the zero-shot and out-of-domain performance assessment of the models.

We evaluated the performance of the models, grouping their scores by the written language of the test sets in NPSC and NST. Models trained on the Bokmål subset of NPSC performed not too well on the test set of NST. Similarly, models trained only on NST underperformed on the test set of the Bokmål subset of NPSC. Adding a five-gram language model yielded significant improvements across the board.[10] However, the biggest gain in performance was the addition of extra data. The models fine-tuned on combinations of NPSC and NST produced significantly better results. On the whole NPSC, the new 300 million parameter model using a combination of NST and NPSC outperformed the previous best model by 9.5 points and the previous state-of-the-art NPSC-Bokmål model by 4.16 points. For the other datasets, the one billion parameter model combining NST and the Bokmål subset of NPSC outperformed the rest of the models, yielding increases over the model trained solely on the Bokmål subset of NPSC of 0.6 points and of 14.89 points on NST. Interestingly, the performance of the best 300 million and 1 billion models was very close. For Nynorsk, our newer NPSC-Nynorsk 1 billion model outperformed the NPSC-Nynorsk 300 million model by 1.14 points. Interestingly, the out-of-domain performance of the models was also greatly improved by adding the planned speech in NST to NPSC. Models on both sizes improved their word error rate scores from 12.98 to 9.88 for the 300 million model, and from 13.03 to 9.87 for the 1 billion model.

Despite the improved performance of our models compared to the other baselines, ASR models for Norwegian still face several challenges. One major challenge is the complex phonetics and morphology of the different dialects, which makes it difficult for models to accurately transcribe the phonemes in the input speech to the correct spelling. Another challenge is the limited availability of high-quality datasets for Norwegian speech, which limits the amount of training data for ASR models. Finally, the prospect of training wav2vec 2.0 directly on non-normalised text is an interesting avenue for research, as it would make the models directly usable without having to transform the output of the models to make them more readable.

For these reasons, we created a new labelled dataset of Norwegian speech by combining TV programme subtitles from the Norwegian Broadcasting Corporation, a new dataset of parliamentary speeches from Stortinget and a set of audiobooks. After compiling the data, we trained a series of Whisper models that not only overcame the aforementioned limitations, but also outperformed every existing ASR model for Norwegian, commercial or not. These models were released at the end of 2023 and we are actively working on applying them to our vast collection of radio broadcasting and oral catalogue to make them searchable and easier to discover.

Sámi language technology

The Sámi, Europe's only indigenous people (their territory is shown in Figure 3.11), have nine endangered languages related to Finnish and Estonian, with some mutual intelligibility but different orthographies. Sámi speakers are usually bilingual or multilingual. Lule Sámi is spoken in Norway and Sweden, while North Sámi is spoken in Norway, Sweden and Finland, creating variation among users. South, Lule and North Sámi

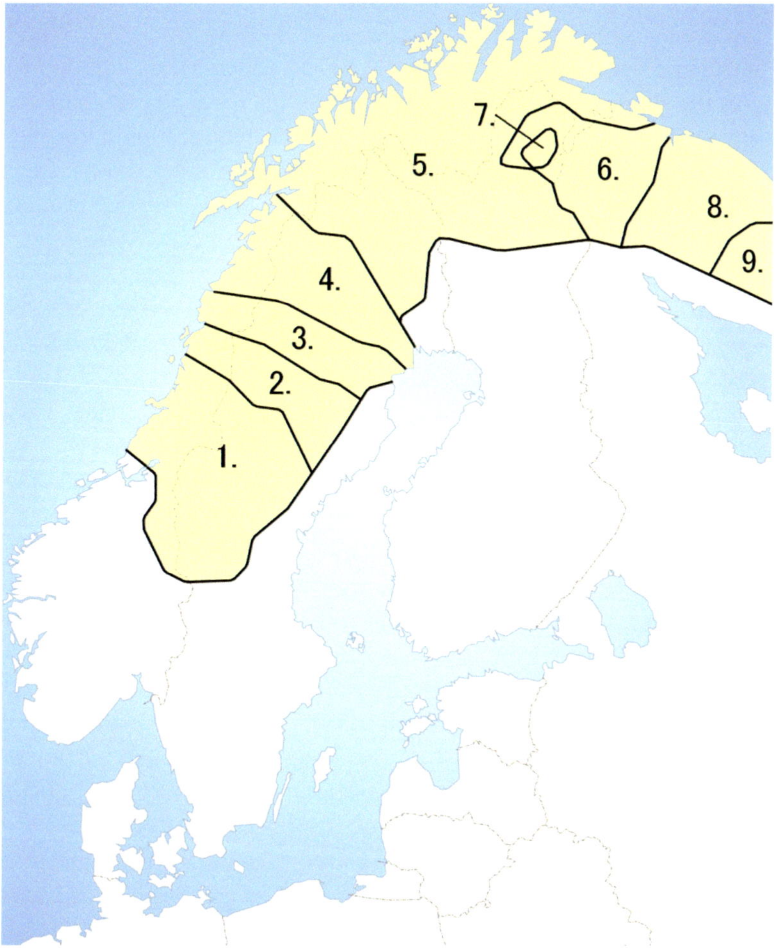

Figure 3.11 A map showing the traditional speaking areas of nine Sámi languages (1. Sør; 2. Ume; 3. Pite; 4. Lule; 5. Nord; 6. Skolt; 7. Enare; 8. Kildin; 9. Ter). Akkala Sámi is not shown on the map since it is considered extinct. Map: Wikimedia Commons, CC BY-SA 3.0.

have official status in Norway, requiring their presence in official contexts alongside Norwegian.

North Sámi has by far the largest number of language users among the Sámi languages: 25,000 in all three countries where it is spoken. Lule Sámi has considerably fewer speakers: a total of 2,000 in both countries in which it is spoken. North Sámi, with a lesser degree of endangerment than Lule Sámi, has the highest number of language users among the Sámi languages, resulting in a greater availability of language resources and a wider variety of tools. An infrastructure of dictionaries, morphological analysers, spell checkers and other language learning tools have been maintained and developed since 2001 by the Divvun[11] and Giellatekno[12] groups. Recently, the NB AI-Lab embarked on a project to boost the support for Sámi languages within the library by establishing a close collaboration with the Divvun and Giellatekno groups. According to the feedback they get from the language communities, there is high demand for a speech-to-text tool like ASR, for example, for making automatic transcriptions or subtitling videos.

Building upon an audiobook read aloud by a single female speaker of North Sámi used as training data for an early prototype of a wav2vec 2.0 system, the NB AI-Lab tried to leverage the more recent Whisper model to increase the performance. Showing exceedingly good results in a variety of languages, the Whisper model is capable of performing well even in noisy environments and providing transcriptions in a readable format without the need for an extra inverse text normalisation process. Unfortunately, the model did not include any of the Sámi languages and thus was not directly usable for our purposes. However, the model included Finnish, a closely related language to North Sámi. In the first experiment of its kind, we were able to reuse the existing weights for Finnish and fine-tune the model with North Sámi annotated speech, wiping out Finnish in the process but providing ASR for North Sámi. We achieved a word error rate score of 24.91% on a held-out test set randomly extracted from the training corpora described above. The Sámi Whisper model, despite being able to generate capitalisation and punctuation marks, did not include any of this data in the training set for Sámi.

We are now in the process of expanding these experiments and producing a readily usable model for ASR based on the Whisper architecture, with the hope of making it multilingual in at least Lule and North Sámi. Our latest experimental ASR model has already been shown to be useful, especially for raw-transcribing large amounts of speech materials.[13] In the near future, we plan to develop the North Sámi ASR further and eventually make it openly available.

Conclusion

The Nasjonalbiblioteket has recognised the potential of machine learning to transform its operations, services and accessibility. By harnessing the power of machine learning to automate processes, enhance information discovery, facilitate digitisation, optimise resource allocation and promote accessibility, the library can fulfil its mission of preserving and promoting Norway's cultural heritage while embracing the digital age. As the library continues to integrate machine learning into its fabric, it positions itself as a forward-thinking institution, adapting to the changing needs of its users and enriching the cultural landscape of Norway for generations to come. Establishing a dedicated unit for AI and machine learning research with access to the library collections offers several advantages. First, the library collections hold a vast amount of diverse and valuable textual and visual data that can be utilised for training and validating AI and machine learning models. This wealth of resources provides researchers with a rich dataset for various research purposes, including text analysis, document classification, sentiment analysis and image recognition. Furthermore, having a dedicated unit for this research allows for focused expertise and collaboration among researchers. By bringing together specialists in AI, machine learning and library sciences, the unit can leverage collective knowledge and skills to explore innovative approaches to information retrieval, data processing and knowledge extraction from the library collections. This interdisciplinary collaboration enhances the quality and depth of research outcomes and encourages cross-pollination of ideas and techniques. In addition, the establishment of such a unit enables the development and refinement of AI and machine learning algorithms specifically tailored to the needs of the Nasjonalbiblioteket. By applying advanced techniques, researchers can automate various tasks, such as metadata generation, content indexing and recommendation systems, thereby improving the efficiency of library operations and enhancing user experiences. This not only streamlines processes within the library but also opens up opportunities for enhanced discovery and accessibility of library resources to the public.

However, it is important to acknowledge potential challenges and disadvantages associated with such a dedicated unit. One potential concern is the ethical use of AI and machine learning technologies in the context of library collections. Safeguarding user privacy, ensuring unbiased algorithms and addressing issues of algorithmic transparency are critical considerations that must be addressed to maintain public trust and protect sensitive information. Moreover, establishing and maintaining a dedicated

AI and machine learning unit requires significant investment in infrastructure, computational resources and ongoing training for researchers. Adequate funding and support are necessary to ensure the sustainability and long-term success of the unit. Additionally, the integration of AI and machine learning technologies within a traditional library environment may require careful planning, change management and user education to foster acceptance and effective utilisation of these technologies by library staff and patrons.

In conclusion, the establishment of a dedicated unit for AI and machine learning research with access to the library collections at the Nasjonalbiblioteket offers numerous advantages, including access to rich and diverse datasets, interdisciplinary collaboration and the potential for innovative applications. However, careful attention must be given to ethical considerations, resource allocation and organisational challenges to fully harness the benefits of AI and machine learning in the library context.

Notes

1. https://ai.nb.no/.
2. http://ai4lam.org/.
3. www.cenl.org/networkgroups/ai-in-libraries-network-group/.
4. https://bibsys-almaprimo.hosted.exlibrisgroup.com/primo-explore/search?vid=SAMISK.
5. https://huggingface.co/NbAiLab/nb-bert-base-sami-relevant.
6. See also https://huggingface.co/NbAiLab/nb-maken.
7. See https://huggingface.co/NbAiLab/nb-bert-base and https://huggingface.co/NbAiLab/nb-bert-large.
8. https://huggingface.co/NbAiLab/nb-gpt-j-6B.
9. See https://huggingface.co/NbAiLab/nb-wav2vec2-1b-bokmaal, https://huggingface.co/NbAiLab/nb-wav2vec2-300m-bokmaal, and https://huggingface.co/NbAiLab/nb-wav2vec2-300m-nynorsk.
10. See https://huggingface.co/NbAiLab/nb-wav2vec2-kenlm.
11. https://divvun.no.
12. https://giellatekno.uit.no.
13. https://huggingface.co/NbAiLab/whisper-large-sme.

References

Amdal, I. and Ljøen, H. 1995. 'TABU.0 – en norsk telefontaledatabase', *Scientific Report*, 40:95.

Amdal, I., Holter, T. and Svendsen, T. 1999. 'Maximum likelihood pronunciation modelling of Norwegian natural numbers for automatic speech recognition'. In *Proc. Norwegian Signal Processing Symposium (NORSIG)*, 145–50.

Babu, A., Wang, C., Tjandra, A., Lakhotia, K., Xu, Q., Goyal, N., Singh, K., von Platen, P., Saraf, Y., Pino, J. et al. 2021. 'XLS-R: Self-supervised cross-lingual speech representation learning at scale'. arXiv:2111.09296.

Baevski, A., Zhou, Y., Mohamed, A. and Auli, M. 2020. 'wav2vec 2.0: A framework for self-supervised learning of speech representations', *Advances in Neural Information Processing Systems*, 33:12449–60.

Bommasani, R., Hudson, D. A., Adeli, E., Altman, R., Arora, S., Arx, S. von et al. 2021. 'On the opportunities and risks of foundation models'. Available at: https://crfm.stanford.edu/assets/report.pdf.

Bowman, S.R., Angeli, G., Potts, C. and Manning, C.D. 2015. 'A large annotated corpus for learning natural language inference'. In *Proceedings of the 2015 Conference on Empirical Methods in Natural Language Processing*, 632–42. Lisbon, Portugal, Association for Computational Linguistics. doi: 10.18653/v1/D15-1075.

Chicco, D. and Jurman, G. 2020. 'The advantages of the Matthews correlation coefficient (MCC) over F1 score and accuracy in binary classification evaluation', *BMC Genomics*, 21:1–13.

Common Crawl. No date. Accessed 27 June 2023. https://commoncrawl.org/.

Conneau, A., Ma, M., Khanuja, S., Zhang, Y., Axelrod, V., Dalmia, S., Riesa, J., Rivera, C. and Bapna, A. 2022. 'FLEURS: FEW-shot learning evaluation of universal representations of speech', 2022 IEEE Spoken Language Technology Workshop (SLT), 798–805.

De La Rosa, J., Braaten, R.-A., Kummervold, P. and Wetjen, F. 2023. 'Boosting Norwegian automatic speech recognition'. In *Proceedings of the 24th Nordic Conference on Computational Linguistics (NoDaLiDa)*, 555–64. Tórshavn, Faroe Islands. University of Tartu Library. https://aclanthology.org/2023.nodalida-1.55.

Devlin, J., Chang, M.-W., Lee, K. and Toutanova, K. 2019. 'BERT: Pre-training of deep bidirectional transformers for language understanding'. In *Proceedings of the 2019 Conference of the North American Chapter of the Association for Computational Linguistics: Human Language Technologies, Volume 1 (Long and Short Papers)*, 4171–86. Minneapolis, Minnesota. Association for Computational Linguistics. doi: 10.18653/v1/N19-1423.

Dosovitskiy, A., Beyer, L., Kolesnikov, A., Weissenborn, D., Zhai, X., Unterthiner, T., Dehghani, M., Minderer, M., Heigold, G., Gelly, S., Uszkoreit, J. and Houlsby, N. 2021. 'An image is worth 16×16 words: Transformers for image recognition at scale'. https://doi.org/10.48550/arXiv.2010.11929.

Duhaime, D. 2023. 'PixPlot', Yale Digital Humanities Lab. https://github.com/YaleDHLab/pix-plot.

Gao, L., Biderman, S., Black, S., Golding, L., Hoppe, T., Foster, C., Phang, J., He, H., Thite, A., Nabeshima, N., Presser, S. and Leahy, C. 2020. 'The Pile: An 800GB dataset of diverse text for language modeling'. arXiv:2101.00027.

Hoge, H., Tropf, H.S., Winski, R., van den Heuvel, H., Haeb-Umbach, R. and Choukri, K. 1997. 'European speech databases for telephone applications'. In 1997 IEEE International Conference on Acoustics, Speech, and Signal Processing, 1771–4.

Intersoft Consulting. No date. 'General Data Protection Regulation (GDPR), official legal text'. Accessed 8 June 2023. https://gdpr-info.eu/.

Johansen, F.T., Amdal, I. and Kvale, K. 1997. 'The Norwegian part of SpeechDat: A European speech database for creation of voice driven teleservices'. In Proceedings of NORSIG-1997, 40–43.

Kummervold, P.E., De la Rosa, J., Wetjen, F. and Brygfjeld, S.A. 2021. 'Operationalising a national digital library: The case for a Norwegian transformer model'. In *Proceedings of the 23rd Nordic Conference on Computational Linguistics (NoDaLiDa)*, Reykjavik, Iceland (Online), 20–29. Linköping, Sweden: Linköping University Electronic Press. https://aclanthology.org/2021.nodalida-main.3.

Kummervold, P., Wetjen, F. and de la Rosa, J. 2022. 'The Norwegian Colossal Corpus: A text corpus for training large Norwegian language models'. In *Proceedings of the Thirteenth Language Resources and Evaluation Conference*, 3852–60. Marseille, France. European Language Resources Association. https://aclanthology.org/2022.lrec-1.410.

Kvale, K. 1996. 'Norwegian numerals: A challenge to automatic speech recognition'. In *Proceeding of Fourth International Conference on Spoken Language Processing. ICSLP'96*, 2028–31. IEEE.

Kvale, K. and Amdal, I. 1997. 'Improved automatic recognition of Norwegian natural numbers by incorporating phonetic knowledge'. In *Proc.* 1997 IEEE International Conference on Acoustics, Speech, and Signal Processing, 1763–6.

Library of Congress. 2022. 'ALTO: Technical metadata for layout and text objects'. Accessed 25 June 2023. www.loc.gov/standards/alto/.

Lovdata. 2018. 'The Copyright Act'. Accessed 14 January 2023. https://lovdata.no/dokument/NL/lov/2018-06-15-40.

Lovdata. 2022. 'Norwegian Language Act'. Accessed 14 January 2023. https://lovdata.no/dokument/NL/lov/2021-05-21-4.

Malmsten, M., Haffenden, C. and Börjeson, L. 2022. 'Hearing voices at the National Library – A speech corpus and acoustic model for the Swedish language'. arXiv:2205.03026.

Martens, J.-P. 2000. *Final Report of COST Action 249: Continuous speech recognition over the telephone*. Belgium: Ghent University, Electronics & Information Systems.

Mikolov, T., Chen, K., Corrado, G.S. and Dean, J. 2013a. 'Efficient estimation of word representations in vector space'. http://arxiv.org/abs/1301.3781.

Mikolov, T., Sutskever, I., Chen, K., Corrado, G.S. and Dean, J. 2013b. 'Distributed representations of words and phrases and their compositionality'. In Advances in Neural Information Processing Systems 26. Curran Associates, Inc. Accessed 8 June 2023. https://papers.nips.cc/paper_files/paper/2013/hash/9aa42b31882ec039965f3c4923ce901b-Abstract.html.

Nordisk Språkteknologi. 2020. 'NST Norwegian ASR database (16 kHz) – Reorganised', The Language Bank: oai:nb.no:sbr-54. https://www.nb.no/sprakbanken/en/resource-catalogue/oai-nb-no-sbr-54/.

Norwegian Digitalisation Agency. 2023. 'Norwegian licence for open government data (NLOD) 2.0'. Accessed 26 June 2023. https://data.norge.no/nlod/en/2.0.

Øvrelid, L., Mæhlum, P., Barnes, J. and Velldal, E. 2020. 'A fine-grained sentiment dataset for Norwegian'. In *Proceedings of the Twelfth Language Resources and Evaluation Conference*, 5025–33. Marseille, France. European Language Resources Association. https://aclanthology.org/2020.lrec-1.618.

Paliwal, K.K. 1992. 'On the use of line spectral frequency parameters for speech recognition', *Digital Signal Processing*, 2(2):80–87.

Raffel, C., Shazeer, N., Roberts, A., Lee, K., Narang, S., Matena, M., Zhou, Y., Li, W. and Liu, P.J. 2019. 'Exploring the limits of transfer learning with a unified text-to-text transformer'. https://doi.org/10.48550/arXiv.1910.10683.

Rehurek, R. and Sojka, P. 2011. 'Gensim – Python framework for vector space modelling', NLP Centre, Faculty of Informatics, Masaryk University, Brno, Czech Republic.

Schneider, S., Baevski, A., Collobert, R. and Auli, M. 2019. 'wav2vec: Unsupervised pre-training for speech recognition'. In *Proc. Interspeech 2019*, 3465–9.

Snydman, S., Sanderson, R. and Cramer, T. 2015. 'The International Image Interoperability Framework (IIIF): A community & technology approach for web-based images'. In Proc. Archiving Conference, 16–21. Society for Imaging Science and Technology.

Solberg, P.E. and Ortiz, P. 2022. 'The Norwegian parliamentary speech corpus'. arXiv:2201.10881.

Språkbanken. 2022. 'Norsk aviskorpus'. Accessed 5 February 2024. www.nb.no/sprakbanken/ressurskatalog/oai-nb-no-sbr-4/.

Suárez, P.J.O., Sagot, B. and Romary, L. 2019. 'Asynchronous pipelines for processing huge corpora on medium to low resource infrastructures'. In *Proceedings of the Workshop on Challenges in the Management of Large Corpora (CMLC-7) 2019*, Cardiff, 22nd July, edited by P. Bański, A. Barbaresi, H. Biber, E. Breiteneder, S. Clematide, M. Kupietz, H. L"ungen and C. Iliadi, 9–16. https://doi.org/10.14618/ids-pub-9021.

Svendsen, T., Paliwal, K.K., Harborg, E. and Husoy, P. 1989. 'An improved sub-word based speech recogniser'. In *International Conference on Acoustics, Speech, and Signal Processing*, 108–11. IEEE.

Szegedy, C., Vanhoucke, V., Ioffe, S., Shlens, J. and Wojna, Z. 2016. 'Rethinking the inception architecture for computer vision'. In *2016 IEEE Conference on Computer Vision and Pattern Recognition (CVPR)*, 2818–26.

Young, S.J. and Young, S. 1993. 'The HTK Hidden Markov Model Toolkit: Design and philosophy'. Technical report CUED/F-INFENG/TR.152. Cambridge: University of Cambridge, Department of Engineering.

Part II

Text and beyond: AI applied to text, images and audiovisual archives

4

From preservation to access and beyond: the role of AI in audiovisual archives

Julia Noordegraaf and Anna Schjøtt

About 30 minutes outside of Amsterdam, you find the Netherlands Institute for Sound and Vision – a large multicoloured building that manages one of the largest collections of audiovisual content in Europe and now also hosts the newly reopened Media Museum. Once you enter the revolving doors to the building, you are immediately greeted by employees in bright blue shirts who scan your museum ticket and tell you to take the stairs to the second floor of the building. Arriving at the top of the stairs on the second floor, you encounter an intriguing circular room with a red floor, flashing video screens, large round chairs and booths featuring the numbers one to ten. This is the 'tune-in' area where visitors are asked to first download the Sound and Vision app and then to sit down and go through the steps that will help personalise your experience in the museum. First, you are shown a video explaining how the museum will collect and use the personal data you provide in the app. Using a clip of a burning trashcan, it also shows how your data will be destroyed when you leave. Once the video is over, you receive a chat message in the app that says, 'Welcome, we are happy that you are here'. The app offers you an automatic message to reply with that states, 'Thank you, but what is this really?', which then appears as a reply message. From here the app goes on to explain a bit more about the museum and, in a joking and casual tone, asks you about your age and where you live. It gives you the option to type in your birth year and zip code but also the option to not enter your personal data. You are then asked to play two mini-games. In the first, you are presented with a movie genre and can slide left to state that this is not for you or right if this is a genre you like. In the second, you are asked to choose five interests out of several options presented on the screen. Last, the app asks you to go into one of the numbered photo booths to have your photo taken. When entering the photo booth, you are greeted, by name, by a screen. After taking your photo, you are finally ready to enter the museum. You walk up another set of stairs, and the first thing you see is yourself. Your photo and name are featured on a large screen together with other visitors' faces. You are the exhibition.

This is a snapshot of a visit to the Media Museum at the Netherlands Institute for Sound and Vision (from here on, Sound & Vision), the Dutch national broadcasting archive (see Figures 4.1 and 4.2). The museum, which opened its doors in February 2023, uses facial recognition technology and simple forms of explicit personalisation[1] in the exhibition to tell its story of how we are all 'living in the media' in today's societies (based on the work of Mark Deuze: Deuze et al 2012; Deuze 2016). In this chapter, we use the museum of this audiovisual archive (AV) as an illustrating example of how digitisation and the introduction of AI into archival practices are transforming the role of the archive, the role of the archivist and the archival object itself. Specifically, we highlight how the museum embodies and illustrates the current shifts towards increasingly datafied and participatory archival practices, which are driven by an emphasis on the facilitation of access to the archive. We illustrate how the use of AI has evolved over time and become more and more active in the construction of the archive, as it becomes a tool for storytelling and visitor engagement. The application of AI in the Media Museum exemplifies this by changing the role of the technology from a simple facilitator to making it an active part of the exhibition. In turn, this use of AI transforms the archival workflow as it places the user at the centre of the archival process.

To sustain this argument, we trace the evolution and expanding use of AI within AV archives, using Sound & Vision to exemplify these changes. Then we turn to the recently opened museum to discuss how placing AI on display represents a shift from spectatorship to participation, which in turn reshapes the archival workflow. This last section is based on insights from three months of ethnographic fieldwork conducted by the second author inside the museum in the months following its opening, including retrospective interviews with employees who were involved in the conception and execution of the museum. Before turning

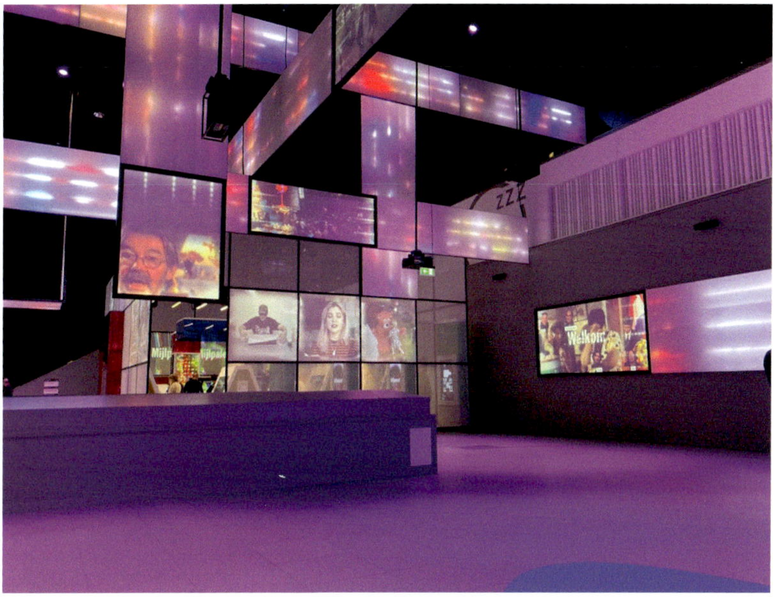

Figure 4.1 Entrance area of the Media Museum of Sound and Vision, which features the so-called Media Reactor that presents a stream of media content – also featuring the users themselves, Hilversum, the Netherlands. © Anna Schjøtt.

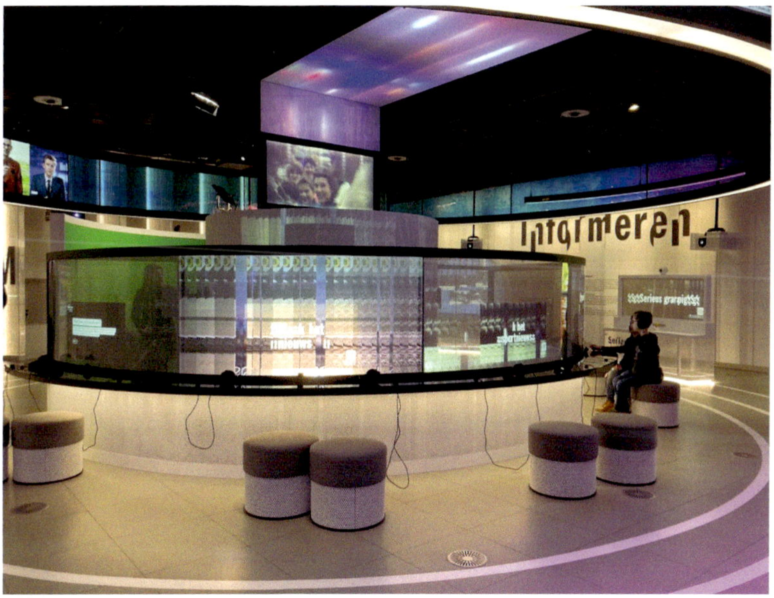

Figure 4.2 News area of the Media Museum of Sound and Vision, also titled 'Inform', Hilversum, the Netherlands. © Anna Schjøtt.

to the historicisation of AI in archival practices, we first introduce some key conceptual ideas that frame our understanding of the archive.

Dynamic conceptions of the archive

Archives serve an important role in society by providing a record of the activities of individuals, social groups and organisations in the past that allow future users to retrace and interpret past events. As a result of this function archives can be understood as 'the documentary by-products of human activity' (International Council on Archives n.d.). When these records of human activity are deemed to be of societal relevance, they are collected, appraised, described and made accessible in publicly or privately funded institutional archives. These institutional archives serve the role of keepers of the evidence of past human activity and, therefore, as museums and libraries, serve as important repositories for a society's cultural memory (Assmann 2010). To be a trusted repository for the evidence of human activity they hold, the archival institutions have developed professional practices and archival workflows that ensure the authenticity, reliability, integrity and usability of archival records (International Council on Archives n.d.).

While these definitions of the archive help us to understand the broader role of the archive in society, they do not address the discursive power of archival knowledge. For Foucault, the archive plays an immensely important role by taking part in defining what counts as knowledge. As a result, he defined the archive in a conceptual sense as 'the general system of the formation and transformation of statements' or 'set of rules' that govern a particular episteme (Foucault 1972, 148, 146; Lowry and McNeal 2021). At the dawn of the digital age, Jacques Derrida, in a famous lecture held in 1994, traced the etymology of the word archive as closely related to those in power (Derrida 1995). His conception of the archive inspired a strong trend of critical archival theory that pays attention to the ways in which the archival processing of the documentary heritage of individuals, social groups and organisations shapes what can be remembered and how those events are interpreted (e.g., Ketelaar 2001; Schwarz and Cook 2002). This critical approach to archival practice also emphasises what is forgotten or repressed either by neglecting to document human activity or by actively destroying existing records (e.g., overlooking the documentary evidence of minorities, or ignoring alternative perspectives on the meaning of the records that are collected and preserved; Assmann 2010).

As a result of this critical conception of archiving as a technique embedded in practices of knowledge and power, scholars in the domain of archival studies have developed more holistic views on the whole continuum of archival practices. Such practices include the creation, capturing, organising and pluralising of records as well as the actors and processes that underlie and affect their creation, management, organisation and use. This perspective has become known as the 'records continuum' model (Upward 1996; Upward et al 2018). Such a holistic conception of the production and circulation of archival records invites a social constructivist perspective on the archival record and how its meaning is constructed throughout the archival process and actors (see, e.g., Bowker and Star 2000).

In today's society, which is pervaded by digital technology, the ontology of the archive is changing, and new actors are intervening in the way that archival records are produced, captured, appraised and used. Digital AV archival objects exist in an online, cross-media landscape, where they achieve their meaning partly via their circulation on social media platforms but also through intertextual references to other intellectual property rights or privacy-protected media content (e.g., social media posts, Marvel film clips, etc.). The consequence of this change has been a need for a more dynamic conception of the notion of archiving and of what its 'object' is (Ernst 2013). However, as Edwards (2002) has argued, digital infrastructures tend to be invisible: 'The most salient characteristic of technology in the modern (industrial/post-industrial) world is the degree to which most technology is not salient for most people, most of the time' (Edwards 2002, 185). As the infrastructure for processing archival records is not neutral but heavily invested with power dynamics, it becomes crucial to detect how and where exactly it generates knowledge, of what kind, and whose perspective(s) it represents. MacKenzie (2017), for example, illustrates that the human and technological actors involved in machine learning systems produce knowledge (MacKenzie 2017). Colavizza et al (2021) have also illustrated how the use of AI in archival processes transforms the archival workflow in unexpected ways, posing both new possibilities and challenges.

When exploring this exact change in this chapter, namely the digitisation and AI augmentation of the AV archive, we use these understandings of the archive to sensitise our conceptual discussion to consider both ideas of power and politics of archival knowledge production, the uniqueness of the digital collection, and how the infrastructures and technological affordances of AI take part in (re)constructing the archive. In the following, we illustrate how AI has intensified existing shifts in archival practice that had already been brought on by digitisation and the emergence of digital archives. We do so by following Sound & Vision's journey from an analogue institution to a highly datafied and AI-augmented institution, before turning to the museum as an embodiment of this transformation, which alters the very understanding of what the archive, its objects and its role is. In this way, we hope to add to the dynamic understanding of archives in the age of AI.

From the analogue to the digital and beyond: towards the datafied and AI-augmented archive

As discussed above, the advances in the development of digital technology in the past two decades have significantly transformed the workflow and function of cultural institutions and induced a shift from the preservation of heritage to the prioritisation of access – what is also referred to the digital turn in archiving (Fossati 2012, 2017). While digitisation represented a new way to preserve fragile materials for years to come, it also, as Prelinger (2007) argues, shifted the focus of archival practices towards access and the need to activate the archival content (see also Paalman et al 2021). Prelinger (2007, 2009) highlights the role of the wider digitisation of society and emergence of alternative 'archives' such as YouTube in this shift, as these developments greatly expanded the scope of born-digital information and created the expectation that collections of cultural heritage are generally accessible online. The Open Images platform created in 2015 by Sound & Vision exemplifies this ambition of accessibility and of activating the archive, as it made part of the collection available for reuse under an open licence and engaged several artists to experiment with the collection (Markus et al 2019) .

The digital turn has induced significant changes in the archival workflow and both blurred and extended the boundaries of the archive (Noordegraaf 2010a, 2011). On the one hand, it has led to a transformation of the role of the archivist, who is no longer the gatekeeper of the knowledge produced within the archive. Rather, the archivist now has the role of an editor or asset manager who must assess whether the information (see also Barok et al 2019), which is generated by a variety of actors outside the walls of the archive, can be deemed heritage and as a result should be archived (Noordegraaf 2010a). This extension of the archival processes beyond the walls of the archive itself has, on the other hand, produced an increased need to involve users in the practices of archival description. This need arises because preserving born-digital information requires the collection of objects and metadata at the moment of production and the involvement of users to interpret them meaningfully (Noordegraaf 2011). As Wolfgang Ernst has pointed out, in a context where archival records exist in the form of digital data, they become indistinguishable from the descriptive metadata that has become essential to retrieve objects from a digital archive (Ernst 2013). The growing focus on the accessibility of the collection has also reinvigorated existing questions of the political role of archives and archivists in curating memory as only parts of collections were made accessible, often at the expense of minority groups (Brunow 2017; Cordell 2020; Brennan 2022).

The emerging experimentations with AI in AV archives are also often framed as enabling accessibility to the archive by enhancing the searchability, creative reuse and analysis of the collections (Wactlar and Christel 2002; Rehm 2020; Cecchine 2021). A survey of the current literature has shown that AI is used to augment the processes of acquiring, storing, preserving and making accessible the documentary heritage of societies (Colavizza et al 2021). Cecchine (2021) has also surveyed the use of AI across different forms of AV institutions and highlighted the challenges and current limitations to AI experimentations in AV archives. By looking at different AV archives with different institutional histories and missions, she also illustrates how these institutional values shape how AI is implemented and how these values are transformed in the process. These findings highlight that the use of AI introduces new questions and transformations in AV archives beyond the processes of digitisation. So, while the use of AI is often seen as an extension of the digitisation of the archive, we here argue that it also enables transformations that move beyond the digital turn and warrant new conceptualisations (see also Fosatti 2017).

In the following, we use Sound & Vision's experimentations with AI as an illustrative case, while also drawing on other examples from other AV archives to highlight that this is not unique to Sound & Vision. By tracing the developments at Sound & Vision, we illustrate how AI induces increased processes of datafication, which is often defined as 'the process of rendering into data aspects of the world not previously quantified' (Kennedy et al 2015, 1). Mayer-Schönberger and Cukier (2013), in their conceptualisation, highlight that datafication is uniquely different from digitisation in which materials are converted into new digital formats because it is via the process of datafication that these digitised objects become indexable and searchable (see also Mejias and Couldry 2019). As the use of AI in AV archives is increasingly aimed at increasing searchability by producing metadata, we argue that AI induces a new datafied turn in archival practices and ultimately changes both the archival object and the archivist's role. Furthermore, we illustrate how the experimentations with AI also enable an intensification of the already emerging participatory turn (illustrated, for example, with crowdsourcing practices; see Noordegraaf 2010a, 2011) as users are giving an increasingly central role in the archival processes as both verifiers and creators of content.

The metadatafication of archival practices and objects

Archival description has historically been a key part of archival practice, also in AV archives, and is aimed at facilitating archivists and users in navigating the collections via these descriptions (Edmondson 2004; Delaney and De Jong 2015). These descriptions are carried out based on long-established principles of cataloguing with the aim of providing consistent and precise descriptions (Edmondson 2004). While archival description remains central in AV archive production processes (Delaney and De Jong 2015), the production of metadata is increasingly being delegated to AI applications. Born-digital content, such as video clips on Facebook or YouTube, come with automatically produced descriptions regarding, for example, time of upload, geographic location of the video and, more recently, often also automated transcriptions of audio and image content. For existing collections, the generation of such more fine-grained metadata would be highly resource intensive if done by human describers, which is why metadata production has been one of the main areas of experimentations with AI in AV archives.

There are several AI technologies that are used to produce different forms of metadata, such as automated transcriptions, object or speech recognition and segmentation tools (see Cecchine 2023 for a full overview). These technologies have also been part of the journey at Sound & Vision. For example, in 2011, they partnered with Dutch company SpraakLab for a project to use speech recognition technology for automatically labelling over three thousand known speakers on Dutch public television listed in the Common Thesaurus of Audiovisual Archives (GTAA) in the collection of radio and television broadcasts. With the help of these time-coded speaker labels, known Dutch people can now be traced at the level of the instance they appear in the overall programme (Cecchine 2021). In 2021 Sound & Vision was part of the Europeana Subtitled project, which aimed to use automatic speech recognition and machine translation technologies to produce automated English subtitles and captions for 6,000 pieces of AV content. Such automatically generated descriptions provide new access points by making possible the equivalent of full text search for audio and video content.

The use of AI to produce more metadata about archival content is a key part of making the archive more accessible because, as Wachtlar and Christel write: 'Without metadata, a thousand-hour digital video archive is reduced to a terabyte or greater jumble of bits; with metadata, those thousand hours can become a valuable information resource' (2002, 81). The digitisation process of previous analogue items enables a transformation of the archival object into 'bits' that can be separated and reused in highly different ways than analogue carriers of AV content. This fragmentation of the archival object as, for example, a complete film is facilitated by this datafication process in which bits of data are produced about the individual bits of the content. The increasingly datafied content has highly different affordances in terms of searching for specific segments of interest, but it also drastically changes our understanding of the archival object, which becomes increasingly decontextualised. Scholars have discussed the importance of introducing measures of recontextualisation in such cases to ensure that users are supported in their interpretation of the content (Brunow 2017; Efrat and Casimiro 2022). In a different project, Sound & Vision also experimented with colourising old black-and-white video footage from the so-called 'Polygoon' newsreel collection from the twentieth century using deep learning approaches (Marsman et al 2017). The aim was to allow new forms of engagement with the collection by making it easier to interact with the content but also more relevant and current for a wider audience. In this process, the footage is separated into each frame, which is then colourised, producing thousands of new images that in the end become a new version of the archival object. Here, the emphasis on accessibility rather than simply preservation, which could have included improving the quality of the existing footage, becomes part of a practice of generating archival objects that were not collected but produced. Such experiments raise new questions about what constitutes an archival object and how to understand their relation to the original content.

These datafication processes also change the role of the archivist, as they yield their role as the primary 'descriptor' that provides the contextualisation of the archival object via standardised processes of recordkeeping to an automated description workflow. With many of these AI tools, rather than actively producing description (e.g., who is in the clip) the archivist's role becomes that of the human-in-the-loop, accepting or declining the proposed description. In more and more cases, this task is also delegated to users of the system, who will be able to provide direct feedback into the system if they, for example, see a falsely labelled speaker in the example given above. In the context of born-digital data, the role of the archivist in describing the object also becomes much more distributed because the data is constituted via external actors who have made decisions on what data is collected and how that data is constructed (e.g., what counts as a geolocation). Equally, the users also begin to play a much more prominent role, as this type of content requires actively crowdsourcing the task of meaningfully interpreting the content to others (Noordegraaf 2011). This user involvement in the descriptive practices also highlights how the users become more and more central actors in the archival workflow and how the archival processes and decisions on how to provide descriptions become distributed across a multitude of actors (human and non-human). This distributed descriptive process, therefore, challenges archival control over how objects are catalogued, as they no longer have full oversight over the principles that guide the description. Both Feinberg (2017) and Drucker (2010) have highlighted the importance of recognising the constructed nature of data and how each decision regarding the composition of data conditions the decisions that follow (e.g., the way things are measured must be taken into account for what forms of analysis are possible). Therefore, the distribution and delegation of these decisions require new reflective practices over how to use this data in the archival workflow.

Making the archive user-facing

The increasing production of metadata enables increased searchability in the archive and new forms of creative search interfaces that users can engage with. An example of this is 'VPRO Backlight', which was released in 2022 and developed by VPRO Medialab, design agency Sudox and Sound & Vision (VPRO Tegenlicht 2022). The 'Archive of the Future' as it is also referred to is an online archive in which 500 broadcasts of the TV show *VPRO Backlight* are made accessible and searchable in new ways via AI. Concretely, the project leveraged image recognition and speech and text analysis techniques to transform the 500 broadcasts into 'bits' of data so that users can search at a highly granular level, for example for specific clips, shots or quotes. Furthermore, the online archive presents a highly browsable interface in which still images from the broadcasts are presented with coloured bars underneath, signalling different themes, such as health. This interface is to enable a more exploratory search approach within the archive while still being predominantly semantically focused via keywords. More sensory and abstract approaches to browsability can be found in the Sensory Moving Image Archive (SEMIA), in which AI was used to produce connections between items based on specific sensory features (Masson and Olesen 2020).

There are also more and more AI tools that directly focus on analysis and research within the archive by enabling researchers to, for example, explore certain characteristics across collections. The CLARIAH Media Suite, which is part of the Dutch national research infrastructure for digital humanities and developed and hosted by Sound & Vision, represents this growing emphasis on not only accessibility to but also the analysability of the archive (CLARIAH Media Suite 2023). The Media Suite is a research environment in which researchers can access AV collections (as datasets), use specific AI-powered tools to explore these collections, and get access to other more experimental tools, such as Jupyter Notebooks and computer vision algorithms (Ordelman et al 2019; Wigham et al 2018; Noord et al 2021). As part of the work within the European AI4Media project (AI4Media n.d.), Sound & Vision are also currently developing a new analytical tool for partial audio matching, which will allow users to explore how a piece of audio (e.g., a clip of a politician) was reused and circulated in the media after its initial airing. This can allow the novel analysis of both circulation patterns and how the clip is (re)framed throughout its lifetime, reception analysis of iconic clips, as well as the ability to track illegal uses of content. These projects represent a move towards a much more user-facing archive in which interfaces with underlying AI tools are built to ease the ability to explore and analyse the archive. The users in many cases also become co-producers of the archive either by participating in annotating parts of the collection or by publishing their analyses of the collections.

This emphasis on the user as a co-producer of archival content becomes even more evident in the use of AI for creative reuse. As an example of this, Thunderboom Records in collaboration with Sound & Vision are currently developing and experimenting with Waive Studio, an AI-infused DJ system (WAIVE 2022). The system uses sounds from Sound & Vision's digitised collections to create new music samples, beats and loops. A similar project in the United States is the Citizen DJ project which allows users to resample audio samples from the Library of Congress collections (Citizen DJ n.d.). Similar to the colourisation project described above, the aim of Waive is to make the collections accessible to new audiences who might be enticed by the ability to creatively play around with the collections.

Again, the use of AI changes the role of the archive from the producer of contextual descriptions of the archival object to becoming a co-producer of novel objects that remediate the existing archival objects. Thereby, the use of AI is extending the archival cycle by enabling new objects to circulate that refer back to the archive. As a result, the participatory role of the user in the archival processes is becoming more central in implicit ways, for example, providing system feedback, but also much more directly in terms of actively engaging with the archival content via analysis or creative reuse. This resonates with the cyclical nature of the 'records continuum' model of archiving discussed above (Upward 1996).

With these many developments, which Sound & Vision has served to illustrate here but that can be generalised to practices at other AV archives, we have highlighted two trends that have emerged with an increased focus on accessibility via the use of AI. These include the increasing datafication of the archive, where objects become increasingly granular, which also induces the need for 'bits about bits' (Negroponte 1996), or metadata, as we have referred to it here, to make the granularity useful. The second is an increased focus on opening the archive via interfaces that users can interact with and where they also become co-producers of archival objects and descriptions. These trends are uniquely embodied in the new Media Museum, which we now turn to before discussing the implications of these developments.

From spectator to participant

In addition to opening up the archive through metadata creation and reuse by producers and various groups of reusers, AV archives have also been experimenting with exhibitions of their collections to showcase their holdings and the stories they tell to broader user groups. Traditionally, archives have provided access to users via reading rooms and/or viewing booths, often by appointment. Increasingly, archives have discovered the temporary or permanent museum exhibition as a format for increasing their public outreach (Reed 2007). AV archives, such as Sound & Vision, occupy a position in between archives and museums. Their core role is to archive audiovisual recordings (and related materials), which, in the case of broadcasting materials, should be ready for reuse by the broadcasting corporations. At the same time, especially in the case of publicly funded institutions, AV archives have a responsibility to inform broader audiences about the history of public service media and use their collections to educate citizens about the way we are living in and with media (Deuze 2016).

Hence, audiovisual archives, while primarily servicing the public broadcast producers, have long since used museum exhibitions to show parts of their collections. The history of the museum of Sound & Vision and its predecessors shows a clear trend, moving from an object-centred, classical model of museum display to an almost fully digitised, data-driven multimedia experience. This development is characterised by a parallel change in the implied conception of the visitor, which has shifted from a spectator who takes in what is being communicated by the authoritative museum, to a participant who actively co-creates the exhibition and its meaning. In the following section, we introduce the new media museum of Sound & Vision, analysing the way it exemplifies this trend towards participatory engagement. Referencing theory on spectatorship, we analyse the transformations in the way the relation between the objects and the visitor is conceptualised in this setting.

The audiovisual archive on display: from media experience to media museum

Sound & Vision is a unique institution, both in terms of its large collections and innovative projects but also due to its double function. Having been founded in 1997 as the Dutch National Audiovisual Archive, as a merger of various public broadcasting and documentary film collections and the national broadcasting museum, it has functioned both as a working AV archive and host for an exhibition that showcases the archival collections to the wider public. Since 1983, the national broadcasting museum had showcased a sample from the collection of radio and television equipment to tell the story of broadcasting in the Netherlands (Knot n.d.). Housed at different locations, these exhibitions were examples of the classical museum exhibition format, which displays physical objects with accompanying text panels explaining their role and function. As Bal (1992) has argued, such a combination of objects and explanatory texts and the suggested 'routing' turn the museum display into a sign system that produces the viewer's knowledge. The specific layout of the exhibition 'addresses an implied "focalizer" whose tour is the story of the production of the knowledge taken in and taken home' (Bal 1992, 561). In the exhibitions of the national broadcasting museum, visitors were conceptualised as passive receivers of a predetermined narrative that focused on the institutional and technical development of broadcasting as becoming increasingly refined.

This conception of the visitor as a passive recipient of a predefined message changed when in December 2006, Sound & Vision opened the doors of its new 'Media Experience' to the public. Here, visitors were given a ring containing a chip, which was used to activate each of the 14 thematic exhibitions that included radio and television content from the 1950s to the present (for a full analysis, see Noordegraaf 2010b). The Media Experience was a unique exhibition as the majority of the 'objects' were presented virtually through screens, while some physical objects, such as cameras and clothing worn in famous Dutch TV shows for example, were also on display. Upon arrival at the Media Experience, visitors were asked to provide their name, date of birth and email address as well as choose a virtual guide – one of 12 famous Dutch media personalities – who would provide context at the exhibitions. These data entries and the choice of the guide were linked to the ring so that the visit felt personalised because the content shown would consider the age of the visitor, so that, for example, at the pavilion showcasing children's TV would show visitors clips from the time they were children and likely watched those programmes. Besides, some of the exhibits invited visitors to step into the shoes of media producers, such as reading the news from an autocue or experimenting with editing and special effects. Thus, in the Media Experience, visitors actively 'performed' the radio and television archive: to a certain extent, their input determined which kind of material was shown and seen. In that sense, the visitor acts as a more active spectator who is invited to actively compose and make sense of the objects on display (Noordegraaf 2010b, 206). This coincides with theories on television spectatorship that, in line with the increased control viewers have obtained over what they view, see a shift 'from a passive position to a more interactive one, from an observer separate from the apparatus to a participant' (Friedberg 1994, 144).

'You can no longer be a spectator, only a participant'

The heading of this section is a quote from an elderly male visitor in the new Media Museum, who did not want to use his mobile phone to engage with the museum and had chosen a strategy of looking over the shoulder of other visitors as a way of engaging or remaining in the spectator role within the museum. So, to follow the quote by Friedberg, this shift is radically intensified in the new museum, as becoming a participant is no longer a luxury, it is a prerequisite for engaging with the museum's exhibits. As described briefly in the introduction, the new Media Museum, which opened in February 2023, aims to be even more interactive and personalised than its predecessor in the way in which it tells its story of 'living in media' by using facial recognition and forms of explicit personalisation. These technologies help to mimic how the media is distributed today and are part of the more critical story the museum aims to tell, namely, to make the otherwise often hidden and opaque processes of algorithmic recommender systems visible to the visitor. Beyond this, the new Media Museum does not solely rely on the archival collection but also includes social media content and other external pieces of content to tell its story. This curatorial choice was considered necessary to ensure that the museum reflected the changed media landscape and the broad collection policy of the institute, which, in addition to radio, television and film, now also includes websites, social media and written press content and computer games. The emerging dynamic understanding of archiving we have outlined above is, therefore, highly visible in the ways the museum puts the archive on display.

The use of AI in activating the archive in the museum, therefore, embodies this participatory turn described above, as the use of AI in the museum infrastructure not only contributes to reconstructing the archive, it also reconstructs the visitor as an engaging participant who performs media. This is the case in the Media Museum, as visitors become datafied participants at the centre of the exhibition. The visual presence of the visitor's face, which appears both on the welcome screen and on every screen in the exhibition when the user approaches, means the user is met with their own image and a named greeting. More invisibly, this presence is apparent in the data infrastructure, because when each visitor touches the many interfaces in the museum, they produce new data, which the museum staff hope to use to further personalise the museum in the future. Such data could also help tailor access to the archive by sending a personalised selection of additional clips from the wider archive after visitors have left.

With this approach, the Media Museum places the user at the centre of the archival practices. As the user's preferences guide their experience of the archive, their data traces after leaving the museum spaces become tools to interpret the collection, forming an amplified user interface, as discussed above. This approach represents a new shift in conceptualising the role and practices of the museum; the previously rather controlled process, aimed at ensuring the authenticity, reliability, integrity and usability of archival records, is opened up not only via the inclusion of digital content, but also by placing the user at the heart of the curational process. This presents new questions, because as Feinberg (2017) and Drucker (2010) teach us, data is like the archive itself: situated, partial and constructed. Decisions in the archival process are, therefore, not necessarily in the hands of the archivists; rather, they move into the domain of the data scientists who produce methods for metadata collection or operationalise the personalisation in the museum. At Sound & Vision these decisions remain collaborative as archivists, museum staff and data scientists work together, but nonetheless, they require scholars of archives to move their analytical attention towards new locations in the museum when exploring the transformation of AV archives in the age of AI.

Conclusion

In this chapter, we have discussed the current shift in cultural heritage organisations from the preservation of heritage to the prioritisation of access and beyond – highlighting the impact of the uptake of AI. We argue that this technology-induced attention to new forms of access and reuse has led to an increased datafication of the archival collections and to a renewed conception of user engagement as participation. Our analysis of the use of digital technology and AI in the archival workflow and the transformations of the museum at Sound & Vision serves as an example of how the shift towards datafication and participation occurs in AV archives.

In the archival workflow, employing AI technologies such as speaker labelling, speech transcription, keyword extraction, subtitle generation and object detection leads to a process of 'automated metadatification'. Such automatically generated metadata are crucial for making the archive accessible and the archival records visible, as without such metadata digital artefacts cannot be recalled and thus cease to exist. The fact that a human interpretation of archival records is replaced by an automated computational reading of the content affects the status of the archival holdings as a source of knowledge about the mediated past. At the same time, it enables the emergence of a variety of different access points to the collections via different interfaces that allow various users to both engage with but also actively contribute to both the interpretation of existing content and extend the archive by producing new content through creative reuse.

We argue that the choices you make when creating, capturing, organising and pluralising data in an artificially intelligent environment turn the archival process into a cycle in which producers, archivists and users interact in a constant redesign of the archival object and the construction and interpretation of its meaning. This becomes specifically clear in the media museum, where the visitor is placed centre stage. In the AI-enhanced museum, the visitor becomes a participant who not only triggers what is shown but becomes part of what is exhibited. Their behaviour potentially also shapes which parts of the archive are put on display in the future, as the archive may use the visitor data to inform the curatorial choices for the future iterations of the exhibition. In this way, the datafied AV archive and museum raise interesting new questions about who has what agency in the archival process: placing the user at the centre means that the AV archive now starts collecting data on media *behaviour* instead of only media objects. As such, the artificially intelligent archive of the future democratises access to and engagement with the storage space of our collective cultural memory, while it poses new challenges to ensure that it will not amplify existing inequalities and blind spots.

Note

1. The personalised features in the museum can be characterised as 'explicit personalisation', where the user actively provides their preferences and then are presented with content based on those preferences. This is contrary to 'implicit personalisation' in which the recommendations to the user are not based on given preferences, but on inferences based on behavioural data (e.g., clicks on a website) (Bodó 2019). The latter is generally used to power Machine Learning (ML) systems, while the explicit personalisation uses more simple filtering systems.

References

AI4Media. No date. 'AI4Media'. Accessed 30 June 2023. www.ai4media.eu.

Assmann, A. 2010. 'Canon and archive'. In *A Companion to Cultural Memory Studies*, edited by A. Erll and A. Nünning, 97–107. Berlin; New York, NY: De Gruyter.

Bal, M.G. 1992. 'Telling, showing, showing off: A walking tour', *Critical Inquiry*, 18(3): 556–94.

Barok, D., Noordegraaf, J. and de Vries, A.P. 2019. 'From collection management to content management in art documentation: The conservator as an editor', *Studies in Conservation*, 64(8): 472–89.

Bodó, B. 2019. 'Selling news to audiences – a qualitative inquiry into the emerging logics of algorithmic news personalization in European quality news media', *Digital Journalism* 7(8): 1054–75.

Bowker, G.C. and Star, S.L. 2000. *Sorting Things Out: Classification and its consequences*. Cambridge, MA: MIT Press.

Brennan, M. 2022. '"The custodian of the BBC archives": The future of BBC Four as an archive channel', *Critical Studies in Television*, 17(2): 201–7.

Brunow, D. 2017. 'Curating access to audiovisual heritage: Cultural memory and diversity in European film archives', *Image [&] Narrative*, 18(1): 97–110.

Cecchine, R. 2021. 'AI in audiovisual archives: What kinds of analysis are possible?', Sound & Vision, 28 May. Accessed 12 May 2023. https://beeldengeluid.nl/en/knowledge/blog/ai-audiovisual-archives-what-kinds-analysis-are-possible.

Cecchine, R. 2023. Audiovisual Archives, AI, and Values: A web of relationships. Master's Thesis, University of Amsterdam.

Citizen DJ. No date. 'Homepage'. Accessed 12 May 2023. https://citizen-dj.labs.loc.gov/.

CLARIAH Media Suite. 2023. 'CLARIAH Media Suite'. Accessed 15 May 2023. https://mediasuite.clariah.nl/about.
Colavizza, G. et al. 2021. 'Archives and AI: An overview of current debates and future perspectives'. arXiv:2105.01117.
Cordell, R. 2020. *Machine Learning + Libraries: A report on the state of the field*. LC Labs, Library of Congress.
Delaney, B. and De Jong, A. 2015. 'Media archives and digital preservation: Overcoming cultural barriers', *New Review of Information Networking* 20(1–2):73–89.
Derrida, J. 1995. 'Archive fever: A Freudian impression', *Diacritics* 25(2): 9–63.
Deuze, M. 2016. 'Living in media and the future of advertising', *Journal of Advertising* 45(3): 326–33.
Deuze, M., Blank, P. and Speers, L. 2012. 'A life lived in media', *Digital Humanities Quarterly*, 6(1). Available at: www.digitalhumanities.org/dhq/vol/6/1/000110/000110.html.
Drucker, J. 2011. 'Humanities approaches to graphical display', *Digital Humanities Quarterly*, 5(1). Available at: www.digitalhumanities.org/dhq/vol/5/1/000091/000091.html.
Edmondson, R. and Edmonson, R. 2004. *Audiovisual Archiving: Philosophy and principles*. Paris: UNESCO.
Edwards, P.N. 2002. 'Infrastructure and modernity: Force, time, and social organisation in the history of sociotechnical systems'. In *Modernity and Technology*, edited by T.J. Misa, P. Brey and A. Feenberg, 185–226. Cambridge, MA: MIT Press.
Efrat, L. and Casimiro, G.G. 2022. 'Transformative heritage: Open source, insurgent nationalism, and augmented memories', *Culture Unbound*, 14(2):133–52.
Ernst, W. 2013. *Digital Memory and the Archive*. University of Minnesota Press. https://www.jstor.org/stable/10.5749/j.ctt32bcwb.
Feinberg, M. 2017. 'A design perspective on data'. In Proceedings of the 2017 CHI Conference on Human Factors in Computing Systems, 2952–63.
Fossati, G. 2012. 'Found footage filmmaking, film archiving and new participatory platforms'. In *Found Footage: Cinema Exposed*, edited by Giovanna Fossati and Jaap Guldemond, 177–84. Amsterdam: Amsterdam University Press.
Fossati, G. 2017. 'Film heritage beyond the digital turn'. Inaugural lecture.
Foucault, M. 1972. *The Archaeology of Knowledge*. New York: Pantheon Books.
Friedberg, A. 1994. *Window Shopping: Cinema and the Postmodern*. Los Angeles: University of California Press.
International Council on Archives. No date. 'What are archives?' Accessed 30 June 2023. https://www.ica.org/en/what-archive.
Kennedy, H., Poell, T. and van Dijck, J. 2015. 'Data and agency', *Big Data & Society*, 2(2).
Ketelaar, E. 2001. 'Tacit narratives: The meanings of archives', *Archival Science*, 1: 131–41.
Knot, H. No date. 'Herinneringen aan het Omroepmuseum', MediaPages.nl. Accessed 30 June 2023. https://www.mediapages.nl/muziek-a-media/339-herinneringen-aan-het-omroepmuseum.
Lowry, J. and MacNeil, H. 2021. 'Archival thinking: Archaeologies and genealogies', *Archival Science*, 21(1):1–8.
Mackenzie, A. 2017. *Machine Learners: Archaeology of a data practice*. Cambridge, MA: MIT Press.
Markus, G., Brinkerink, M. and Jansen, B. 2019. 'Be engaged: Facilitating creative reuse at the Netherlands Institute for Sound and Vision'. In *The Routledge International Handbook of New Digital Practices in Galleries, Libraries, Archives, Museums and Heritage Sites*. London: Routledge.
Marsman, R. et al. 2017. 'New life for old media: Investigations into speech synthesis and deep learning-based colorization for audiovisual archives'. New European Media Summit.
Masson, E. and Olesen, C.G. 2021. 'Digital access as archival reconstitution: Algorithmic sampling, visualization, and the production of meaning in large moving image repositories', *Signata. Annales des sémiotiques / Annals of Semiotics*, 12. https://doi.org/10.4000/signata.3011.
Mayer-Schönberger, V. and Cukier, K. 2013. *Big Data: A revolution that will transform how we live, work, and think*. Boston: Houghton Mifflin Harcourt.
Mejias, U.A. and Couldry, N. 2019. 'Datafication', *Internet Policy Review*, 8(4).
Negroponte, N. 1996. *Being Digital*. First edition. New York, NY: Vintage.
Noord, N.V. et al. 2021. 'Automatic annotations and enrichments for audiovisual archives'. In *Proceedings of the 13th International Conference on Agents and Artificial Intelligence –Volume 1: ARTIDIGH. Special Session on Artificial Intelligence and Digital Heritage: Challenges and*

Opportunities, 633–40. https://www.scitepress.org/PublicationsDetail.aspx?ID=DgZjO6HYYTA=&t=1.
Noordegraaf, J. 2010a. 'Who knows television? Online access and the gatekeepers of knowledge', *Critical Studies in Television*, 5(2):1–19.
Noordegraaf, J. 2010b. 'Experiencing TV: The screen space of the media museum'. In *The Cinematic Experience: Film, contemporary art, museum = film, arte contemporanea, museo*, edited by A. Autelitano, 201–11. Pasian di Prato, Italiy: Campanotto.
Noordegraaf, J. 2011. 'Crowdsourcing television's past. The state of knowledge in digital archives', *Tijdschrift voor Mediageschiedenis*, 14(2): 108–20.
Ordelman, R., Melgar, L., Martinez-Ortiz, C., Noordegraaf, J. and Blom, J. 2019. 'Media Suite: Unlocking archives for mixed media scholarly research'. In *Selected Papers from CLARIN Annual Conference 2018, Pisa, 8–10 October 2018*, edited by I. Skadina and M. Eskevich, 133–43. Linköpings universitet, Linköping Electronic Conference Proceedings. https://ep.liu.se/en/conference-article.aspx?series=ecp&issue=159&Article_No=14.
Paalman, F., Fossati, G. and Masson, E. 2021. 'Introduction: Activating the archive', *The Moving Image*, 21:1–25.
Prelinger, R. 2007. 'Archives and access in the 21st century', *Cinema Journal*, 46(3): 114–18.
Prelinger, R. 2009. 'Points of origin: Discovering ourselves through access', *The Moving Image: The Journal of the Association of Moving Image Archivists*, 9(2):164–75.
Reed, M. 2017. 'Blurring the boundaries: Collaborative library and museum exhibitions in Los Angeles', *RBM: A Journal of Rare Books, Manuscripts, and Cultural Heritage*, 8(1): 45–50.
Rehm, G. 2020. 'The use of artificial intelligence in the audiovisual sector'. In *Concomitant Expertise for INI Report, Research for CULT committee*. Brussels: European Parliament, Policy Department for Structural and Cohesion Policies.
Schwartz, J.M. and Cook, T. 2002. 'Archives, records, and power: The making of modern memory', *Archival Science*, 2(1): 1–19.
Upward, F. 1996. 'Structuring the records continuum part one. Post-custodial principles and properties', *Archives & Manuscripts*, 24(2): 268–85.
Upward, F. et al. 2018. *Recordkeeping Informatics for a Networked Age*. Clayton, Victoria: Monash University Publishing.
VPRO Tegenlicht. 2022. 'VPRO Tegenlicht en Beeld en Geluid creëren "Archief van de Toekomst"', Beeld & Geluid newsroom. Accessed 12 May, 2023. https://nieuws.beeldengeluid.nl/209816-vpro-tegenlicht-en-beeld-en-geluid-creeren-archief-van-de-toekomst.
Wactlar, H.D. and Christel, M.G. 2002. 'Digital video archives: Managing through metadata'. In *Building a National Strategy for Digital Preservation: Issues in digital media archiving*, 80–95. Washington DC: Council on Library and Information Resources Washington, D.C. and Library of Congress.
WAIVE. 2022. 'Thunderboom Records – WAIVE'. Accessed 15 May 2023. www.thunderboomrecords.com/waive.
Wigham, M., Melgar, L. and Ordelman, R. 2018. 'Jupyter Notebooks for generous archive interfaces'. In *2018 IEEE International Conference on Big Data (Big Data)*, 2766–74. https://doi.org/10.1109/BigData.2018.8622203.

5

Digital mapping and cultural heritage

Claire Warwick and Katherine Aske

Maps represent one of the most complex categories of archival records, and a rich source for research. In both their born-digital and physical forms, what information maps contain and represent can vary massively. Maps can present bias and misinformation, national priorities and global perceptions – they represent time and space, creating endless avenues for analysis. However, combinations of image and text, complex layouts, varying sizes, scales and formats, and fluctuations in the quality and accuracy of data records mean that preserving and making these records accessible has been, and remains, a challenge.

In this case study, we examine how maps are being made more accessible, either through digitisation or the availability of born-digital map data; what they are being used for and how they are being used; and where AI is being or can be employed to make digital maps machine-readable. With a focus on current preservation initiatives, collaborative projects, methodologies and approaches through AI tools, this study examines the uses and potentials of digital mapping, while also underlining key cautions regarding issues of transparency and AI algorithms.[1]

Digital mapping has long been used for geographical information systems (GIS) and the Global Positioning System (GPS), such as those applied to Google Maps and OpenStreetMap, and as a way to preserve cultural heritage. Digital maps can also act as an interface for connecting disparate information. Exploring cultural heritage organisations in the UK and Ireland, this case study examines the interdisciplinary research enabled by digital and computer-generated mapping within cultural heritage, and beyond. We examine approaches to the digital preservation of maps used within six legal deposit libraries (Bodleian Library; British Library; Cambridge University Library; the Library of Trinity College,

Dublin; the National Library of Scotland; and the National Library of Wales), with an extended look into the work of the National Library of Wales (NLW). We also offer guidance for research methodologies and approaches to preservation, digitisation and the creation of linked data and enriched metadata for cultural heritage organisations.

Maps are significant tools in our everyday lives, from searching for directions, to shaping our view of the world. Throughout recorded history, maps have provided us with a sense of place in time and space. From the earliest sketches to the most accurate satellite imaging, maps have documented the movements, explorations and discoveries of humankind. While the earliest maps may have been crude imaginings, by the sixteenth century they began to gain practical and political meaning as techniques for land surveying improved. But maps often demonstrate more information about culture than any geographical location. Even now, despite advances made through platforms like Google Maps, there remain significant biases in the way the information from maps is used and visualised. As multimedia sources, maps present endless opportunities, but without accurate metadata and transparent archival processes, these records, whether digitised or born-digital, can, ironically, be difficult to navigate.

The accuracy of a map also has a direct impact on how it can be used, what it can show us and how it can help us to visualise the world. Historical maps are littered with inaccuracies or may be entirely fictitious. However, thanks to modern surveying, we now tend to assume that the information presented on maps is correct (Keates 1996, 97). But what is *correct* locational information? Does it relate to precise coordinates or geographical features such as roads and rivers? Is it information about the locality, such as shops and facilities, or all of the above? Maps can store infinite amounts of information, so how are we using them in the digital age?

Digitised and born-digital maps

As Jen Jack Giesking (2018) argues, there is a long history of the use of digital mapping technologies in digital humanities. This includes both the digitisation and analysis of historical map collections, and also the use of digital techniques such as GIS to create maps of place or time-based specific phenomena. GIS, originally a military technology developed in the 1960s, was quickly adopted by social scientists, such as geographers. It allows database entries to be linked to geographical coordinates that identify their geographical location, allowing them to be output as a map, or other visual representation. Its use became widespread in archaeology from the 1980s onwards and began to be adopted in disciplines such as history and literary studies in the early 2000s (Gregory and Healey 2007; Murrieta-Flores, Donaldson and Gregory 2017). One of the most high-profile uses of such technologies in digital humanities was by Franco Moretti (2007) whose book, *Graphs, Maps and Trees*, was based on his use of digital technologies, including GIS, to interrogate what were at the time very large datasets of literary texts in 2007. This pioneering use of big data methodologies demonstrated that the frequency of literary phenomena could be plotted not only over time, but in space. GIS-based projects now number in the thousands: over two hundred of them can be accessed directly from the Anterotesis blog.[2]

Large-scale map digitisation projects, however, have a shorter history than the use of GIS itself. Printed maps are large documents which may become delicate with age. This means that specialist equipment and careful handling are required for their digitisation. The files created in the process were also too large for the limited storage capacity of early digital repository systems (Novak and Ostash 2022). Libraries, therefore, only began to digitise maps at scale in the early 2000s (Knutzen 2013; Woods et al 2016; Damoor 2019).

Once digital images of historical maps became available, they were used in digital humanities research to enrich the information provided by a spatial database; for example, the Salem Witch Trials and Boston Back Bay Fens projects carried out at the University of Virginia's Institute for Advanced Technology in the Humanities in the early 2000s. The Salem Witch Trials project combined GIS with digitised historical maps to demonstrate how accusations of witchcraft spread through the area around Salem, Massachusetts, in 1691 like an epidemic of disease.[3] Boston Back Bay Fens used GIS, historical maps and images of Boston to investigate the relationship between the development of the city and its environment in the late nineteenth century.[4] Both of these projects, and the work of Moretti and the Spatial History Lab at Stanford, demonstrated the potential of spatial digital humanities to make possible novel, visual representations of literary and historical phenomena (Shnayder, 2010; White, 2010).

Nevertheless, the coordinates for geographical features still had to be entered into GIS databases by hand, using information from a geographical dictionary or gazetteer (Weinman et al 2019). This was a laborious process, which might take up to six hours for a standard-size map (Knutzen 2013). It is therefore not surprising that, since the early 2020s, a significant amount of research has been undertaken into the possibility of developing digital systems for the automatic recognition of map features (Chiang, Leyk and Knoblock 2013). However, maps still presented a challenge to such systems, since the data they contain is both textual and visual, including topographical features, symbols and textual description (Hosseini et al 2021). This means that researchers have to decide whether to use automated optical character recognition on textual labels, or to use computer vision techniques to automatically recognise visual features, such as road junctions, by their shape (Chiang et al 2020). The advent of Google Earth in 2001 was an important step forward in the study of digital maps: it made automatic recognition of some topological features possible for users without high levels of technical expertise (Knutzen 2013). As computer vision technologies have improved in the last decade, these systems have become increasingly powerful. However, humans still have to check that the system has correctly identified topographical features and add any that are missing (Chiang et al 2020). This is why libraries are so vital as custodians of digital maps. As Hosseini (2021) argues, the intervention of library professionals is most critical in the application of complex item-level metadata, which allows users to search effectively for the map data that they need. Maps of the same area may also be created to different scales and at different times. Therefore, accurate georeferencing services, usually provided by librarians, are vital in ensuring that the same places or features are correlated with each other despite differences in size and age of digitised maps.

The need for human input, however, has meant that the creation of digital map corpora has been very time-consuming. It is partly for this reason that citizen science and crowdsourcing have proven vital in digital mapping. In 2010, the New York Public Library (NYPL) launched a project to encourage the public to contribute their knowledge to their newly created map database. Their web interface allowed users without expertise in GIS to curate their own collections from the corpus of digitised maps, and to annotate the names of places and features. This benefitted users and librarians alike, resulting in a larger map corpus without information having to be manually entered from a gazetteer (Knutzen 2013).

Such an enterprise may have been inspired by the success of the OpenStreetMap (OSM) initiative.[5] This was founded in London in 2004 and encouraged volunteers to contribute mapping data to a central database using small, inexpensive, mobile GPS units, which were newly available. OSM's aim was to produce free, open, geospatial data that anyone could use. It also provided free software to allow non-expert users to create their own maps via a web interface. The initiative proved so successful that it is now a global phenomenon, used in numerous spatial apps and software packages (Jacobs and Mitchell 2020).

Crowdsourcing of spatial data has also been used successfully in education. For example, in 2015, David Wrisley and his students at the American University in Beirut began a project to map the linguistic cultures of this polyglot city. Students used their mobile phones to take photographs of features such as shop signs that demonstrated which language was being spoken in different parts of Beirut. The images were then plotted on a map, using GIS coordinates. As with the NYPL's mapping project, this utilised the knowledge of those living in a city to create an accurate spatial representation of its linguistic and historical culture (Waddell 2017; Wrisley 2020).

There are now numerous projects which combine mapping and GIS technologies to study historical and cultural heritage objects using spatial data. The Pelagios Network[6] unites several international historical mapping initiatives, including studies of the place names of ancient Greece, global occurrences of bubonic plague since the Black Death and maps of the Horn of Africa from the eighteenth century onwards. The Pelagios project also produces open-source software, such as Recogito,[7] a tool which allows users without specialist knowledge of GIS or programming to create maps of historical phenomena (Simon et al 2015, 2017). These include documents from the Ottoman Empire in the 1570s, which were annotated by postgraduate students taking the 'Spatial History' seminar at the Department of History of Boğaziçi University in Istanbul, thus forming the basis of a new Ottoman Gazetteer.[8] Once again, this demonstrates the potential of utilising community and volunteer efforts to create and populate historical maps.

Recogito is making an extremely important contribution to digital humanities. However, data still has to be entered by hand, and thus the scale of the corpora that can be handled is necessarily limited. Pelagios is, therefore, currently investigating the use of data science methods to make possible the use of visualisation and analytical technologies at a larger scale (Rees and Gadd n.d.). This is becoming necessary because, as in other areas of cultural heritage, the amount of digital map data has increased massively over the last decade (Novak and Ostash 2022). This means that very large map corpora can now be constructed, but that such corpora are too large for manual analysis. AI tools are, therefore, increasingly necessary.

Digital mapping at the national legal deposit libraries (UK and Ireland)

In Great Britain and Ireland, the largest source of digital map data is the Ordnance Survey of Great Britain (OS).[9] The OS began in the mid-eighteenth century, when military maps of the Scottish Highlands were created following the rebellion of 1745. The whole of the UK was then gradually mapped during the nineteenth century and completed in 1869. However, it has only recently become possible to conduct computational data analysis of the data recorded on such maps, thanks to the efforts of the UK and Ireland's national legal deposit libraries (Bodleian Library; British Library; Cambridge University Library; the Library of Trinity College, Dublin; the National Library of Scotland; and the NLW), who are preserving, digitising and producing sheet-level metadata for their map collections.

Since 1998, the OS has deposited an annual snapshot of its large-scale map data (scales of 1:1,250, 1:2,500 and 1:10,000) in these libraries.[10] These digital maps and geospatial data are allowing national libraries to open up new avenues for research, not only in linked data and visualisation, but as primary sources of research (Hosseini et al 2021). However, as we have seen, the creation of map corpora is costly and labour-intensive for libraries and archives, and only possible for those with the resources to undertake high-quality and large-scale photography for large physical maps. Cartographic materials therefore require a unique set of approaches, and below we examine how the six legal deposit libraries are preserving and opening up their digital map collections for users.

Library of Trinity College, Dublin

The Library of Trinity College, Dublin (TCD) holds over half a million printed maps and atlases in the Glucksman Map Library, ranging from rare older materials to modern maps, from Ireland, Great Britain and the rest of the world, making it the largest collection in Ireland. At the time of writing, there are 36 items in the digitised cartographic collection, dating from 1560 to 1838; the remaining physical collection must be consulted in the library or may be scanned on demand.[11] The Fagel Library's map collection, although little known beyond academia, is one of the highlights of TCD's holdings. Collected over five generations of the Dutch Fagel family from the late seventeenth to the early nineteenth centuries, the Fagel Map collection is one of the finest in the world and is the only extant collection of its size to be assembled as materials were published, rather than retrospectively. These mostly eighteenth-century maps are global in scope, coloured and intricately detailed, and an invaluable source for researchers. The Fagel Project, which began in 2015, aims to digitise the entire collection, particularly the maps, to make it more accessible to the public. So far, 28 titles in the collection have been made freely available online (with the option to download their metadata), and six of these contain maps.[12] Librarians are also working with computer scientists to create three-dimensional streetscapes and overlay battle plans onto modern topography.

Bodleian Library, Oxford

The Bodleian Library holds 1.5 million sheet maps, 20,000 atlases and a selection of geospatial data, dating from medieval times to the present day. Their OS materials provide an almost complete collection of maps for Britain, dating from the eighteenth century onwards. Around 500 items from the Bodleian's map collection have been digitised so far and are available on their digital database accompanied by catalogue metadata, including brief descriptions, dates, scales, cartographers and links to physical records in the library's catalogue.[13] The library also provides access to two GIS software packages: ArcGIS,[14] a mapping and spatial analytics tool that allows users to view maps in 3D and share data through ArcGIS Online, and Quantum GIS (QGIS),[15] an open-source GIS package used for creating, editing, visualising, analysing and publishing geospatial information.

Cambridge University Library

Cambridge University Library's (CUL) Map Department holds 1.3 million maps and more than 40,000 atlases and books on cartography. Most of their physical cartographic resources, ranging from early manuscripts and printed maps to those from the modern day, can only be viewed in the library's Map Room. However, 300 of these maps have now been digitised and can be downloaded, with their metadata, from the Cambridge Digital Library database.[16] This marks a shift towards the availability of 'large-scale' digital collections of unique mapping, which provides the opportunity for general interest and new avenues for research 'on a wide range of subjects: not just cartography, but also landscape change, social history, local and family history, art history and much more' (Smith 2021).

Between 1998 and 2005, CUL received maps of Great Britain in the OS Land-Line® data format which is structured around 'tiles' (squares of varying extent, similar to conventional map sheets). However, since 2006 the library has received this data in OS MasterMap® format, which is based on features (buildings, roads, railways, etc.) and dates, allowing a more specific record of landscape change; they can also be coloured to create a more intuitive and clearer map.[17] With some exceptions, CUL hold digital copies of every Ordnance Survey map 'ever published'.[18] These can be accessed in the Map Room, or via the Digimap Service, an online map and data delivery service, available by subscription to UK Higher and Further Education establishments, which includes OS, historical, geological, LiDAR and marine maps and spatial data.[19]

The map collections at the National Library of Scotland (NLS), the British Library (BL) and the NLW operate at an even larger scale. With facilities to digitise large and highly detailed records, as well as developing, exploring and applying new technologies to make their collections more accessible and usable, these libraries are also applying innovative approaches to their map data.

The National Library of Scotland, Edinburgh

Of all the national deposit libraries, the NLS has the largest collection and most accessible digital map database.[20] The NLS's collection of digital maps and its online database are extensive, and the NLS has been working with several partners to encourage the use of machine learning and computational research methods using its digital map collections. These include the 'Living with Machines' and 'Machines Reading Maps' (more details below) projects in partnership with the University of Minnesota and the Alan Turing Institute in London.[21] These projects aimed to create born-digital maps 'whose design mimics the style of historical map sheets', to help make embedded text within historical map collections searchable (Fleet et al 2021). Using OS data and georeferencing, the NLS's OS digital platform now allows users to search across map collections for specific places, as well as to view maps side by side, and even in 3D, making research into geographical, as well as historical and industrial, changes to the landscape far more accessible.[22]

By 2019 the NLS held over 220,000 online maps with georeferenced layers of mapping. In 2011, it had already begun to use early versions of Klockan Technologies' Georeferencer to allow the blank edges of printed maps to be cut away and the remaining data to be placed in layers using the map's longitude and latitude. MapTiler was then used to create a seamless layer for online presentation. Many of the tools that are employed by the NLS, including GeoServer and OpenLayers, have been created by the web-mapping communities, as part of collaborative code development activities, and are provided on GitHub (Fleet 2019). The release of the library's geospatial data through the Historic Maps API in 2011 allowed a historical georeferenced map of England, Scotland and Wales from the 1920s to be embedded inside another website. This improved user accessibility and, according to Fleet's 2019 study, saw 6.7 million sessions and 10.8 million page views over seven years (2011 to 2018). The website 'was also used by a broader range of institutions than the NLS's traditional online user base' (Fleet and Pridal 2012). The increased user engagement from the NLS's accessible map data and the online platform begins to demonstrate the potential of improving map usability.

British Library, London

The BL has a collection of maps, plans and views that numbers nearly 4.5 million records – one of the largest collections in the world. Their OS collections from the UK and Ireland, which date back to the mid-nineteenth century, are available in the library's dedicated Reading Rooms, and some of these collections are still available on BL's online exhibition pages through the UK Web Archive.[23] The BL's collection of digital maps and geospatial data deposited under non-print legal deposit are available to readers through a digital map viewer in the Maps Reading Room. Those that have been digitised or scanned from a physical source can be accessed online,[24] and through the BL's Georeferencer interface,[25] which has over 50,000 online map images. They can also be searched via Old Maps Online,[26] a geographic search interface from numerous historic map collections.

Researchers at the Alan Turing Institute have used the BL's collections to develop computer vision techniques to analyse historical maps as part of the 'Living with Machines' project.[27] The AHRC-NEH funded project, 'Machines Reading Maps'[28] – a collaboration between the BL, the Alan Turing Institute, the University of Southern California, the Austrian Institute of Technology, the Library of Congress and the NLS – is seeking to treat map text as a 'new kind of data' (Dotson 2020). Building on the 'Linked Maps' project and the text extraction tool Strabo, the project utilises fully georeferenced digitised historical OS maps to create prototypical methods of annotating text on maps using the Recogito tool (Li et al 2021).[29] They nevertheless recognise the need for human correction and curation of automatically extracted map text.

The project aims to invent a new method for historians to work with large map collections and has been designed as a platform to help researchers understand the role map data can play in historical research. The team has used data from approximately 130,000 map sheets to discover how many maps the British OS made, as well as the date and location of creation to discover how much has been digitised, and which maps may be missing from the collection. Using dates and coordinates, the project team have been able to leverage time and space as interdependent points of information, providing an interface that analyses the shape of large-scale polygon datasets. Data visualisation has allowed the project to show how the OS collection was built, and the team are hoping to add data from non-OS records to tell the stories of maps, bringing maps and timelines together to aid accessibility for humanities researchers.

The project has also created MapReader, a free, open-source software library written in Python for analysing large digital map collections.[30] Aimed at users with little expertise in computational research methods, MapReader enables researchers to work at scale, putting visual markers into machine-readable data (Hosseini et al 2021b). The team that created MapReader has also investigated the feasibility of automatic recognition of what they have called 'rail spaces' in maps from the nineteenth century. Using a corpus of maps digitised by the NLS, they are looking for evidence of the presence of rail transport in the landscape, including not only stations, but structures such as sidings, goods yards and the kinds of industrial premises associated with rail transport. Their aim is to automate the detection of such features so that they can be studied at scale, rather than individually or in small groups. This will make possible an analysis of how railways affected the landscape of the UK as a whole and how this changed over time – a task which would be massively time-consuming if performed on individual maps. This does not mean that the close reading of historical maps is in any way rendered obsolete, but, as with distant reading of other types of text, it makes possible a different, quantitatively driven method of understanding historical data (Hosseini et al 2021b).

National Library of Wales, Aberystwyth

The NLW has several digital mapping outputs, many of which can be consulted online, and their digital team is investigating ways in which maps can be used to present their collections through linked and machine-readable data.

The NLW holds one of the largest collections of maps in the British Isles, and the largest in Wales, consisting of over a million sheets of maps, charts and plans, and thousands of atlases. Not surprisingly, the collection is particularly focused on maps of Wales, but also includes material relating to the Welsh diaspora in Patagonia, and areas with Welsh connections, such as Brittany. As a legal deposit library, since 1911 the NLW has been entitled to a copy of every map published in the UK – a collection which it has also supplemented with purchased material.[31] The Library undertook a major map digitisation exercise as part of the 'Cynefin: Mapping Wales Sense of Place' project, which ran from 2014 to 2017 and was funded by Heritage Lottery Fund Wales, the Welsh Government and Archives and Records Council Wales. During this project, the NLW digitised more than 1,100 of their Welsh tithe maps.[32] The process of digitisation followed the NLW's workflow, whereby images are digitised in-house, the file is then checked for accuracy, and metadata is then added using Archivematica software. Once this process is complete, the digitised image is uploaded into the NLW's Fedora repository (McInnes n.d.).

Crowdsourcing techniques were also used during the Cynefin project. Using a web interface, volunteers georeferenced each map and transcribed around 27,000 entries in the accompanying tithe apportionment documents, linking them to the relevant field numbers on the maps. Six smaller projects were also undertaken across Wales, overseen by local archives. Each project was embedded in communities that chose the aspects of the tithe maps that were of greatest interest to them. These included a study of Dwygyfylchi parish before the railways arrived; an investigation of rural land use in The Hiraethog area; the creation of a spatial database of more than a thousand pubs in Ceredigion; an exploration of the ancient woodland on the Gower peninsula; a recreation of the local history of the Valleys Garw and the Llynfi Valleys, north of Bridgend, through the creation of new textile art; and an investigation of the trials in Gwent. The range and variety of the Cynefin project's local initiatives is a potent demonstration of the potential use of mapping and spatial data to engage the public and local communities (none of whom were technical experts) and to create a connection with the places of Wales. Many of the projects also involved school children, showing the potential of digital crowdsourcing to contribute to education.

Digital mapping, accessibility and AI

As part of this case study, we talked to archivist Sally McInnes, Head of Unique Collections and Collections Care at NLW, and Jason Evans, the first permanent Wikimedian to be given a role at a UK cultural institution.

McInnes and the NLW have been working on forming a trusted digital repository, which, considering the bilingual elements of the NLW's record data, is a significant step.[33] According to McInnes, the NLW has been working closely with the University of Aberystwyth, which has a particular strength in AI and is currently leading the collaborative AHCR project 'Towards a National AI-Enabled Repository for Wales'.[34] The NLW is investigating how techniques such as computer vision could be used to extract information from their map database by automatically identifying features in the map images themselves, rather than by searching the metadata. The aim of using such techniques would be to make searching the database easier and more efficient for users.

The usability of their collections will become increasingly important in the context of the 'Towards a National Collection' (TaNC) initiative in which NLW is participating. As its name suggests, this programme aims to link together digital collections held in different repositories across the UK, allowing for unified searches across very large, linked databases.[35] NLW already uses the International Image Interoperability Framework (IIIF), the international standard for sharing and annotating digital images, to display its visual digitised sources. However, Evans commented that NLW's participation in TaNC has caused a 'real shift' in their work: 'unifying and aligning catalogues and data on a huge scale' means that AI is a 'natural avenue' for the processing of record data, which can no longer be processed manually.[36] Evans explained that the Library is also employing user-generated content, and crowdsourced materials to improve search and retrieval of material from the map collection using Wikidata – a vast online database that anyone can contribute to and use (Evans 2021). It contains hundreds of millions of items of user-generated data, including text and images, and uses linked data to allow users to search the entire collection. The NLW has shared thousands of its images and their attendant IIIF manifests on Wikimedia, allowing users to find NLW content without having to access it through their web interface, or even be aware that it is part of their collection. Wikidata is now a stable platform around which community-building tools can be constructed. Indeed, in recent years the Wikidata community has developed several tools that make use of IIIF functionality to allow users to add additional information to images, or to highlight aspects of an image that are of interest, information which is then stored within the IIIF manifest.

NLW have used this functionality to enable further crowdsourcing activity, which is especially significant in the case of spatial data. Tools such as Wikidata Image Positions make it possible for a user to tag an image in the NLW's crowdsourcing platform and add a place name and spatial coordinates. Such functionality is especially useful when annotating an image of a building or topographical feature that is also recorded on digitised maps. The annotation made by the user can be fed back into Wikidata and compared with other information stored there about the same item, identified by its geotag. This allows the accuracy of the information to be cross-referenced using identifiers from other organisations, and also allows for multilingual tagging of place names in both English and Welsh. Evans suggested that open data sources have been particularly helpful in the generation of a Welsh-language map of Wales and the standardisation of Welsh place names. This is in marked contrast to the experience of the OS, which encountered significant problems identifying place names on Welsh language maps due to variants in their spelling (Vane et al 2021). In this sense, the NLW's development of a Welsh-language map will inform future research and the development of commercial applications, such as GIS apps. In its current form, Wikidata offers an alternative to the use of AI as a means of making searches of large map databases more effective. However, Evans hopes that in future, the two methods may be combined by using AI for data verification and reconciliation. It also seems likely that crowdsourced data will still be necessary, even if image recognition is automated, since, as Evans argues, AI can identify features such as lakes, but, at present at least, human intervention would be needed to identify the name of a specific lake in a given location.[37]

Ultimately, the NLW would like to push spatial functionality further and consider ways of utilising maps as a means of displaying different kinds of data. At present, the library's collections can only be accessed using a conventional textual search interface. However, Evans observed that 'People love maps … never underestimate the power of dots on a map, because people really connect with and relate to that'.[38] Users evidently enjoy working with maps and often wish to organise their search for material around geographical places such as those where they or their family have lived and worked. The NLW is therefore working on a map-based interface, which, in addition to the more conventional search functionality, would allow users to access their collections by geographical location. A user would, for example, be able to see all the material in the collection that relates to Aberystwyth displayed visually on a map of Wales. Such a development is particularly timely, since the Welsh school curriculum has recently been revised to stress the importance of identification with a sense of place – the quintessentially Welsh concept of 'Cynefin', a word which, significantly, has no direct English translation.

However, unlike annotation methods that make use of citizen science and crowdsourcing methods, the use of large-scale methods of analysis has the potential to move spatially based scholarship away from users without technical expertise. As we have seen, humanities students may be able to collaborate on projects to map historical phenomena using software such as Recogito or even the slightly more complex ArcGIS, with a relatively small amount of technical instruction. Yet, a significant amount of technical expertise is required to use the AI-based analytical methods used in computer vision. It is, therefore, relatively more difficult for users to understand how the results of a search using AI have been achieved, and whether they should trust them (Spiegelhalter 2020).

As part of our conversation with the NLW, we asked whether their users were aware of the potential use of AI as a method of accessing the library's collections. We wondered whether there was any demand for its use, or, conversely, whether any fears had been expressed about its deployment. Evans and McInnes stressed the importance of keeping users informed about the methods the library has been using, for example by being open about levels of reliability when crowdsourced data is being used. It is clear that academic researchers in areas such as information studies, digital humanities and computer science are keen to explore the potential of AI in a cultural heritage setting, and that funders wish to see greater use of such methods in the context of initiatives such as TaNC. However, at present there appears to be no immediate demand from users themselves for information about the data they are using, or the methods that are being used to retrieve it. NLW have seen little evidence of awareness of the use of such methods in their user community, nor had information professionals who attended an AEOLIAN workshop in 2022, at which we asked the same question.

This might not be a matter of significant concern. As Schmidt, Klein, Gold et al (2016) argue, it is not essential that non-experts, such as humanities scholars, understand the computational detail of the algorithms that are used to search the data that they are interested in. However, if such techniques have the potential to skew the results that are achieved from such analysis, but users are unaware of how, why or even that this has happened, then it does become significant, because the application is no longer sufficiently transparent, and the means of accessibility is cloaked by invisible boundaries. In many cases, humanities scholars can work in collaboration with computer and data scientists on such projects, and thus consult them about such matters, but it is far less likely that members of the public, using systems which are based on complex AI or other algorithmic methods, have access to computer scientist collaborators with whom to discuss them. Most users find it difficult to conceptualise the extent of the vast datasets that are used in data science or understand the mathematics that underlies the methods of analysis. As a result, few of us know whether to trust algorithms, or understand the criteria we should use to evaluate their effectiveness (Spiegelhalter 2020).

In terms of accessibility and use, there have been claims dating back to the 1990s that researchers, especially in the humanities, need to understand the extent of collections, and be able to compare the scale of the information that they have already found to what remains to be discovered (Bates 1996). An increasing body of research also demonstrates that users tend to trust algorithms only when their rationale has been made clear. They want to know what the algorithm is doing and why it is doing so, and to be assured that the results are as unaffected as possible by biases (Shin and Park 2019). If users perceive the results of the use of algorithmic methods to be unfair or unethical, they are unlikely to support the use of such systems, even if they are more accurate than human processing of the same data (Kieslich, Keller and Starke 2022). This tendency was amply demonstrated by the controversy about UK A-level results in the summer of 2020. Such was the public discontent about the use of algorithmic methods to allocate grades that, under massive political pressure, the government cancelled their use, reverting instead to teacher-allocated grades (Kolkman 2020, 2022). It was clear that students and their parents perceived human decision-making to be fairer than 'The Algorithm' even though up to 75% of the A-level grade predictions made by teachers are known to be inaccurate (Murphy and Wyness 2020). As cultural heritage organisations become increasingly reliant on AI and algorithmic methods of data processing, how can we ensure that the results are as comprehensible and apparently trustworthy as those we gather from crowdsourcing and other human inputs?

Mapping the future

Concerns about fairness and bias may seem exaggerated in terms of the use of AI in historical mapping data. But it is important to be aware of the possibility that algorithms developed on historical maps might also be used on modern cartographic data in systems used for decision-making about social welfare, the justice system or healthcare, areas in which AI-based recommender systems are already being used. Thus, it is important that the techniques that we develop now are fit for purpose in any system.

More prosaically, perhaps, libraries and other cultural heritage organisations have spent, and will spend, significant amounts of time and money on digital map creations. It is, therefore, important that users trust the systems and want to use them again. Therefore, such systems should be as transparent as possible, something which could be achieved by providing documentation that users can easily access and understand. The use of explainable AI systems (XAI) whose design makes it possible for humans to understand the rationale for their operation is also a promising option, though XAI is still in its relative infancy, and it is not clear whether it will make AI explicable to non-technical experts.

Nevertheless, Nakao and colleagues (2022a; 2022b) have shown that if users are involved in the design of explainable AI systems, they are far more likely to trust in its fairness. This is an important step towards ensuring that communities that will be affected by AI have a voice in discussions about its use. However, as is usual for research in human–computer interaction, Nakao's studies rely on either university students or well-educated professionals as participants. Members of the communities who may be most at risk from the negative consequences of the use of AI systems in education, social welfare, criminal justice and healthcare are seldom represented in such studies, although arguably these are the very people with whom designers should be working. This is somewhat ironic, given that digital methods are sometimes seen as a means by which cultural heritage institutions can reach the kind of underserved audiences who do not attend museums or libraries in person (Pratty 2018; Murphy 2022).

Initiatives such as the NLW's 'Tithe Maps' project have demonstrated that communities can and do collaborate with crowdsourcing projects.[39] Yet there is a danger that communities will have no voice in the design of the AI systems that may, in future, make available the information they themselves contributed, or that provide them with information about the places they live and work in. This is surely a matter of concern, in terms of social justice, and of AI system design. The potential threat of the use of AI in cultural heritage contexts may seem relatively low, compared to areas such as welfare or healthcare. However, as the Welsh government's stress on the concept of Cynefin demonstrates, the ability of citizens to identify with their homeland and their heritage is an important factor in national culture and wellbeing. The cultural heritage organisations which deploy AI systems in future, therefore, surely have a responsibility to include users in their design, and to keep them informed about such functionality.

Librarians, archivists and other information professionals are therefore key players in debates about the future use of AI in cultural heritage. For decades they have helped users to understand the potential and effects of a wide range of digital technologies. They have also contributed to technical discussions about the creation of trusted digital repositories, and, more recently, about the appropriate uses of AI. It is probably not realistic to expect users who are not already computational scientists to undertake training courses to enable them to understand the nature of AI or data science. The role of information professionals is therefore of critical importance in this context, both to support and to inform users of AI-based systems, but also to advocate for the inclusion and consideration of users when such systems are being designed. The more users can be informed about the potential and drawbacks of such technologies, the less they are likely to fear or mistrust them. Funders also have an important part to play in this context. Some of the impetus for the use of AI in cultural heritage is coming from those who fund collection development in national and international contexts, such as UKRI, the USA's National Endowment of the Humanities (NEH) and the European Research Council. Such bodies could consider using their influence to insist that the organisations they fund are as transparent about the use of AI technology as possible and demonstrate that users and local communities are being included in project planning and, if applicable, activities that emerge from them.

Conclusion

The projects we have discussed, intended to make map collections more usable, demonstrate the innovative and creative approaches being applied to these complex data forms. While preservation remains a main concern for many map-holding libraries, the technologies and tools that are being used to make maps and map data more accessible have much broader applications in the ways cultural heritage organisations can present their collections in a visual interface, and through linked data. In turn, these efforts are enabling new areas of research that were not possible before. Where the large digital-based cultural heritage projects like 'Living with Machines' and 'Towards a National Collection' are fuelling these technological advancements, the hands-on approach to data collection and crowdsourcing through collaborations at local and national levels have an equally important role. Indeed, the collaborations evident in these projects, spanning disciplines, locations and expertise, public as well as academic users, are the key to their success. While more can be done to improve the relationships between developers, users and automated technologies, and to ensure that technologies are being employed with a level of transparency and inclusivity across cultural heritage organisations, positive steps are being taken. The widespread implementation of AI technologies across the cultural heritage sector may still be many years away, but with the use of open-source data platforms such as Wikimedia Commons, Wikidata and IIIF, the potential to do more with digital maps, images and other complex digitised and born-digital records, and open up these significant cultural resources to more users, is already very promising.

Notes

1. We would like to acknowledge the information provided by interviewees at The National Library of Wales, Sally McInnes and Jason Evans.
2. Anterotesis, 'DH GIS Projects'. Accessed 15 June 2023. https://anterotesis.com/wordpress/mapping-resources/dh-gis-projects/.
3. The Salem Witchcraft GIS. Accessed 22 June 2023. https://salem.lib.virginia.edu/gis/index.html.
4. Evolutionary Infrastructure: Boston's Back Bay Fens. Accessed 22 June 2023. http://www2.iath.virginia.edu/backbay/.
5. OpenStreetMap. Accessed 15 June 2023. www.openstreetmap.org.
6. Pelagios Network. Accessed 15 June 2023. https://pelagios.org.
7. Recogito. Accessed 29 June 2023. https://recogito.pelagios.org.
8. Pelagios, 'Creating Ottoman Gazetteer'. Accessed 15 May 2023. https://pelagios.org/case-studies/creating-ottoman-gazetteer/.
9. Ordnance Survey. Accessed 29 May 2023. www.ordnancesurvey.co.uk/.
10. Cambridge Library Map Collection. Accessed 18 July 2023. www.lib.cam.ac.uk/collections/departments/maps/digital-maps.
11. TCD, Glucksman Map Library digital collection. Accessed 18 July 2023. https://digitalcollections.tcd.ie/collections/1831cm56h?locale=en.
12. See 'An introduction to the Fagel project'. Accessed 29 May 2023. https://digitalcollections.tcd.ie/collections/b5644r52v?locale=en&page=2&view=masonry; and an introduction to the Fagel project: www.tcd.ie/library/fagel/maps/.
13. Bodleian Map Collection catalogue. Accessed 30 May 2023. https://digital.bodleian.ox.ac.uk/collections/maps/.
14. ArcGIS. Accessed 13 June 2023. www.esri.com/en-us/arcgis/products/index?rmedium=esri_com_redirects01&rsource=/en-us/arcgis/products; https://www.qgis.org/en/site/.
15. Bodleian 'Making Maps'. Accessed 29 May 2023. www.bodleian.ox.ac.uk/maps/making-maps.
16. See Cambridge Digital Library Map Collections. All Accessed 18 June, 2023. https://cudl.lib.cam.ac.uk/collections/maps/1; CDL catalogue, https://idiscover.lib.cam.ac.uk/; CUL 'Finding Maps'. www.lib.cam.ac.uk/collections/departments/maps/finding-maps.
17. OS Mastermap. Accessed: 18 June 2023. www.ordnancesurvey.co.uk/business-and-government/products/mastermap-products.htm.
18. CUL OS Digital Maps. Accessed 18 June 2023. www.lib.cam.ac.uk/collections/departments/maps/ordnance-survey-digital-maps.
19. Digimap. Accessed 18 June 2023. https://digimap.edina.ac.uk.
20. NLS Map Database. Accessed 18 June 2023. https://maps.nls.uk.
21. More on the 'Machines Reading Maps' project and further partners. Accessed 18 June, 2023. www.turing.ac.uk/research/research-projects/machines-reading-maps.
22. NLS Spy. Accessed 18 June 2023. https://maps.nls.uk/geo/explore/spy.
23. BL Online Gallery. Accessed 20 June, 2023. www.webarchive.org.uk/wayback/archive/20210615110537/http://www.bl.uk/onlinegallery/onlineex/.

24. BL Maps. Accessed 28 May 2023. www.bl.uk/subjects/maps.
25. Georeferencer. Accessed 28 May 2023. https://britishlibrary.georeferencer.com/start.
26. Old Maps Online. Accessed 28 May 2023. https://britishlibrary.oldmapsonline.org/start.
27. Living with Machines. Accessed 29 May 2023. https://livingwithmachines.ac.uk.
28. Machines Reading Maps (GitHub). Accessed 15 June 2023. https://machines-reading-maps.github.io.
29. Machines Reading Maps. Accessed 28 May 2023. www.turing.ac.uk/research/research-projects/machines-reading-maps.
30. The *MapReader* library is released under the MIT License. Its source code is on GitHub, available at: https://github.com/Living-with-machines/MapReader. There are also Jupyter Notebooks on GitHub.
31. NLW Maps. Accessed 28 May, 2023. www.library.wales/collections/learn-more/maps.
32. NLW Cynefin Project. Accessed 28 May 2023. www.library.wales/discover/projects/end-of-project/cynefin/cynefin-local-projects.
33. Sally McInnes. 2022. Interview with authors (15 June).
34. 'Towards a National AI-Enabled Repository for Wales' is funded by an AHRC National Infrastructure for Digital Innovation and Curation in the Arts and Humanities (iDAH) Scoping Grant. Project lead: Aberystwyth University. Project partners: National Library of Wales, and Royal Commission for the Ancient and Historical Monuments of Wales (lead project collaborators); Archives and Records Council Wales; Cadw; Canolfan Bedwyr; Dictionary of the Welsh Language; Digital Preservation Coalition; Eisteddfod Genedlaethol Cymru; Wales Higher Education Libraries Forum; and Welsh Government. Academic project supporters: Bangor University; Cardiff Metropolitan University; Cardiff University; Open University in Wales; Swansea University; and University of South Wales. Accessed 15 August 2023. https://gtr.ukri.org/projects?ref=AH%2FW007487%2F1.
35. Towards a National Collection (UKRI). Accessed 15 June 2023. www.ukri.org/what-we-offer/browse-our-areas-of-investment-and-support/towards-a-national-collection-opening-uk-heritage-to-the-world/.
36. Jason Evans. 2022. Interview with authors (15 June).
37. Evans. 2022. Interview (15 June).
38. Evans. 2022. Interview (15 June).
39. NLW Tithe Maps of Wales. Accessed 15 June 2023. https://places.library.wales.

References

Bates, M.J. 1996. 'The Getty end-user online searching project in the humanities: Report no. 6: Overview and conclusions.', *College and Research Libraries*, 57(6):514–23.

Chiang, Y.-Y., Leyk, S. and Knoblock, C.A. 2013. 'Efficient and robust graphics recognition from historical maps'. In *Graphics Recognition. New trends and challenges*, edited by Y.-B. Kwon and J.-M. Ogier, 25–35. Berlin, Heidelberg: Springer.

Chiang, Y.-Y. et al. 2020. 'Historical map applications and processing technologies'. In *Using Historical Maps in Scientific Studies: Applications, challenges, and best practices*, edited by Y.-Y. Chiang et al, 9–36. Cham: Springer International Publishing.

Damoor, P. 2019. 'History of digital maps', Medium, 3 November. Accessed 29 June 2023. https://medium.com/@prem.damoor19/history-of-digital-maps-b45e94ca45fa.

Dotson, B. 2020. 'NEH and AHRC support transatlantic machine learning project with historical maps', USC Libraries, 17 December. Accessed 2 June 2023. https://libraries.usc.edu/article/neh-and-ahrc-support-transatlantic-machine-learning-project-historical-maps.

Evans, J. 2021. 'IIIF, open data and drowdsourcing'. Accessed 25 July 2023. www.youtube.com/watch?v=m7nC7772if4.

Fleet, C. 2019. 'Creating, managing, and maximising the potential of large online georeferenced map layers', *e-Perimetron*, 14(3):140–49.

Fleet, C. and Pridal, P. 2012. 'Open source technologies for delivering historical maps online – Case studies at the National Library of Scotland', *LIBER Quarterly: The Journal of the Association of European Research Libraries*, 22(3):240–57.

Fleet, C. et al. 2021. 'Maps with a sense of the past: What are synthetic maps, and why do we love them?', National Library of Scotland Blog, 4 October. Accessed 2 June 2023. https://blog.nls.uk/maps-with-a-sense-of-the-past/.

Gieseking, J.J. 2018. 'Where are we? The method of mapping with GIS in digital humanities', *American Quarterly*, 70(3):641–8.

Gregory, I.N. and Healey, R.G. 2007. 'Historical GIS: Structuring, mapping and analysing geographies of the past', *Progress in Human Geography*, 31(5):638–53.

Hosseini, K. et al. 2021a. 'Maps of a nation? The digitized Ordnance Survey for new historical research', *Journal of Victorian Culture*, 26(2):284–99.

Hosseini, K. et al. 2021b. 'MapReader: A computer vision pipeline for the semantic exploration of maps at scale'. https://doi.org/10.48550/arXiv.2111.15592.

Jacobs, K.T. and Mitchell, S.W. 2020. 'OpenStreetMap quality assessment using unsupervised machine learning methods', *Transactions in GIS*, 24(5):1280–98.

Keates, J.S. 1996. *Understanding Maps*, 2nd edn. Harlow: Longman.

Kieslich, K., Keller, B. and Starke, C. 2022. 'Artificial intelligence ethics by design. Evaluating public perception on the importance of ethical design principles of artificial intelligence', *Big Data & Society*, 9(1):1–15.

Knutzen, M.A. 2013. 'Unbinding the atlas: Moving the NYPL map collection beyond digitization', *Journal of Map & Geography Libraries*, 9(1–2):8–24.

Kolkman, D. 2020. '"F**k the algorithm"?: What the world can learn from the UK's A-level grading fiasco', Impact of Social Sciences, 26 August. Accessed 19 April 2023. https://blogs.lse.ac.uk/impactofsocialsciences/2020/08/26/fk-the-algorithm-what-the-world-can-learn-from-the-uks-a-level-grading-fiasco/.

Kolkman, D. 2022. 'The (in)credibility of algorithmic models to non-experts', *Information, Communication & Society*, 25(1):93–109.

Li, Z. et al. 2021. 'Synthetic map generation to provide unlimited training data for historical map text detection'. In Proceedings of the 4th ACM SIGSPATIAL International Workshop on AI for Geographic Knowledge Discovery (GEOAI '21), 17–26. New York: Association for Computing Machinery. https://doi.org/10.1145/3486635.3491070.

McInnes, S. No date. 'Preserving the Welsh record: A bit at a time'. Digital Preservation Coalition. Accessed 25 July 2023. www.dpconline.org/blog/a-bit-at-a-time-arcw.

Moretti, F. 2007. *Graphs, Maps, Trees: Abstract models for a literary history*. Paperback edition. London: Verso.

Murphy, A. 2022. 'Digitally deprived communities are a key audience for museums to reach', MuseumNext. Accessed 28 July 2023. www.museumnext.com/article/digitally-deprived-communities-are-a-key-audience-for-museums-to-reach/.

Murphy, R. and Wyness, G. 2020. 'Minority report: The impact of predicted grades on university admissions of disadvantaged groups', *Education Economics*, 28(4):333–50.

Murrieta-Flores, P., Donaldson, C. and Gregory, I. 2017. 'GIS and literary history: Advancing digital humanities research through the spatial analysis of historical travel writing and topographical literature'. Accessed 29 June 2023. https://chesterrep.openrepository.com/handle/10034/620256.

Nakao, Y. et al. 2022a. 'Towards involving end-users in interactive human-in-the-loop AI fairness', *ACM Transactions on Interactive Intelligent Systems*. https://doi.org/10.1145/3514258.

Nakao, Y. et al. 2022b. 'Towards responsible AI: A design space exploration of human-centered artificial intelligence user interfaces to investigate fairness', *International Journal of Human–Computer Interaction*, 39(9): 1762–88.

Novak, A. and Ostash, V. 2022 'Digitizing historical maps and their presentation in online map collections', *e-Perimetron*, 17(1):33–44.

OpenStreetMap. Accessed 6 June 2023. www.openstreetmap.org/about.

Pratty, J. 2018. 'Can arts and heritage digital projects tackle deprivation in Hastings?', The RSA. Accessed 28 May 2023. www.thersa.org/blog/2018/07/can-arts-and-heritage-digital-projects-tackle-deprivation-in-hastings.

Rees, G. and Gadd, S. No date. 'PA visualisation & analysis activity charter v4', Google Docs. Accessed 28 May 2023. https://docs.google.com/document/d/1auz-efYqWhhIZiNC05W1mvE3awdhcnu-7qb4VfkOfCc/edit?usp=embed_facebook.

Schmidt, B.M. 2016. 'Do digital humanists need to understand algorithms?'. In *Debates in the Digital Humanities 2016*, edited by L.F. Klein and M.K. Gold. Minneapolis: University of Minnesota

Press. Online publication. Accessed 20 June 2023. https://dhdebates.gc.cuny.edu/read/untitled/section/557c453b-4abb-48ce-8c38-a77e24d3f0bd#ch48.
Shin, D. and Park, Y.J. 2019. 'Role of fairness, accountability, and transparency in algorithmic affordance', *Computers in Human Behavior*, 98(C):277–84.
Shnayder, E. 2010. 'A data model for spatial history: The Shaping the West geodatabase', Stanford Spatial History Lab. Accessed 15 May 2023. https://web.stanford.edu/group/spatialhistory/media/images/publication/railroad_geodatabase_pub.pdf.
Simon, R. et al. 2015. 'Linking early geospatial documents, one place at a time: Annotation of geographic documents with Recogito', *e-Perimetron*, 10(2):49–59.
Simon, R. et al 2017. 'Linked data annotation without the pointy brackets: Introducing Recogito 2', *Journal of Map & Geography Libraries*, 13(1):111–32.
Smith, Z. 2021. 'Mapping the world – one digitisation at a time', Cambridge University Library, 20 January. Accessed 2 June 2023. www.cam.ac.uk/stories/maps.
Spiegelhalter, D. 2020. 'Should we trust algorithms?', *Harvard Data Science Review*, 2(1).
Vane, O. et al. 2021. 'Maps in time: Visualising the historical Ordnance Survey'. Information+ conference 2021. Accessed 2 June 2023. https://vimeo.com/598429189.
Waddell, K. 2017. 'Mapping the many languages of Beirut', Bloomberg.com, 20 November. Accessed 28 May 2023. www.bloomberg.com/news/articles/2017-11-20/mapping-the-many-languages-of-beirut.
Weinman, J. et al .2019. 'Deep neural networks for text detection and recognition in historical maps'. In 2019 International Conference on Document Analysis and Recognition (ICDAR), 902–9. https://doi.org/10.1109/ICDAR.2019.00149.
White, R. 2010. 'What is spatial history?', Stanford Spatial History Lab. Online publication. Accessed 2 June 2023. https://web.stanford.edu/group/spatialhistory/media/images/publication/what%20is%20spatial%20history%20pub%20020110.pdf.
Woods, C. et al. 2016. 'Historical map digitization in libraries: Collaborative approaches for large map series', *Association of Canadian Map Libraries and Archives Bulletin*, 152:11–28.
Wrisley, D.J. 2020. 'Digital spatial practices and linguistic landscaping in Beirut', *ILCEA*, 39.

6

Making more sense with machines: artificial intelligence at the HathiTrust Research Center

Glen Layne-Worthey, J. Stephen Downie, Janet Swatscheno, Nikolaus Parulian, Jill Naiman, Benjamin Schmidt, Peter Organisciak, Ted Underwood and Ryan Dubnicek

The HathiTrust Digital Library includes books in over 400 languages on a staggering variety of subjects, including the humanities, arts, natural and social sciences, and government information. Its immense scope and broad heterogeneity (of languages, writing systems, topics, genres, legal accessibility, etc.) represent fundamental challenges for traditional research methods, but are ideal for the highly scalable computational research approaches created and enabled by the HathiTrust Research Center (HTRC) and its affiliated researchers.

We begin this chapter with the historical, organisational and legal underpinnings of the HTRC's publicly available tools, services and data that allow computational access to the entire Digital Library corpus, including in-copyright works. These methods and data are united under the concept of copyright-compliant 'non-consumptive research', which we also describe briefly.

Subsequent sections of the chapter describe several case studies of AI-enabled approaches that the HTRC research community is currently using to do research in our digital library. These use cases appear in order of fine-grained (sub-page-level) to all-encompassing (the entire digital library collection):

- Machine detection of non-textual objects (e.g., figures, tables, captions, mathematical formulas, etc.) in digitised legacy scientific literature.
- Automatic detection of book front-matter containing largely factual, as opposed to creative, content, and which thus lacks copyright protections.
- Large language predictive models to identify fictional works (which are often not indicated as such in library-provided metadata) in the vast corpus.
- Using neural network classifiers to identify and characterise relationships among books (e.g., duplicate detection).
- Creating reliable, highly reduced feature representations intended to make sense of an otherwise unfathomable collection; in other words, making big data small.

The HathiTrust Digital Library and Research Center

The 2008 creation of HathiTrust was the academic community's most immediate and visible response to the Google Library digitisation project, and it quickly grew to embrace other library efforts, both mass-digitisation ones in partnership with third parties such as the Internet Archive, and smaller, more localised ones. HathiTrust is not only a partnership of now over 150 member libraries, but also a collective preservation repository and digital library comprising over 17.6 million digitised library volumes, including some duplicates; these are catalogued as about eight million book titles and some half-million serial titles. Altogether it constitutes 736 terabytes of data.

Although the digital library is extremely large, it is admittedly imperfect in several significant ways. For example, it reflects the physical, operational and computational realities of bulk scanning operations: minimal human intervention in page-image or other error correction, and imperfect optical character recognition (despite being state of the art). Given the extremely wide range of dates, material types and quality, and language, these errors are not distributed evenly. For some research uses, the sheer size of the corpus may compensate for its imperfections, but researchers are wise to be aware of them.

Despite its size and ambitions, the HathiTrust collection should also not be considered comprehensive: it mirrors the print collections from which it was scanned, which are primarily large, well-resourced academic libraries in the United States. This means that centuries of publishing trends and library acquisition patterns have had major impacts on the kinds of materials found in the collection. For example, there are many copies of many editions of *Pride and Prejudice*, but one is less likely to find examples of popular fiction such as romance novels or speculative fiction.

The publication dates for items in HathiTrust range from the fifteenth century to the present. Genres and topics span the entire range of what one would find in major research libraries – indeed, these (primarily but not exclusively in the United States) are the source of all materials in the HathiTrust Digital Library (HTDL). About six and a half million of these volumes are in unambiguously the US public domain, which means that the other approximately 63% of the collection is potentially protected by copyright and is thus not available for either reading (at least, human reading) or download.

The question of copyright is, of course, a crucial one. For public domain or copyright-free materials, HathiTrust offers an open reading platform (to all readers) and free download (to users of member libraries). For all materials, including copyright-restricted items, basic full-text search is enabled for everyone in the world, but reading access is unfortunately not. At the same time, the sheer scope and nature of the collection lead us to ask new questions that are appropriate to data-intensive research; its mixed copyright profile further complicates such research. In response to these two forces, the HTRC was founded in 2011 by agreement among the University of Illinois Urbana-Champaign, Indiana University Bloomington, and the HathiTrust consortium itself.

HTRC's mission is to enable computational analysis of the HathiTrust corpus, and it offers multiple methods for computationally 'reading' the millions of books to meet a range of required skills and research needs, and to comply with the requirements of copyright law. Compliance with that law was the subject of a set of lengthy legal proceedings in the United States which concluded both in a resounding victory for HathiTrust and with an important operative legal concept that continues to define our work: 'non-consumptive' (sometimes known as 'non-expressive') access to, and use of, digital textual materials. Non-consumptive research is a broad term describing computational analysis that is performed on text during which the researcher does not read or display that text in amounts sufficient to understand the expressive content presented in it.

To enable scholarly access to *data* representing its collection, HTRC has created tools, environments and datasets in three broad categories: partial access to original data, limited access to data in protected 'data capsule' environments, and full access to transformed, 'extracted' data. All of these provide access to data in ways that are computable while remaining non-consumptive. In all of these categories, complete texts from the corpus are preprocessed to quantify statistical features such as word counts, linguistic features such as parts of speech, and page-layout features such as headers and footers; all are identified, calculated and compiled into a form which researchers can manipulate computationally. Machine learning methods are essential at nearly every stage of this processing, and are likewise essential to much of the research that uses this data.

The HTRC Extracted Features[1] (EF) constitute our most versatile derived dataset. It was created by compiling and analysing all the full-text data and library catalogue records in the HTDL, structuring and presenting the results in JSON format, and including information about each volume in the collection, and about every page and every word in each of those volumes. There is one extracted features file for each of the 17.6 million volumes in HathiTrust.

The EF dataset is a staple of our text-mining work, but it does not actually contain 'text' as normally defined. Instead, it consists solely of metadata *about* the digital library's volumes, including its substantial number of in-copyright books. Even though the books thus described may be restricted by copyright, because this metadata consists only of *facts about* these texts, it is not a violation of copyright for us to extract them or to share them with others; in fact, courts in the US have found that precisely this sort of use is a *Fair Use*. In order to promote its adoption and use (and reuse, experimentation, etc.), HTRC publishes the data under a Creative Commons licence.

Most of the specialised case studies that follow make use of the EF dataset, but its research uses are much more general and accessible than may be apparent here. In addition to writing their own code for such uses, as was done for these case studies, researchers may also rely on a rich suite of tools in the 'HTRC Feature Reader' Python library,[2] or using an API framework and lightweight analytic tools soon to be released under the 'Tools for Open Research and Computation with HathiTrust: Leveraging Intelligent Text Extraction' (TORCHLITE) project, funded by the National Endowment for the Humanities.[3]

Case study: page layout analysis for figure and caption extraction

Motivation

Much of the science communicated through academic literature includes page components that are not pure text – mathematical formulas, figures, tables, etc. – and these information-rich objects are of particular interest to scientists and those who study science communities and processes (Maltese, Harsh and Svetina 2015).

While most newer 'born-digital' articles are stored in formats such as XML that make page objects easy to extract, this is not true for articles that were published in print and digitised later. This ease of page object extraction can sometimes extend to vector-based, that is, 'rule-based' PDFs whose file types contain the instructions for rendering article pages. If the vector-PDF format is known, then text and images can potentially be extracted with heuristics which search for keywords (Choudhury et al 2013; Clark and Divvala 2016) and tables/figures and their captions can be extracted as pairs (Clark and Divvala 2016; GROBID 2008). However, heuristic extraction and indexing of figures from vector-based PDF documents can often be non-trivial, leading to erroneous or missing page objects (Bhatt et al 2021).

A variety of deep learning methods (Bhatt et al 2021; Saha, Mondal and Jawahar 2019; Yang et al 2017) have more recently been employed to extract page objects from both born-digital and scanned documents. In the cases of born-digital documents, these deep learning methods are combined with heuristically derived results in post-processing steps (Siegel et al 2018). However, for historical scanned documents, such as the wealth of digitised legacy science in the HathiTrust collections, these methods present many challenges for extraction and categorisation of objects on pages (Yashwant et al 2021; Kahu 2020; Naiman, Williams and Goodman 2022a). In what follows, we focus on one major issue in the document layout analysis: the generalisability of both heuristic and deep learning models, and the fact that models trained on a particular type of page (e.g., electronic theses and dissertations) do not tend to perform well on other types of page (e.g., academic articles).[4]

The problem of generalisability

The lack of generalisability is a known and pervasive problem in the field of document layout analysis (e.g. Bhatt et al 2021; Pfitzmann et al 2022). Changes in publication type and even publication year can drastically lower the accuracy of page object extraction methods for models that are not explicitly trained on this type of document (Yashwant et al 2021; Naiman, Williams and Goodman 2022a, 2022b).

Our prior work was aimed at the extraction of figures and their captions from a subset of the 'predigital' astrophysical literature holdings of the Astrophysics Data System (ADS)[5] using both greyscale and OCR features of article pages. Our model produced a high level of accuracy on our dataset – for an intersection-over-union metric of 0.9 we found F1 scores of ≥ 90%[6] (Naiman, Williams and Goodman 2022a, 2022b).

A natural extension of our work would be the extraction of figures and their captions in other scientific fields or journals. As the HathiTrust contains potentially millions of such article pages, a possible fruitful endeavour would be the application of our model to such articles.

The answer is always more data

Given that seemingly slight differences in font size and page object spacing can result in drastic drops in the accuracy of machine learning models, one natural solution might be to increase the size, scope and representatives of training datasets. While simple in theory, increasing training dataset size in practice is dogged by several issues: inconsistent object definitions, prohibitively expensive data annotation and insufficient historical synthetic data.

Inconsistent page object definitions

Page-object definitions themselves are surprisingly variable. For example, captions can be included or excluded in figure box definitions; each panel of a figure might be annotated as its own figure, or the panels may be considered elements of a single figure (see Figure 2 of Naiman, Williams and Goodman 2022b).

Different annotators can also disagree on class definitions, which leads to inconsistent data within the same dataset (Pfitzmann et al 2022; Younas 2019). While there have been attempts to standardise page object class definitions (e.g., Younas 2019), these have yet to be fully adopted by the various communities involved with document layout analysis.

Finally, object class definitions may depend on a particular use. In the work presented in (Naiman, Williams and Goodman 2022a, 2022b), we create the class definitions of figure and figure caption based on our ultimate goal – hosting historical figures and their captions on the Astronomy Explorer (AIE),[7] as is automatically done with newly published articles. Thus, even if consistent annotation 'codebooks' can be developed (as was done in this work), these definitions may not suit the needs of all document layout analysis applications.

Expensive human annotation

Assuming there is agreement within a group or field as to the definitions of page object classes, one option for generating data is to employ a large group of annotators to hand-classify article pages. One such effort is the DocLayNet dataset (Pfitzmann et al 2022). This large-scale annotation effort illustrates many of the logistical and resource requirements for the generation of a large and diverse set of documents annotated for use with machine learning models.

The dataset, which contains over 80,000 manually annotated pages and is arguably one of the state-of-the-art human-annotated datasets for document layout analysis, took ~40 supervised annotators and a small group of experts over six months to produce, with only a 'small fraction' of the pages being seen by more than one annotator. Additionally, while the annotation process included a >100-page annotation guide and a 12-week training period, the resulting intercoder agreement was only 80–85% for their 11 page object categories in the 'small fraction' of double- and triple-annotated pages. This is an indicator of how difficult it is to scale such hand-annotation tasks. Relevant to our work, this dataset does not even include scanned legacy documents which, as the DocLayNet authors point out, are often more warped or non-uniformly coloured than their annotated set, which obviously introduces even more uncertainty and error into the annotation process.

Minimal historical synthetic data

Another option for enlarging training sets is to generate 'synthetic data' which can be built from article source files. Such large 'benchmark' datasets have been created by mining XML (e.g., PubLayNet, Zhong 2019) and LaTeX source files with or without weak supervision (e.g., TableBank and DocBank, Li et al 2019, 2020). However, the majority of articles included in such datasets are recently published. To compensate for this dearth of historical synthetic datasets, efforts were made to artificially 'age' these newer documents by adding effects such as artificial warping, rotation and simulated dust and random noise on the page. While much focus has been placed on the ageing of articles in downstream tasks such as the mining of historical event-related OCR text (Boros 2022) or named-entity recognition (Hamdi 2022), some recent work has focused on the effects of the ageing process on the localisation of page objects (Yashwant 2021; Kahu 2020) and the generation of new training sets for historical documents (Bartz 2021).

Synthetic historical data is certainly a promising avenue for increasing training dataset sizes; however, many datasets are still relatively small and constructed for a particular type of historical document (e.g., predominantly books, as in Monnier 2020).

... Unless the answer is better models?

Because there are issues in training data collection and generation, another path to investigate is the creation of better models to use with the limited training data available.

One possibility is the use of models that have been trained on large document layout analysis or object detection datasets that are 'fine-tuned' to a particular historical document set through transfer learning. There are several document layout analysis works that adopt this strategy (Boukhers et al 2021; Schreiber et al 2017; Dong et al 2022). However, for historical documents, there is some evidence that transfer learning may add little to page object localisation accuracy (Kahu 2020). Additionally, this requires the format of each page to be the same, making the addition of novel features to the training process more difficult to incorporate (Naiman, Williams and Goodman 2022a).

Models that move beyond translating object detection to document layout analysis tasks are those that include the text data as training features (Naiman, Williams and Goodman 2022a, 2022b; Younas 2019). Often these models are 'multi-modal' in that they draw from the fields of machine learning methods for image classification and segmentation and the processing of text with natural language processing or similar techniques (Boukhers 2022).

Additionally, models are being developed that explicitly deal with a dearth of training data. These 'one-shot' or 'few-shot' models have the potential to drastically decrease the amount of time and logistics that must be resourced to create a specialised document dataset for a particular field (Singh et al 2020).

The combination of models that can make use of transfer learning and textual document components, and only require a small number of training instances, could potentially drive down the cost of analysing the historical literature of a particular field. However, at present, most of the state-of-the-art models have difficulty meeting the high levels of accuracy that are present in other object detection applications (Bhat et al 2021; Pfitzmann et al 2022).

Just kidding! Of course the real answer is all the things!

Because there is presently no 'magic bullet' to perfectly localise page objects across diverse domains, it is likely that increasing the accuracy of document layout analysis will require some combination of the multiple approaches discussed here into a process.

In our own work translating a model tuned on astrophysical literature to the wider historical scientific corpus within the HathiTrust, we are approaching the generalisation problem with three major prongs: document-specific machine learning models, citizen science to scale the annotation process, and the generation of large synthetic datasets with appropriate page-ageing processes applied.

Our current model detects figures and their captions with a modified object detection model which makes use of OCR, linguistic and greyscale features (Naiman, Williams and Goodman 2022a, 2022b). Its YOLO-based architecture gives it a low false positive rate, and combining it in an ensemble with models like detectron2[8] (which is Mask/FasterRCNN-based) with different error profiles likely increases our model's accuracy. We also plan to investigate transfer learning options such as few-shot models (e.g., Singh et al 2020) to decrease the number of training instances required to fine-tune our model to new domains.

To curate a gold-standard annotated training dataset, we are currently designing an annotation interface on the Zooniverse[9] platform, which hosts over one million citizen scientists who help professional scientists with their work. Through tools like tutorials, talk forums and the ability to help citizen scientists 'test' their knowledge with gold-standard datasets (Eisner et al 2021), much of the work to train annotators can be performed at scale. With a larger group of people performing annotations, metrics like intercoder agreement and tolerance for machine learning models can be more fully quantified (Lintott et al 2008; Schwamb et al 2012; Johnson et al 2015).

Finally, we are studying the ageing process of scientific article documents in more detail. While this work is preliminary and ongoing, we plan to make use of synthetic datasets in order to train our models once the quantification of the page ageing process is complete. While past work has typically focused on one of the main methods of increasing document layout analysis accuracy (models, curated datasets and synthetic data), recent work from the community has illustrated the importance of combining all three. We aim to publish not only the results of these efforts, but also our thought processes and guiding principles, in the hope that they prove useful for others in the document layout analysis community.

Case study: automatic front-matter detection

Motivation

As described above, approximately one-third of HathiTrust books are in the public domain and are open to the general public for reading, unlike the remaining two-thirds of copyright-protected works; under current policy, all volumes are either entirely viewable or entirely closed to view. However, even books under copyright include important pages of factual content (which is generally exempt from copyright protections), particularly in their front matter, and these could potentially be opened for public viewing.

Information contained in the opening pages of a volume can often help both scholars and casual readers better understand it. Even though much of the information on a title page is typically included in a book's catalogue record, other front-matter information, such as copyright pages, tables of contents, acknowledgments, etc., is typically not. At the same time, many volumes include in their opening pages creative materials that do have copyright protection, such as photographs and illustrations (including advertisements), poetic epigraphs, or even the main text itself (which begins after an unpredictable number of factual front-matter pages). Manually distinguishing which pages contain purely factual content and which are creative would be vastly prohibitive for the more than ten million in-copyright volumes in the collection.

We thus investigated machine learning approaches to distinguish factual content from creative content in the initial pages of a given HathiTrust volume, within a reasonable level of confidence and tolerance for risk, in order to expand public access wherever possible.[10]

Methods

Our first stage was an evaluation of various machine learning methods using the EF dataset described above. Word-level features such as word and part-of-speech counts are typically useful for a variety of common textual analysis problems, but we found that the many page-level features included in the EF dataset were even more useful in distinguishing 'fact-heavy' pages from 'creative-content' pages. These features include:

- the number of lines on a page;
- the number of tokens on a page;
- the number of sentences on a page;
- the number of tokens on a page that are capitalised;
- the number of tokens on a page that are numeric;
- the percentage of lines on a page beginning with capital letter;
- the percentage of lines on a page ending with a number; and
- the percentage of tokens on a page that have all letter capitals.

The overall workflow of the machine learning model relied on our manually labelled dataset with Extracted Features to be used on training prediction models. We developed and evaluated four prediction models: random forest, logistic regression, support vector machine, and stochastic gradient descent. Figure 6.1 shows the evaluation results of the predictive models. The results suggest that the random forest models have the highest accuracy compared to the other models in using EF statistical features for page-level creative content prediction.

A study of the types of misclassification revealed that most of the errors occurred when the classifier failed to detect creative content, which turns out to be a failure of detecting images on the page (which are a highly relevant type of creative content).

Although the random forest model performed quite well on textual statistical features, concern remained about the percentage of misclassification of creative pages, especially ones that contained images and had little or no textual content (which makes sense, our having used only textual features in the first place).

To rectify this gap, we supplemented our textual data with page images, and trained an image object detection model using YOLO-v3. We then combined the results of this image model with those obtained for text features. This combination of image and text features resulted in a substantial improvement in the predictive model's accuracy, particularly in one most important category of errors, which we now describe.

Accurate identification of creative content is more important to one of our overall goals: not to open pages potentially protected by copyright. Thus, it is better to have a false positive (i.e., a page falsely identified as creative) that keeps the page hidden from view than it is to have a false

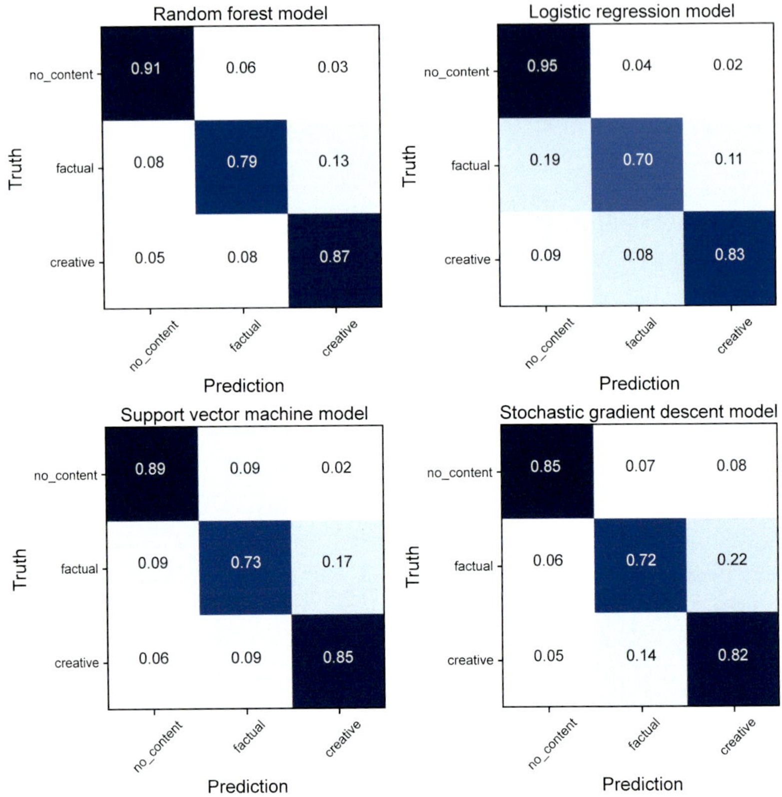

Figure 6.1 Evaluation confusion matrix for the page-level creative/expressive content prediction models. The *y*-axis depicts truth labels, the *x*-axis predicted labels. © Nikolaus Parulian, Glen Layne-Worthey, J. Stephen Downie.

negative and open the page (and open HathiTrust to liability). Analysing the probability distribution of such errors across content types, we chose an optimal probability threshold for identification of the 'creative content' class. When combined with our previous text-based classifier, the new image + text workflow increased the confidence level for creative content from 87% to 96% (see Figure 6.2).

Our work is well on its way toward making more content in the digital library – and more useful, factual content from other closed, in-copyright works – openly available.

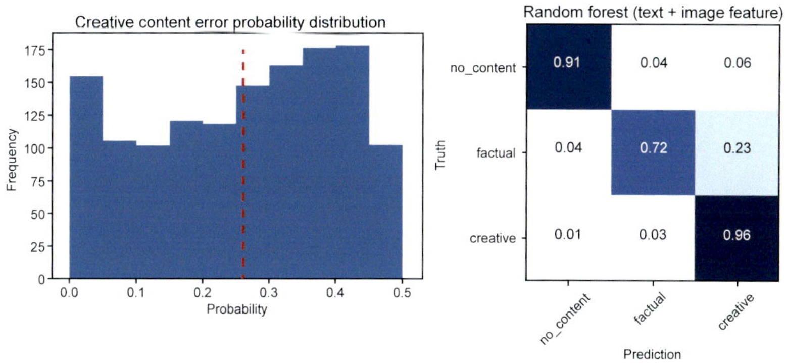

Figure 6.2 (Left) Choosing a probability threshold for identification of creative content. (Right) Confusion matrix for random forest combined text + image model. Note particularly the result in the lower right-hand cell compared with the same position in the random forest confusion matrix for text features alone in Figure 6.1. © Nikolaus Parulian, Glen Layne-Worthey, J. Stephen Downie.

Case study: automatic detection of English-language fiction

Motivation

As more text becomes open to text and data mining, finding and assembling corpora of relevant items remains a challenge. In large, general digital libraries such as the HathiTrust, metadata alone is often not sufficient to identify items of interest. While this is true for all volumes in the collection thanks to uneven cataloguing quality and completeness, it is particularly challenging for fiction volumes, for which legacy metadata standards are often too broad for specific analysis tasks (Miller 2000). This has led researchers to devise novel methods of classifying text, including stylometrics, textual feature analysis (Bucher 2018), and predictive modelling (Short 2019; Gupta 2019). This case study leverages the latter, together with HTRC's EF dataset (Jett et al 2020), to build on successful classification efforts done as part of prior research, seeking to identify and classify English-language volumes as fiction from among the larger collection. This section outlines the methodology, results and planned future work in generating this dataset.[11]

Methods

This work builds on that of the international 2013–2019 NovelTM project (.txtlab 2023), improving the process and accuracy of the NovelTM Datasets for English Language Fiction (Underwood, Kimutis and Witte 2020) that resulted from it. That project used the HTRC's EF dataset to train a predictive model for English-language fiction. We differ from the NovelTM classification process by making predictions at the volume level, using the combined tokens for each volume as input features for the model along with metadata records as ground truth, supplemented by a more accurate manually tagged subset of 2,730 volumes (Underwood, Kimutis and Witte 2020). Three different statistical models were tested for the classification process: logistic regression (LR), support vector machine (SVM) and random forest (RF) using 120 trees, each implemented via the scikit-learn Python library (Pedregosa et al 2011). To test the best model and process, we first assembled three samples of approximately nine to ten thousand volumes each; then gathered the HTRC EF data for each volume; and then split each set into 80% training and 20% test volumes. The three samples were:

- Sample 1: 10,108 random volumes, matching the distribution of items by decade added to the HT digital library since 2016, yielding 1,605 fiction and 8,503 not-fiction volumes.
- Sample 2: 9,969 random volumes, with the same selection logic as Sample 1, but incorporating as many manually verified fiction volumes from the NovelTM dataset as possible, yielding 1,580 fiction and 8,389 not-fiction volumes.
- Sample 3: 8,876 volumes, including 53 fiction and 211 non-fiction volumes for every decade represented in items added to HathiTrust since 2016, creating training and test sets with equal numbers of volumes for each decade, yielding 1,279 fiction and 7,597 non-fiction volumes.

After initial runs of each sample, we also benchmarked a model that incorporates corrected ground truth for each sample, where about half of the initial classification errors were incorrect fiction or non-fiction classifications. The LR, SVM and RF models were all benchmarked for precision, recall and F1 scores against each sample described above, as well as for the corrected samples. The results for each model are shown in Table 6.1, with RF, LR and SVM yielding the highest values of precision, recall and F1, respectively, illustrating that each statistical model is viable for a high-level classification task. However, a corrected Sample 2

Table 6.1 Precision, recall and F1 scores for each sample and statistical model, logistic regression, support vector machine and random forest. Bold indicates the highest value for each column

	Logistic regression			**Support vector machine**			**Random forest**		
	P	**R**	**F1**	**P**	**R**	**F1**	**P**	**R**	**F1**
Sample 1	0.7838	0.9755	0.8692	0.8384	0.9205	0.8776	0.8665	0.8930	0.8795
Sample 2	0.8589	0.9470	0.9008	0.8885	0.9238	0.9058	0.8824	0.8940	0.8882
Sample 3	0.8804	0.9199	0.8997	0.9286	0.8750	0.9010	0.9697	0.8889	0.9275

performed overwhelmingly the best for all metrics and models, indicating that sampling has greater importance than choice of statistical method when training a classifier.

Table 6.2 shows mean F1 scores over five-fold cross-validation for each sample and model to evaluate whether our model overfitted our training data. Scores were again generally high, indicating this was not the case. Sample 2, both before and after error correction, continued to yield the highest levels of accuracy.

Initial results

Each model performed to a generally high level, and in line with the original NovelTM dataset, which had potential error rates up to 14%. However, Sample 2, the training and test sample that had the most accurate (manually verified) ground truth and most reflected the distribution of publication dates of materials we are seeking to find, yielded large gains in the model's accuracy, with an F1 score of 0.9670. This was nearly 10% higher than the other samples achieved for LR, the best-performing model. Though LR outperformed both SVM and RF by about 6% (F1), both models would be viable to replicate the accuracy of the original NovelTM dataset. However, since there were no advantages to implementation, LR is the preferred model for our classification task.

Table 6.2 Mean F1 scores, by model and sample, after five-fold cross-validation

	LR	**SVM**	**RF**	**Rank**
Sample 1	0.8815	0.8876	0.8744	3
Sample 2	0.9123	0.9125	0.9111	2
Sample 3	0.9023	0.8963	0.8989	4
Sample 3 (corrected)	0.9217	0.9180	0.9164	1

Error review was conducted by human annotators, and each sample's errors were annotated by multiple coders to achieve higher levels of accuracy. During review, four main error types surfaced:

- Incorrect ground truth. These are volumes incorrectly tagged as fiction or non-fiction in their library-supplied metadata. Example volumes: Stephen Crane's *The Red Badge of Courage* and Emily Bronte's *Wuthering Heights* were not catalogued as fiction.
- Genres that blur the lines between fiction and non-fiction, such as memoir, biography, and travel narrative. These may share many features with typical fiction or non-fiction volumes, but are incorrectly identified as their inverse. Examples in our data are Daniel Defoe's *Robinson Crusoe* and John Hanning Speke's *Journal of the Discovery of the Source of the Nile* (the first fiction, the second allegedly non-fiction).
- Non-prose fiction. Volumes that are fiction but are not standard prose, particularly verse and drama. Though also fictional, this project sought specifically to identify *prose* fiction.
- True errors. These were the least frequent errors: volumes the model simply got wrong. Some examples are annotated scholarly volumes, compilations of historical news stories, and bound anthologies of serial publications.

In addition to accuracy, this project revealed a number of important lessons for fiction classification. Generally, it is sampling logic, rather than the sophistication of machine learning tools, that is the most important factor in successful fiction classification. While deploying more complex models and techniques may also pay off in results, effort may be better spent in compiling training data that best resembles the items of interest. Similarly, training data should also seek to match the date distribution of the sought-after materials in order to achieve higher levels of accuracy, a finding that accords with the date sensitivities of other NLP methods such as named entity recognition and topic modelling. Next, human-provided ground truth is generally accurate in library records (when these exist), but it still contains some errors. Correcting these errors, though tedious, presents a chance to easily improve accuracy of classification. Lastly, it is important to remember that classifying texts with broad labels like 'fiction' and 'not fiction' is a challenging task, even for humans. It is unlikely that an algorithm alone will ever overcome such a challenge that is linked to larger philosophical and literary debate.

Future work

This project has identified an accurate and easy-to-implement process for English-language fiction classification of HathiTrust Digital Library materials. This process will be implemented on the large set of volumes added to the HTDL since the original NovelTM dataset was generated, yielding a larger set of fiction to make open for computational research. As part of that release, this reproducible process will be fully documented and our code will be released in the hope of larger uptake in the cultural analytics community in service of new insights into our shared cultural history.

Case study: similarity and duplicate detection in HathiTrust

Motivation

This case study introduces the Similarities and Duplicates in Digital Libraries (SaDDL) project,[12] which applies machine learning applications using the HTRC EF dataset to identify works with varying degrees of sameness and similarity to other works within the HathiTrust Digital Library. SaDDL addresses the challenges of duplication and duplicate detection in the collection, presenting a classification workflow and set of datasets that seek to identify near-duplicate and similar-work relationships among the collection's scanned books. In doing so, it also serves as a demonstration of working within the constraints of non-consumptive access for machine learning, as well as one set of approaches for working with the large scale and long document lengths of a bibliographic digital library.

The research goals of this study were to identify near-duplicate relationships in the HathiTrust Digital Library, suggest preferred copies of duplicated works and provide content-based book recommendations for each book in the collection.

The problem of duplicates

Due to the HTDL's consortial collection development it includes a highly uneven representation of works, for example resulting in multiple independent scans of the most common works. Identifying duplication is challenging due to the complex and diverse nature of the printed word, including the ways it is written, compiled, printed and reprinted. This complexity has also led to inconsistent metadata cataloguing practices, making duplicate identification difficult without examining the content of the books themselves.

A manual evaluation in Organisciak et al (2019) highlights these challenges. Upon reviewing randomly sampled target books and their algorithmically similar candidate books, we encountered many more metadata complexities and errors than anticipated. In many cases, books containing the same works had differing OCLC record numbers, titles and even volume numbers. Thus, metadata alone is insufficient for identifying duplicates. Another issue is the frequent reiteration of texts, as exemplified by *Robinson Crusoe*. Initially published in 1719, this work has been repeatedly rewritten using new language as publishers sought to differentiate their editions or modernise the text (Lovett and Lovett 1991).

In sum, addressing duplication in large digital libraries like HTDL requires a comprehensive understanding of publishing history; catalogue metadata alone cannot adequately identify duplicates. The SaDDL project tackles this problem by using the textual content of books and employing a combination of computational and machine learning methods to identify same-work relationships, encompassing both exact duplications and variant texts.

Methods

In this discussion, we adopt the terminology of the 'Functional Requirements for Bibliographic Resources' study (Riva et al 2017): a work refers to the underlying conceptual entity, realised through various expressions (edits, editions, versions), and committed to a particular format as a manifestation. Traditional cataloguing has focused on manifestation-level relationships, even while newer standards allow for representing work-level relationships (e.g., different editions of the same work).

To identify same-work relationships in the HathiTrust collection, the SaDDL project developed a multi-step workflow tailored to the legal and technical challenges of large digital libraries, including copyright restrictions and the unique profile of a large collection of very long texts.

The SaDDL workflow involved three key steps:

1. Identifying a computationally efficient text and document representation, and transforming the texts accordingly.
2. Performing a fast, first-pass algorithm to detect potential work relationships.
3. Utilising a more accurate, albeit slower, neural network classifier to confirm candidate relationships.

SaDDL was conducted exclusively on publicly accessible data, including the HathiTrust's 'Hathifiles' metadata[13] and the Extracted Features dataset. The project analysed 9.8 million English-language works (and excluded government documents). Additionally, some evaluations made use of a corpus of 143,000 books, randomly sampled by the author to preserve the redundancies present in the larger collection.

Document and text representation

SaDDL's text representation involved two key aspects: dividing books into smaller subunits and converting those subunits into static vector representations. These steps were necessary due to the challenges of scale and long document length, and were compatible with the bag-of-words data available in the EF dataset.

Instead of using pages as units of analysis (as presented in the EF dataset), SaDDL employed a book chunking approach, dividing books into sequences of around five thousand or ten thousand words, depending on the stage of the tagging workflow. This approach allowed for a balance between representing within-book context and managing computational complexity, while maintaining similar document sizes. To work within the constraints of the EF dataset, chunks were compiled by gathering runs of pages together, so chunks were rarely the exact target size, but averaged around the target size with some variance. The same principle can be applied more exactly with full-text (i.e., non-bag-of-words) files. The chunking process prioritised the creation of full-size chunks in the middle of the book and split any remainders between the front- and back-matter chunks.

Beyond the document frame, the way that texts are formalised as features for computation is an important choice. Same-work relationship tagging is a document similarity challenge: seeking to measure the distance between texts or subunits of texts. SaDDL predominantly represented materials as vector embeddings, where a distance could be calculated between two documents. It specifically used the GloVe (Pennington et al 2014) word embedding model. Each word in a chunk was represented by a 300-dimensional vector, and the vectors for all words in a chunk were averaged to derive a single address for each chunk.

Current state-of-the-art natural language processing generally relies on transformer-based models (Devlin et al 2018), a type of deep neural network. These models are an evolution of recurrent neural networks, which learn sequences of input data but can rapidly increase in complexity when dealing with longer sequences. To address this issue, transformers use a concept called attention (Vaswani et al 2017), which selectively determines which information in the input sequence is most relevant for a particular task.

During the time of the SaDDL project, transformers were considered inadequate for a few reasons. Firstly, they demand significant computational resources, making large-scale document-to-document comparisons challenging. Even today, embeddings are commonly used for document similarity tasks because of this issue, although transformer-trained embeddings such as sentence transformers and Sentence-T5 now exist (Reimers and Gurevych 2019; Ni et al 2021). Secondly, transformers typically require sequential full-text data, while the EF dataset provides unordered bags of words. However, recent research suggests that these models can perform well with bags of words for some tasks (Hessel and Schofield 2021). Lastly, transformers have traditionally been limited in their input frame. For instance, BERT could only handle up to 512 words (Devlin et al 2018). This limitation has gradually improved, with newer transformer models like GPT-4 supporting up to 8,000 tokens. As a result, these models could potentially work with a chunking approach or an incremental summarisation technique.

In summary, document and text representation is where the SaDDL implementation was driven by practical scale considerations over pure performance. SaDDL simplified book representations into vector embeddings representing smaller chunks of the book. Thus, the books were represented as 108 million book-chunk subunits. A word embedding model was used to represent text as embeddings because it is performant for projection and does not require full sequence data, allowing it to work with sensitive datasets that are shared non-consumptively.

Approximate nearest neighbour

Efficiently comparing book relationships in the very large HTDL poses performance challenges due to the scale of the collection and the length of individual documents. To address this, a two-pass process was employed: in the first pass, possible relationship candidates were identified with an approximate nearest neighbour (ANN) algorithm, in order to send these to a more nuanced pairwise classifier later. ANN was employed to scale linearly and avoid quadratic scaling from pairwise comparisons. There are various ANN algorithms available, and SaDDL employed a random projection trees system implemented using Annoy (Bernhardsson 2013).

Table 6.3 Per-class recall performance for a variety of work relationships

Judgement	Chunk-and-aggregate	Baseline (book neighbours)
SWSM	0.99	0.98
SWDE	0.94	0.81
DV	0.79	0.62
PARTOF	0.98	0.71
CONTAINS	0.98	0.69

In the SaDDL implementation, ANN functions on book chunks rather than entire books, enabling identification of partial matches and offering tuning options for matching thoroughness and cleanliness. A chunk-and-aggregate strategy was developed to maintain ANN's performance benefits while allowing for fuzzier relationships (Organisciak, Schmidt and Durward 2023). This strategy focuses on high recall in order to identify as many potential relationships as possible for later analysis. Table 6.3 displays the strategy's performance on different relationships. While the baseline worked well for exact matches (same work, same manifestation: SWSM), it fared more poorly with more complex relationships such as different editions (same work, different expression: SWDE), different volumes of the same larger work (DV), and whole–part relationships (PARTOF, CONTAINS).

Ground truth: training data and synthetic data

To create training data, we relied on relationships inferred from metadata. Acknowledging the known fallibility of metadata, only high-confidence relationships were used. For assessing same-manifestation relationships, we focused on identical authors, near-identical titles (using subword vector project similarity), and similar dates and page counts. We also concentrated on instances where enumeration (e.g., volume numbers) and chronology fields were present in the catalogue metadata. This approach reduced the training set size but improved its reliability.

To identify DV, PARTOF and CONTAINS classes, SaDDL again used enumeration and chronology fields. However, the evidence for PARTOF and CONTAINS was insufficient for our training data needs, with only 11,903 book relationship tags occurring across training, cross-validation and test data. To address this, we generated synthetic class examples (Organisciak and Ryan 2024).

Artificial data is often used to enhance classifier robustness. In SaDDL, we generated artificial anthologies by combining multiple books, and artificial multi-volume sets by dividing long books into parts. This synthetic data significantly improved performance, with a 37-point improvement in F1 on classifying PARTOF/CONTAINS, from F1 = 0.41 to F1 = 0.79. Given the success of artificial data, we trained an entirely artificial class called OVERLAPS, representing partially overlapping books observed in the corpus that were difficult to identify from metadata. While challenging to evaluate, manual assessments suggest that the classifier is often correct when disagreeing with ground truth.

In addition to same-work relationships, SaDDL also provided content-based book recommendations. To tag different works as being related, we aligned the UCSD GoodReads dataset[14] with HathiTrust records and used online book recommendations to train a separate 'GRSIM' (i.e., 'Good Reads Similar') class. In our reporting, this class is combined into a broader DIFF class, but it remains disaggregated in the SaDDL dataset. Other DIFF subclasses include AUTHOR (different books by the same author), RANDDIFF (two completely random different books) and SIMDIFF (two different books with topical similarity).

Relationship classification

The SaDDL classifier employs a two-input deep neural network for book-to-book relationship classification. The primary input consists of chunk-to-chunk similarity matrices for two books, which are processed using a convolutional neural network. Dropout and max pooling are incorporated to enhance the classifier's robustness by reducing model complexity and promoting the identification of multiple relationship signals. The secondary input comprises book-level vectors, which compare the topics within the two books not captured in the similarity matrices.

Classification results for the SaDDL dataset are presented in Table 6.4. The overall accuracy reached 85%, with a weighted F1 score of 0.85.

SaDDL focuses on identifying complex work relationships while accommodating digitisation and OCR issues. Future application could improve the results by reintroducing metadata to the classifier to complement the data.

The classifier underwent multiple iterations, and its earlier iterations may be instructive for future computational study of digital libraries. Initially, SaDDL employed deliberate feature extraction to quantify as

Table 6.4 Relationship classification performance (n = 524,288)

	Precision	Recall	F1 score	Support
Same work, same manifestation	0.83	0.84	0.83	131,320
Same work, different expression	0.86	0.82	0.84	122,994
Whole–part, different volume	0.81	0.86	0.83	92,926
Part of	0.91	0.92	0.91	31,922
Contains	0.90	0.92	0.91	32,040
Overlaps	0.83	0.26	0.40	2,167
Different work	0.89	0.89	0.89	110,919
Overall accuracy: 0.85 weighted F1: 0.85				

many notable qualities of a book pair as possible. However, this traditional feature extraction approach did not perform well. Instead, providing the classifier with raw information, such as the book-to-book similarity matrix, and asking it to identify the patterns itself proved more effective. In this case, SaDDL treated the similarity matrix similarly to image pixels, searching for patterns in adjacent page convolutions. A challenge here was that a similarity matrix had already been preprocessed, so some book information did not make it to the classifier. This is why the classifier was a two-input model, where the second input gave some information about the topical space of the books. A Siamese network approach, with parallel full data input for both books being provided, was less successful. Nevertheless, this may require implementation adjustments or further investigation.

The SaDDL dataset,[15] along with its accompanying website,[16] include positive classification results for relationships between items identified as the same work. These relationships include exact duplicates, varying editions, iterative versions, partially overlapping texts and related volumes. To cater to use cases that require more than just item-level information, the SaDDL dataset includes manifestation and work groupings, along with unique identifiers inferred from the individual items using a network clustering technique. Users can access all copies of a particular work or a specific edition.

Furthermore, the classification process employed by SaDDL is well suited to content-based book recommendations, which can supplement the strength of traditional expert and user suggestions with more archival depth than human recommendations typically provide. As a result,

SaDDL provides recommended books for each item in the collection, drawing from user recommendations in the GoodReads dataset.

Conclusion

The SaDDL project showcases the immense potential of machine learning applications in vast digital libraries like the HTDL. By addressing challenges related to intellectual property restrictions, document lengths and duplication, the project's multistep workflow enables the identification of near-duplicate and similar-work relationships within the extensive HathiTrust collection. This information can be used to rectify cataloguing errors, enhance information access and retrieval, infer previously uncatalogued metadata about individual items, and address challenges in corpus text analytics. These analytics aim to study history and culture through the lens of cultural heritage and library materials but may be misled by repeating text.

The SaDDL project not only highlights the value of the HTRC's EF dataset, but also emphasises the importance of developing innovative methodologies to work within non-consumptive access constraints. Moreover, the scale of the HathiTrust collection ensures that the findings are not limited to just its digital library: other library collections, even without digital or digitised content to study directly, can still be aligned with the books found in HathiTrust.

SaDDL demonstrates a machine learning application in the cultural heritage domain, facing several challenges that are more pronounced in such contexts. Specifically, the project works with a large collection featuring exceptionally long document lengths, further constrained by intellectual property limitations. Ultimately, the SaDDL project contributes to ongoing efforts to improve access to knowledge, and to enhance the understanding and boost the utility of digital libraries.

Case study: how small can big data get?

Motivation

The size of the HathiTrust collection is almost unfathomable, and working with it in its native forms is extremely difficult. Currently, the most compact version of the complete 17.6-million-volume collection is the Extracted Features dataset, which is still quite large: about 4 TB compressed. EF's page-level feature counts are easily summed to slightly more compact book-level feature counts, but even these are extremely large. This case study[17] explores new ways of making this big collection 'small enough' to work with in three different computational environments – that is, small enough to work with on a laptop (~100 GB), to load into memory (~10 GB), or to build into a web application (~500 MB–1 GB).

Laptop-sized data

A single 'document vector' for each work would result in a laptop-sized representation of 64 GB. A document vector, also called an 'embedding', is the basic unit of machine learning models. Models can turn anything into a numeric vector consisting of an arbitrary number of values (typically a hundred to a thousand), or *dimensions*, but to achieve the desired size, the number of dimensions must be reduced. This is normally done in one of three ways: principal component analysis on the term–document matrix, top-*n* words or topic models.

Of these methods, the first is probably the best. But there are reasons not to use the best method. First, it is computationally intractable: a full matrix would consist of trillions of rows, and a sparse matrix of billions. Second, it is difficult to distribute: most users at home cannot embed documents in a particular space unless they also download a massive language model. Third, and most importantly, any embedded space is optimal only for the text collection it was trained on. In response to these concerns, I developed and published what I called a 'minimal, universal dimensionality reduction' (Schmidt 2018). Such an algorithm should:

- be domain-agnostic;
- be language-agnostic;
- be capable of accounting for any vocabulary;
- make only general assumptions about human language;
- be capable of working from existing feature-count datasets; and
- be easily implementable across platforms and languages.

The proposed method is called 'stable random projection' of term counts, based on a standard algorithm in applied mathematics. See Schmidt (2018) for a full description of this method.

While this method is not a perfect representation of the works in the collection, it is surprisingly good. In a test of its ability to predict, based on a volume's dimension-reduced document vector, which of 225 Library of Congress subclassifications is appropriate for it, the method has 68% accuracy and an 87% top-three accuracy (meaning that the misses are usually not dramatic: 87% of the time the actual subclassification is within the top three predicted by the classifier).

Memory-sized data

Although these document vectors squash books to much smaller than their word counts, they still take up a fair amount of space: about five kilobytes per book, or about the size of, say, Shirley Jackson's short story 'The Lottery'. Storing millions of books at that size is possible, but still not ideal.

There is, however, a computational trick that can make things much smaller: storing information as bits rather than as floating-point numbers. Each number requires 32 bits of memory; we can reduce the size 32 times by thresholding the random projection at zero. That is, simply reduce the number on each dimension of the stable random projection to zero if its value is less than zero, and to one if it is greater than zero. In this reduction, the vector [134.123, −12.3, 1.423, −312, −4.2345, ...] becomes [10100 ...]. The resulting vector is 32 times fewer bytes, which brings the representation of the entire collection down to about 3.5 GB. These vectors can further be packed as numbers: 10100 is the binary representation of 20. By representing each of the floats as a bit in an integer, we can reduce it even more radically: each book can be represented by just 20 groups of 64 bits each, and those bits can be stored as integers in a database.

Since computers are capable of very fast binary operations, comparing the binary vector representations of book pairs is almost instantaneous. Here, comparing a pair of books to each other means comparing the bits in each position of the books' reduced-dimension vectors to see whether they are similar or different; this is called the Hamming distance in information theory, and it turns out to be surprisingly effective for comparison of book-length documents.

An interactive demonstration of one potential use of such comparisons is available at https://observablehq.com/@bmschmidt/similarity-search-on-millions-of-books-in-browser.

This notebook performs real-time Hamming search in a browser on any subset of the HathiTrust collection, including up to the entire collection. Using text of arbitrary length (including one or more volumes in the collection itself) as a search term, the algorithm returns volumes represented by the most similar vectors. For instance, beginning with any HathiTrust book, the algorithm generates a list of the most similar other books based on their miniature Hamming representations. Perhaps not all of these are precisely on the same topic – although many indeed are – but in a massive collection otherwise searchable only with very limited topic metadata (e.g., an often very generic title, possibly a few subject headings), the ability to use an entire text to find similar texts is genuinely transformative.

Web-sized data

Even the radically reduced representation described above requires a database to be of any use for a HathiTrust-sized collection. But reducing the representation even further, down to just two dimensions, creates data that can be sent directly to a browser. The implications of this are powerful, but how might one produce two-dimensional data that is actually meaningful? The 'uniform manifold approximation and projection' (UMAP) algorithm (Sainberg, McInnes and Gentner 2020) is done by computing a graphical representation of the dataset; then, using stochastic gradient descent (a machine learning algorithm), creating an embedding that preserves the structure of that graph.

This new, highly reduced graph can be visualised using the 'H curve' method (originally developed to represent long DNA sequences; see Hamori and Ruskin 1983) such that similar books are clustered together. Including very basic metadata (for example, Library of Congress classification, language and publication date) allows one to filter, visualise and explore the collection as whole.

Figure 6.3 is an in-browser visualisation of a substantial sample (approximately one-third) of the HathiTrust collection. Points are clustered by text similarity and coloured by language. The large orange cluster represents English-language works; the much smaller green cluster (with metadata highlighted for a randomly selected point) represents Japanese; and so forth. The consistency of colour in each cluster, and the clear separation of clusters, demonstrates that the text-similarity algorithms do indeed reflect reality: any two volumes in the same language are of course more similar, based purely on their text, than any two volumes in different languages.

To verify whether these two-dimensional embeddings might be useful (in addition to being 'true'), we used this visualisation to study where in the visualisation the NovelTM dataset described above is clustered. In Figure 6.4, the volumes included in the 2020 release of the NovelTM dataset of English-language fiction are coloured in orange (naturally, clustering together), and in blue are the books not included in it.

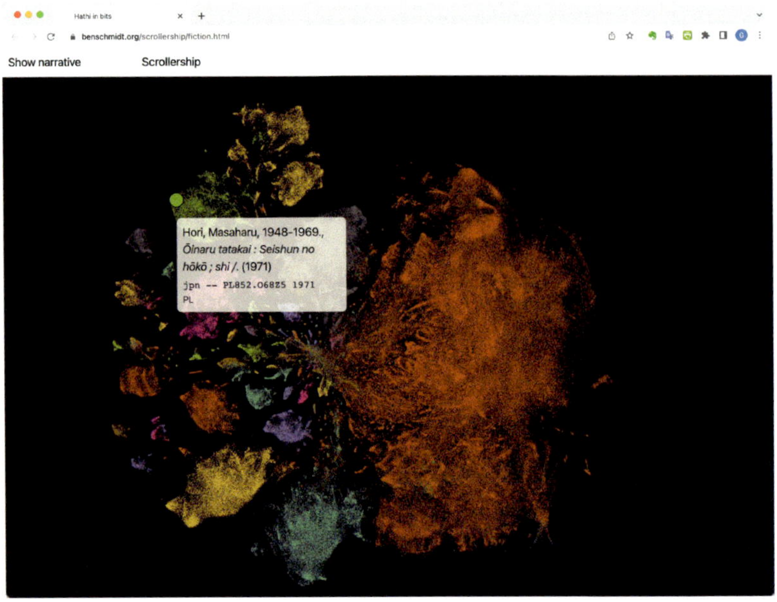

Figure 6.3 Visualisation of approximately 30% of the HathiTrust collection, clustered according to text similarity (represented as highly reduced document vectors) and coloured by language (as identified in volume metadata). © Benjamin Schmidt, Glen Layne-Worthey, J. Stephen Downie.

At a very high level, the clustering and the colouring mutually validate the automatic classification of fiction and the correctness of the visualised embedding space. But more significantly, zooming in on several smaller orange clusters outside the main cluster (and more especially outside the large English-language cluster) allows us to identify either possible mismatches in the fiction classification, or artefacts of the dimensionality reduction. Data visualisation tools like this can be useful in addition to traditional methods for tagging, or on their own as a way to identify and isolate groups of information.

Conclusion

Representing centuries of library collection-building, curation and cataloguing, as well as decades of digitisation activity, the HathiTrust Digital Library, Research Center and their scholar-users rely increasingly on AI and machine learning methods to make more sense of this unique and uniquely massive collection of our shared cultural heritage.

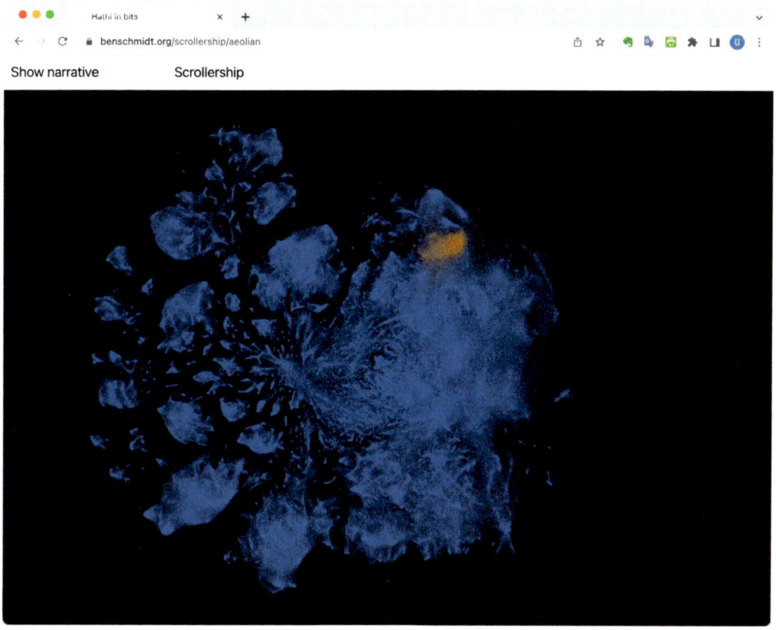

Figure 6.4 Visualisation of approximately 30% of the HathiTrust collection, clustered according to text similarity, and coloured by inclusion in (orange) or exclusion from (blue) the 2020 NovelTM dataset. © Benjamin Schmidt, Glen Layne-Worthey, J. Stephen Downie.

Notes

1. HTRC Extracted Features 2.0. Accessed 4 January 2024. https://doi.org/10.13012/R2TE-C227.
2. https://github.com/htrc/htrc-feature-reader.
3. www.niso.org/niso-io/2022/01/neh-grant-supports-hathitrust-research-centers-torchlite.
4. This case study is largely the work of Jill P. Naiman, and was supported by a University of Illinois Fiddler Fellowship and a NASA Astrophysics Data Analysis Program Grant (20-ADAP20-0225). A much fuller description of the research is available at https://arxiv.org/abs/2301.10781.
5. See https://ui.adsabs.harvard.edu/.
6. The F1 score is a combination metric of precision (prec) and recall (rec) with F1 = 2 × prec × rec / (prec + rec), with prec = TP / (TP + FP) and rec = TP / (TP + FN) as the combination metrics of true positives (TP), false positives (FP) and false negatives (FN).
7. See www.astroexplorer.org/.
8. See https://github.com/facebookresearch/detectron2.
9. See www.zooniverse.org/.
10. This case study is largely the work of Nikolaus Parulian.
11. This case study is largely the work of Ted Underwood and Ryan Dubnicek.
12. This project is the work of Peter Organisciak, and was supported by IMLS #LG-86-18-0061-18, with additional support from the University of Denver.
13. See www.hathitrust.org/hathifiles.
14. https://mengtingwan.github.io/data/goodreads.html.

15. See https://github.com/massivetexts/saddl-dataset.
16. See https://saddl.du.edu.
17. This case study is the work of Benjamin Schmidt.

References

.txtlab. 2023. 'NovelTM'. .txtlab @ McGill. Accessed November 4 2023. https://txtlab.org/category/textminingthenovel/.

Bartz, C., Raetz, H., Otholt, J., Meinel, C. and Yang, H.. 2021. 'Synthesis in style: Semantic segmentation of historical documents using synthetic data'. https://arxiv.org/abs/2107.06777.

Bernhardsson, E. 2013. 'Annoy [C++]'. Spotify. https://github.com/spotify/annoy.

Bhatt, J., Hashmi, K.A., Afzal, M.Z. and Stricker, D. 2021. 'A survey of graphical page object detection with deep neural networks', *Applied Sciences*, 11(12):5344.

Boros, E., Nguyen, N.K., Lejeune, G. and Doucet, A. 2022. 'Assessing the impact of OCR noise on multilingual event detection over digitised documents', *International Journal on Digital Libraries*, 23(3):241–66.

Boukhers, Z. and Bouabdallah, A. 2022. 'Vision and natural language for metadata extraction from scientific PDF documents: A multimodal approach'. In *Proceedings of the 22nd ACM/IEEE Joint Conference on Digital Libraries*, 1–5. Cologne, Germany. ACM. https://doi.org/10.1145/3529372.3533295.

Boukhers, Z., Beili, N., Hartmann, T., Goswami, P. and Zafar, M.A. 2021. 'MexPub: Deep transfer learning for metadata extraction from German publications'. In *2021 ACM/IEEE Joint Conference on Digital Libraries (JCDL)*, 250–53. https://doi.org/10.1109/JCDL52503.2021.00076.

Bucher, R. 2018. 'Classification of fiction genres: Text classification of fiction texts from Project Gutenberg'. Master's thesis, University of Borås. Accessed 5 February 2024. http://urn.kb.se/resolve?urn=urn:nbn:se:hb:diva-16007.

Choudhury, S.R., Mitra, P., Kirk, A., Szep, S., Pellegrino, D., Jones, S. and Giles, C.L. 2013. 'Figure metadata extraction from digital documents'. In *12th International Conference on Document Analysis and Recognition*, 135–9. https://doi.org/10.1109/ICDAR.2013.34.

Clark, C. and Divvala, S. 2016. 'PDFfigures 2.0: Mining figures from research papers'. In *2016 IEEE/ACM Joint Conference on Digital Libraries (JCDL)*:143–52.

Devlin, J., Chang, M.-W., Lee, K. and Toutanova, K. 2018. 'BERT: Pre-training of deep bidirectional transformers for language enderstanding'. https://arxiv.org/abs/1810.04805v2.

Dong, H., Cheng, Z., He, X., Zhou, M., Zhou, A., Zhou, F., Liu, A., Han, S. and Zhang, D. 2022. 'Table pre-training: A survey on model architectures, pre-training objectives, and downstream tasks'. https://arxiv.org/abs/2201.09745.

Eisner, N.L., Barragán, O., Lintott, C., Aigrain, S., Nicholson, B., Boyajian, T.S. et al. 2021. 'Planet hunters TESS II: Findings from the first two years of TESS', *MNRAS*, 501(4):4669–90. https://arxiv.org/abs/2011.13944.

GROBID. 2008. https://github.com/kermitt2/grobid.

Gupta, R. 2019. 'Classifying fiction and non-fiction works using machine learning'. Student Publications & Research, Illinois Mathematics and Science Academy. Accessed 5 February 2024. https://digitalcommons.imsa.edu/student_pr/46.

Hamdi, A., Linhares Pontes, E., Sidère, N., Coustaty, M. and Doucet, A. 2022. 'In-depth analysis of the impact of OCR errors on named entity recognition and linking', *Natural Language Engineering*, 29(2):425–48.

Hamori, E. and Ruskin, J. 1983. 'H curves, a novel method of representation of nucleotide series especially suited for long DNA sequences', *Journal of Biological Chemistry*, 258(2):1318–27.

Hessel, J. and Schofield, A. 2021. 'How effective is BERT without word ordering? Implications for language understanding and data privacy'. In *Proceedings of the 59th Annual Meeting of the Association for Computational Linguistics and the 11th International Joint Conference on Natural Language Processing*, Vol. 2: Short Papers, 204–11. https://doi.org/10.18653/v1/2021.acl-short.27.

Jett, J., Capitanu, B., Kudeki, D., Cole, T.W., Hu, Y., Organisciak, P., Underwood, T., Dickson Koehl, E., Dubnicek, R. and Downie, J. S. 2020. 'The HathiTrust Research Center Extracted Features Dataset (2.0)', HathiTrust Research Center. https://doi.org/10.13012/R2TE-C227.
Johnson, L.C., Seth, A.C., Dalcanton, J.J., Wallace, M.L., Simpson, R.J., Lintott, C.J. et al. 2015. 'PHAT stellar cluster survey. II. Andromeda Project cluster catalog', *The Astrophysical Journal*, 802(2):127.
Kahu, S.Y. 2020. 'Figure extraction from scanned electronic theses and dissertations'. Master's thesis, Virginia Tech.
Li, M., Cui, L., Huang, S., Wei, F., Zhou, M. and Li, Z. 2019. 'TableBank: A benchmark dataset for table detection and recognition'. https://arxiv.org/abs/1903.01949.
Li, M., Xu, Y., Cui, L., Huang, S., Wei, F., Li, Z. and Zhou, M. 2020. 'DocBank: A benchmark dataset for document layout analysis'. https://arxiv.org/abs/2006.01038.
Lintott, C.J., Schawinski, K., Slosar, A., Land, K., Bamford, S., Thomas, D., Raddick, M.J., Nichol, R.C., Szalay, A., Andreescu, D., Murray, P. and Vandenberg, J. 2008. 'Galaxy Zoo: Morphologies derived from visual inspection of galaxies from the Sloan Digital Sky Survey', *Monthly Notices of the Royal Astronomical Society*, 389(3) 1179–89.
Lovett, R.W. and Lovett, C.C. 1991. Robinson Crusoe*: A bibliographical checklist of English language editions (1719–1979)*. Westport, CT: Greenwood Publishing Group.
Maltese, A.V., Harsh, J.A. and Svetina, D. 2015. 'Data visualization literacy: Investigating data interpretation along the novice–expert continuum', *Journal of College Science Teaching*, 45(1):84–90.
Miller, D.P. 2000. 'Out from under: Form/genre access in LCSH', *Cataloging & Classification Quarterly*, 29(1–2):169–88.
Monnier, T. and Aubry, M. 2020. 'docExtractor: An off-the-shelf historical document element extraction', 17th International Conference on Frontiers in Handwriting Recognition. https://doi.org/10.1109/ICFHR2020.2020.00027.
Naiman, J.P., Williams, P.K.G. and Goodman, A. 2022a. 'Figure and figure caption extraction for mixed raster and vector PDFs: Digitization of astronomical literature with OCR features'. In *Linking Theory and Practice of Digital Libraries*, edited by G. Silvello, O. Corcho, P. Manghi, G.M. Di Nunzio, K. Golub, N. Ferro and A. Poggi, 52–67. Cham, Switzerland: Springer.
Naiman, J.P., Williams, P.K.G. and Goodman, A. 2022b. 'The reading time machine figure localization dataset'. Unpublished paper.
Ni, J., Ábrego, G.H., Constant, N., Ma, J., Hall, K.B., Cer, D. and Yang, Y. 2021. 'Sentence-T5: Scalable sentence encoders from pre-trained text-to-text models'. arXiv:2108.08877.
Organisciak, P. and Ryan, M. 2024. 'Improving text relationship modeling with artificial data', *Journal of Information Science*, 50(2):434–46.
Organisciak, P., Shetenhelm, S., Vasques, D.F.A. and Matusiak, K. 2019. 'Characterizing same work relationships in large-scale digital libraries', *International Conference on Information*, 419–25. https://doi.org/10/gg8g2t.
Organisciak, P., Schmidt, B.M. and Durward, M. 2023. 'Approximate nearest neighbor for long document relationship labeling in digital libraries', *International Journal on Digital Libraries*, 24:311–25.
Pedregosa, F., Varoquaux, G., Gramfort, A., Michel, V., Thirion, B., Grisel, O. et al. 2011. 'Scikit-learn: Machine learning in Python', *Journal of Machine Learning Research*, 12(85):2825–30.
Pennington, J., Socher, R. and Manning, C. 2014. 'GloVe: Global vectors for word representation'. In *Proceedings of the 2014 Conference on Empirical Methods in Natural Language Processing*, 1532–43. Doha: Association for Computational Linguistics.
Pfitzmann, B., Auer, C., Dolfi, M., Nassar, A.S. and Staar, P.W.J. 2022. 'DocLayNet: A large uman-annotated dataset for document layout analysis'. https://arxiv.org/abs/2206.01062.
Reimers, N. and Gurevych, I. 2019. 'Sentence-BERT: Sentence embeddings using Siamese BERT-Networks'. In *Proceedings of the 2019 Conference on Empirical Methods in Natural Language Processing and the 9th International Joint conference on Natural Language Processing*, 3982–92. Hong Kong: Association for Computational Linguistics.
Riva, P., Le Boeuf, P. and Zumer, M. 2017. *IFLA Library Reference Model: A Conceptual Model for Bibliographic Information*. The Hague: International Federation of Library Associations and Institutions.
Saha, R., Mondal, A. and Jawahar, C.V. 2019. 'Graphical object detection in document images'. In *2019 International Conference on Document Analysis and Recognition (ICDAR)*, 51– 8. https://doi.org/10.1109/ICDAR.2019.00018.

Sainburg, T., McInnes, L. and Gentner, T.Q. 2020. 'Parametric UMAP embeddings for representation and semi-supervised learning'. https://arxiv.org/abs/2009.12981.
Schmidt, B. 2018. 'Stable random projection: Lightweight, general-purpose dimensionality reduction for digitized libraries', *Journal of Cultural Analytics*, 3(1).
Schreiber, S., Agne, S., Wolf, I., Dengel, A. and Ahmed, S. 2017. 'DeepDeSRT: Deep learning for detection and structure recognition of tables in document images'. In *2017 14th IAPR International Conference on Document Analysis and Recognition (ICDAR)*, 1162–7. IEEE, Kyoto. https://doi.org/10.1109/ICDAR.2017.192.
Schwamb, M.E., Lintott, C.J., Fischer, D.A., Giguere, M.J., Lynn, S., Smith, A.M., Brewer, J.M., Parrish, M., Schawinski, K. and Simpson, R.J. 2012. 'Planet hunters: Assessing the Kepler inventory of short-period planets', *The Astrophysical Journal*, 754(2):129.
Short, M. 2019. 'Text mining and subject analysis for fiction; or, using machine learning and information extraction to assign subject headings to dime novels', *Cataloging & Classification Quarterly*, 57(5):315–36.
Siegel, N., Lourie, N., Power, R. and Ammar, W. 2018. 'Extracting scientific figures with distantly supervised neural networks'. https://arxiv.org/abs/1804.02445.
Singh, P., Varadarajan, S., Singh, A.N. and Srivastava, M.M. 2020. 'Multi-domain document layout understanding using few-shot object detection'. In *Image Analysis and Recognition*, edited by A. Campilho, F. Karray and Z. Wang, 89– 99. Cham, Switzerland: Springer.
Underwood, T., Kimutis, P. and Witte, J. 2020. 'NovelTM datasets for English-language fiction, 1700–2009', *Journal of Cultural Analytics*, 5(2).
Vaswani, A., Shazeer, N., Parmar, N., Uszkoreit, J., Jones, L., Gomez, A.N., Kaiser, L., Polosukhin, I. 2017. 'Attention is all you need'. http://arxiv.org/abs/1706.03762.
Yang, X., Yumer, E., Asente, P., Kraley, M., Kifer, D. and Giles, C.L. 2017. 'Learning to extract semantic structure from documents using multimodal fully convolutional neural networks'. In *2017 IEEE Conference on Computer Vision and Pattern Recognition (CVPR)*, 4342–51. https://doi.org/10.1109/CVPR.2017.462.
Yashwant Kahu, S., Ingram, W.A., Fox, E.A. and Wu, J. 2021. 'ScanBank: A benchmark dataset for figure extraction from scanned electronic theses and dissertations'. https://arxiv.org/abs/2106.15320.
Younas, J., Rizvi, S.T.R., Malik, M.I., Shafait, F., Lukowicz, P. and Ahmed, S. 2019. 'FFD: Figure and formula detection from document images'. In *2019 Digital Image Computing: Techniques and Applications (DICTA)*, 1–7. https://doi.org/10.1109/DICTA47822.2019.8945972.
Zhong, X., Tang, J. and Jimeno Yepes, A. 2019. 'PubLayNet: Largest dataset ever for document layout analysis'. https://arxiv.org/abs/1908.07836.

Part III
Digitised collections and handwritten text: challenges and new methods

7
Distant viewing archives

Taylor Arnold and Lauren Tilton

Facilitating search and discovery is an ongoing challenge for cultural heritage data. The scale and scope of large-scale digitisation has brought exciting possibilities for the public to engage with and learn about the immense holdings of cultural heritage institutions, including archives, libraries and museums. We focus on how practices of looking, specifically computer vision through distant viewing, are facilitating access and discovery of collections through the automated and semi-automated production of metadata. The chapter begins with how the recent scale of digitisation has brought an impressive range to the amount of accessible data. Then, we turn to how metadata shapes access and discovery of collections. Computer vision offers another layer of metadata based on analysis of the computational analysis of the digital image itself. We focus on three methods – colour, image segmentation and image similarity – and how they offer different kinds of information to facilitate discovery. While we are excited about the possibilities, we also highlight challenges, including legal barriers, along with future areas for research. Given that we are US-based scholars, our examples are primarily drawn from collections held by US-based institutions.

Digitisation: scope and scale

Significant work is underway to make archives and collections accessible. While the early 2000s were particularly marked by concerns that digitisation would hurt institutions that held and displayed cultural heritage, the research has proved otherwise (Crow and Din 2010; Bertacchini and Morando 2013). The tides have shifted as cultural heritage institutions, and the publics they engage with, have seen how digital access supports their missions. For example, the Rijksmuseum in Amsterdam made a splash several years ago when they made most of their metadata available for bulk download with clear documentation.[1] The Smithsonian in the United States garnered praise in 2020 when they launched Smithsonian Open Access, which now has over four million images as of 2023 (Bote 2020). These initiatives brought attention to the scope of the materials, and the scale.

Few physical institutions are positioned to display their entire collection, and in many cases only feature a small fraction of their holdings. Underneath many institutions and in storage facilities sit tens of thousands of materials, from government documents to works of art to old technologies. They range in size from a small jewel or coin to cars and planes. In many cases, institutions do not even know all that they have, and the process of preparing an exhibition, providing access to researchers and digitisation reveal priceless holdings. Supporting access and discovery through digital forms has come to be seen as a way of opening the scale and scope of collections, revealing the importance and custodial work of the institution rather than being seen as a threat to the physical institution and in-person visitor numbers. The global pandemic that began in 2019 only hastened the call to support digital access as the world turned to digital technologies in order to learn and connect.

The rapid investment and support for digital access was possible because of several decades of innovation. The first digital scanner in 1957 created by a team at the US National Bureau of Standards was a breakthrough, but it was not until the 1980s and 1990s that their cost and features became amenable to the needs of cultural heritage institutions. This was a particular issue for scanning visual and audio sources. The Library of Congress in the United States in the 1990s was among the earliest institutions pioneering the process for digitisation in photography and film. Working with new technologies, the Library of Congress digitised several photography collections, including the famed FSA-OWI set of photographs from the Great Depression and World War II in the United States. In 1995, they launched the corresponding digital public project 'American Memory' (Rottman 1992; Library of Congress 2003). While the site was simple by today's standards, with the only way of searching through tens of thousands of photographs being through an open search box, 'American Memory' was an important early effort to organise and contextualise aspects of these collections. Following traditional ideas of curation, the site also included special digital exhibits of selected images describing topics such as 'The Evolution of the Conservation Movement, 1850–1920'.[2] Using the site quickly revealed a key challenge that animates the creation of digital collections: making a lot of materials available while finding ways to support sifting through and understanding a collection. In other words, how to make materials accessible *and* discoverable.

Metadata: access and discovery

Access and discovery are connected but not the same. One can have access but not have great ways to move through the materials and understand their scope. Think of the open search box provided by Google. The white background, just waiting for you to type in something … anything. We find that white box daunting, just as we do when we open a new text editor to begin writing a new project. Five minutes later, the page is still blank, and we are staring into the abyss. The open search box has not been a usual way to make archives and collections available to the public over the years. There are many great reasons for this, from financial to technical constraints along with efforts to prioritise just getting materials out there, even if the first pass on making the materials accessible prioritises domain experts. At least the materials are more accessible in their digital surrogate, particularly for fragile materials, including decaying paper or even explosives, such as nitrate film. Yes, one has access. But how does one find what one is looking for, or even know what to look for, if one does not have deep knowledge of the collection already? Information retrieval systems, such as faceted search and recommender systems using metadata, have been a powerful answer.

Metadata offers a way to facilitate access through discovery with the specific features of a source. Let us take a photograph as an example. We might want to search a collection to discover if there are photographs by a specific photographer, taken during a determined time period, addressing certain themes or created with a certain kind of film stock. This data about the data, such as the name of the creator, the year created, a description of the content and the type of material, enables discovery through informational retrieval processes. They draw on over a century of practices, such as the Library of Congress Subject Headings, which have been maintained since 1898.[3] They provide a way to search and find through subjects such as genre, geography and language, and have been adopted by other institutions, including libraries and museums.

Once written on index cards and now strings in databases, these schemas provide a way to sift through collections. This has led to the development of domain-specific vocabularies such as the Getty Union

List of Artists Names and the Art & Architecture Thesaurus (AAT) that offer consistency within and across collections to help with discovery.[4] If one wants to find a photograph by Gordon Parks across collections or a certain feature in an image made from the same material, it is easier when they each spell the name the same way, use an ID that is the same and agree on terminology.[5] There is incredible power in descriptive and provenance metadata, which provides a key layer of information for accessing and discovering collections. The work of experts such as metadata librarians, curators and archivists in collaboration with disciplinary experts in fields such as art history have worked tirelessly to develop these systems that drive information retrieval. After all, it takes someone to create and structure the information in our current data-driven world; the expertise of so many in what is labelled as the 'humanities' provides a major backbone to our current information ecosystem.

Yet, one challenge has been the same condition that made this world possible: labour. It is a time-consuming task to manually look at and add text-based data to each item in a collection. As a result, there have had to be priorities and trade-offs. Using controlled vocabularies offers connections within and across collections, enabling projects like 'Europeana' that connect Europe's digital cultural heritage across physical, political and cultural borders.[6] Yet, standardisation often means reducing nuanced concepts and specificity for a shared concept as well as focusing on popular languages like English. Another challenge is the focus on text-based knowledge with someone looking, reading and describing in words. At the same time, much of the way that we interpret and engage with cultural heritage is through visual elements, which are not always easily captured through text. How might we account for this and expand our approach to access and discovery?

Before we turn to addressing this question, we offer one final note about terms. While we will continue to use the term discovery, we want to flag an issue. Discovery is a bit of a misnomer. While the term is the lingua franca of those who work with cultural heritage, which is composed of a diverse and interdisciplinary community, the term suggests that one is the first to find or observe something. It could be seen as a particularly colonial way of thinking, as if another set of people has not already worked to create, preserve, organise and make available the materials that someone else is 'discovering'. We will use this term, but we think we need to find another term that acknowledges all the labour and work that goes into making something 'discoverable', including the intellectual labour to create schemas for metadata, and the use and interpretation of computer vision to create another 'discovery' layer that we turn to now.

Computer vision: viewing at scale

Computer vision (CV) offers exciting possibilities for the creation of metadata at scale. An area focused on how computers process, analyse and understand digital images, CV is how computers view the digital surrogates of materials such as manuscripts, photographs and works of art that cultural heritage institutions have digitised. This area of AI has been driven by work in areas such as automated cars, surveillance and medicine (Boyd and Crawford 2012). The emphasis on corporate and governmental needs that have shaped the available models combined with the technical needs of CV, such as significant and costly processing power and storage, has made image analysis a bit more challenging to adopt in the digital humanities and cultural heritage, particularly compared to text analysis (Arnold et al 2021). The landscape is changing as CV becomes more attainable, the types of models are expanding, legal roadblocks are slowly coming down, and new methods and theories are bringing an expanded interdisciplinary lens on the possibilities.

Once primarily available to only the most affluent institutions, working with CV has become more accessible due to several developments. One is the emergence of GPUs, graphic processing units designed to work with images, in the 1970s and their lowering cost by the early 2000s. At the same time, personal computers have become much more powerful over the last two decades. It was once challenging to process tens of thousands of images, such as photographs, without access to a high-performance computer, but now a MacBook Pro can run a model in a few hours or days depending on the size and number of images. Cloud services have also made a new space for processing, and one can reduce costs further with efficient code. The relative affordability of these methods is being augmented by powerful institutions working to support better access to machine learning of cultural heritage for the public. Organisations like the Library of Congress's LC Lab have been doing exciting work to figure out the best way to support large-scale cloud-based access and analysis of cultural heritage data through their 'Computing in the Cloud Initiative'. This new landscape is making computer vision more accessible, but how does it help with access and discovery of cultural heritage? We turn to several methods and their possibilities.

Colour offers one way to explore collections. These spectrums of light are an important analytical tool, particularly for fields such as art history, media studies and visual culture studies (Helmreich 2014). Artists might be interested in a certain colour period, such as Yves Klein's blue period. We might be interested in when and how a particular photographer or organisation, such as Magnum, used certain film stocks. Looking at the range of colours in magazine covers offers a lens into aesthetics as well as histories of printing. Others have been interested in moving images and genres, and how colour has changed over time (Manovich 2002; Ferguson 2017). The ability to filter a collection by colour offers one way into and across collections.

A cluster of exciting experimental work by museums made the rounds in 2018 and 2019 that demonstrated the potential for colour to be an informative and fun way into collections. One of the earliest projects in this space was by the Cooper Hewitt in New York City. A museum dedicated to design, they developed the 'Dive Into Color' project in 2018. Drawing on multiple visualisations, users could select a colour from a colour wheel and look at items in the collection over time as a part of the exhibition *Saturated: The allure and science of color* (Vane 2022). They could see a particular colour over time, spurring questions about the use of certain colours and the development of saturation as a colour technique. A prototype by the Swedish National Heritage Board, Malmö Museer, Nationalmuseum, National Museums of World Culture and the Nordic Museum brought together tags and colour to build an exploratory interface based on fashion.[7] Users can select a colour and keep adding combinations to filter through the collection of approximately 5,000 items providing unexpected connections. Laura Wrubel developed colour palettes for collections from the Library of Congress. Even just a cursory glance at the colour range of collections like the Civil War Maps and Sanborn Maps, the former with more saturated darker hues and the latter with a more pastel palette, provides insights into the different aesthetics and process of map creation.[8] While few have implemented these projects at scale, museums like the Cooper Hewitt have integrated colour as a search feature in their Advanced Search.[9] One can type in a colour such as *blue* or use a hex code such as *#b4d9ef* to search results. One can further refine by location, copyright status, period and other facets. Colour becomes just one more way into the collection driven by computer vision.

Region segmentation offers another way to explore collections. Introduced around 2016, the approach extends the ways that we can view images (Caesar, Uijlings and Ferrari 2018). Object detection allows us to identify specific items like a car or animal in an image. However, objects are not all that comprise an image. People interpret images quickly. Let us say we are looking closely at a photograph that a friend is sharing with us. We quickly recognise objects such as a cake, candles, table, people and party hats along with the grass, fence and sky. The combination of elements in the foreground and background indicates that this is a photo of a birthday celebration. Putting the objects that we can count, also known as object detection, along with the elements of the image that are more abstract offers a more complex way to view images.

Bringing together object detection and background/foreground detection, the goal of region segmentation is to assign each of the pixels in the image to a category. It is akin to the idea of tokenisation in text processing, where you are splitting a document into words. But unlike text analysis, it is not as clear where to make the cut in an image. For example, if you have a house in the middle of a photo, you could have one category for the entire house. You could also split the categories into door, windows, wall and roof. This creates regions of adjacent pixels that are assigned to the same category. A further question is what categories you assign to each of these regions. We could even go a bit further. Now that we know it is a door, we might say whether it is a wooden door or a metal door. It is possible to train region segmentation models from a training set with different tagged regions. One of the most well-known pretrained datasets is MS-COCO. Their dataset creates a hierarchy of categories split between 'things' and 'stuff'. 'Things' are concrete objects that we can count, like a door, table and cake. 'Stuff' are concepts that are innumerable such as the sky, snow and water. Image segmentation offers us a way to identify both 'things' and 'stuff'.

Region segmentation offers another layer to build into discovery. One could use features such as things and stuff to add metadata tags that one could search and facet by. Interested in histories of technology? One could search for a collection of photographs or TV news segments that feature cars. Interested in climate change? One could search for elements such as snow, water and dirt across collections. In our own work, we have used region segmentation to look at which photographers took photographs inside or outside to understand more clearly which photographers were focused on the land and outside environment amid the Great Depression in the United States (Arnold and Tilton 2023). In our work for the Library of Congress, we experimented with looking at composition in photography, such as camera angles and styles of portraiture (Arnold, Tilton and Wigard 2022). Image segmentation offers an approach to building more complex metadata that draws on the features of visual culture, such as composition and point of view.

Along with colour and regions, another way of searching for shared features and themes is through image embeddings. They are a way of measuring image similarity, but the challenge is that the results are not as explainable as colour models. Image embeddings map images into a sequence of numbers, often produced by cutting off the penultimate layer of the neural network; this produces a series of numbers that describe the image (see Arnold and Tilton 2021). This is a step right before what we more commonly think about when discussing computer vision algorithms like object detection or face detection. Right before the model is about to interpret and name features of the image with labels such as a chair or car, we stop the process to generate a numeric description. The effect is that this becomes a great way to look at image similarity based on more abstract features. The challenge is that it is unclear which features drive the similarity. It is usually a combination of colour, texture and objects, among other features that drive the pattern recognition. It is up to human interpretation of the results to understand, or at least hypothesise, the connection. While some might find the lack of clarity about the connections daunting, one can also think of this as a powerful approach because it can provide unexpected connections. It introduces a bit of fun, and may support discovering new connections.

Because of the exciting results of this approach, it has quickly become a popular approach to discovery, particularly through recommender systems. Recommender systems are an information retrieval process that provides users with content and connections that they can browse and explore. Rather than the open text search box, image similarity incorporated into a recommender system immediately offers items in the collection to engage with instead of the user having to know what to look for. The added benefit is that the user may be recommended items they did not even know existed in the collection and which may not have been discoverable through a text search. We will use our work on 'Photogrammar' as an example to show how image similarity augments textual metadata as well as ways to explore items in collections that have little to no description (see Figure 7.1).

Photogrammar is a platform for exploring the 170,000 photographs from the Great Depression and World War II taken in the United States by a federal government unit known as the FSA. Along with engaging with the collection through a map, users can facet the results through metadata such as photographer, date and theme. When a user lands on a specific photograph, they are presented with a set of similar photographs through a recommender system (Arnold, Leonard and Tilton 2017). The results are based on cutting off the penultimate layer of the VGG-19 convolutional neural network. The benefits are at least twofold. The first is that the user can see photographs that share a feature with the chosen image. Interested in churches? Here are photos of churches from across the United States. Interested in parades? Here are photos of parades from the late 1930s through the mid-1940s. One may not even know these themes

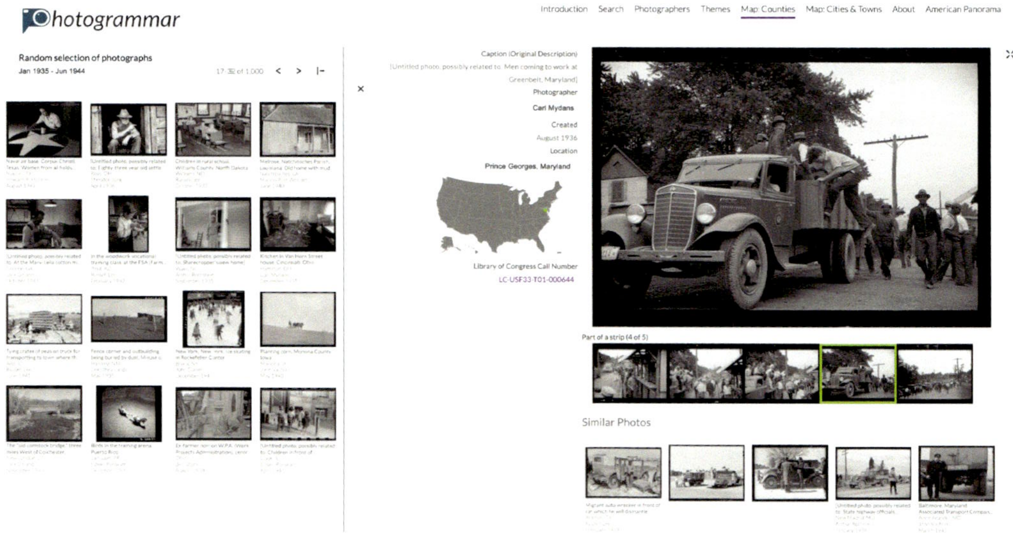

Figure 7.1 Screenshot from Photogrammar showing the use of computer vision to suggest similar photographs using an embedding space. https://photogrammar.org © Taylor Arnold and Lauren Tilton.

were in the collection. With 170,000 photographs, even when they have keywords and descriptions for each image written in text, a text search will still not create all the connections and patterns that the visual similarity is offering. Image similarity built into a recommender system offers another layer of interpretation and a way to move through the collection.

The second benefit is that this approach can also support the discovery of items with no other metadata. In the case of the FSA, approximately 40,000 photographs have no metadata – photographer, caption, date or location. When one goes to the Library of Congress website, the only way to find these photos is to know their LOC number. Users can discover these photos through the image similarity recommender system on Photogrammar. These are photos that only those familiar with the physical collection in Washington DC or the ID number system of the Library of Congress could find. For those familiar with text analysis, image similarity becomes a kind of visual topic modelling that uses shared patterns in the pixels to make connections that can then be used to suggest connections. While one must be careful not to overread into these connections, they often provide connections based on shared themes, aesthetics and formal elements that offer another way to view, explore and interpret the collection.

Image similarity continues to be a popular approach in cultural heritage. Our work on Photogrammar is indebted to projects like 'Ukiyo-e Search' at Ukiyo-e.org. Developed by John Resig in 2012, the project brings together 23,000 Japanese woodblock prints from across 24 institutions to aggregate and facilitate search across holdings in libraries, museums, auction houses and art dealers.[10] Along with using metadata to aggregate work by time, the site offers a visual similarity search.[11] By clicking on a piece, one can see similar prints in the collection. For example, one can see that prints by Katsushika Hokusai are held worldwide and that institutions like the Library of Congress, Minneapolis Institute of the Arts and Tokyo National Museum all hold versions of the same work, but the titles vary slightly. The approach helps with building connections where metadata might include different names or slight variations in names, which is a major issue for forms such as prints and photography, where there are often multiples of the same image. As 'Ukiyo-e Search' demonstrates, image similarity brings another layer of search and discovery within and across collections, enables connections across institutions and holdings, and becomes a strategy when metadata does not exactly align.

The approach has become so popular that there are now tools designed for working with a collection of your choice. From the Yale DH Lab, PixPlot provides a Python-based toolkit for loading the collection of your choice to measure image similarity.[12] Their dynamic interface allows users to move around the clusters in a 3D viewer, offering an exciting way to explore connections and patterns in a collection. The CUDAN Open Lab at Tallin University launched 'Collection Space Navigator' (CSN) in 2023.[13] Like PixPlot, one can load in a dataset and explore image similarity in an interactive environment by zooming in and out. CSN adds the ability to do nested search and highlight data based on categorical metadata such as genre and style. These tools speak to the importance of cultural heritage institutions providing open-source data, where the public can explore collections with computer vision based on their interests.

The methods above are just the tip of the iceberg. Scholars such as Jasmijn van Gorp and the Clariah MediaSuite team have been working to integrate computer vision techniques for searching audiovisual materials held in the Netherlands, while Thomas Smits and Mike Kestemont have shown possibilities with models like CLIP (Smits and Kestemont 2021; Ordelman et al 2019). Melvin Weavers, Bee Lee and Ryan Cordell have looked at how computer vision can find features of newspapers such as photographs and advertisements, while Katherine McDonough and the 'Living With Machines' team have been looking at the use of computer vision to access and study maps (Hosseini et al 2022; see also Chapter 5 in this collection). Estelle Gueville, Kristine Mapes and David Wrisley have been applying computer vision to the study of illuminated manuscripts, while Alexander Dunst and Justin Wigard are forging the computational study of comics (see Arnold, Tilton and Wigard 2023). And, of course, there is the exciting work of the 'EyCon Project: Visual AI and Early Conflict Photography' and the LUSTRE Network led by Lise Jaillant, one of the editors of this collection.[14] These contributions offer further directions for using computer vision to assist in discovering collections and even possibilities for connections across different types of media.

As we look toward the future, there are many opportunities for computer vision to facilitate search and discovery. These many methods offer different ways of adding another layer of information that can be harnessed for information retrieval processes. Along with augmenting contextual metadata such as creator, date and location, they can help with building connections and patterns across collections that we did not know existed or even think to look for in the first place from the actual sets of pixels that comprise a digital image. An added benefit is computational power. We can iterate over a collection as we add new features that we want to view. The scale becomes less of a daunting task given the analytical power of computer vision methods, particularly compared to manually looking at each item repeatedly.

The added layers of information also connect into calls to think more generously and creatively about how we make digital collections accessible. Mitchell Whitelaw's call for 'generous interfaces' responds to the issue that search is unable to communicate the abundance of materials in collections (Whitelaw 2015). He demonstrates how browsing through data visualisation techniques like mosaics, bar graphs and grids harnessing metadata features offers a more giving way to see the abundance that cultural heritage institutions are offering the public. If we think of this as a mode of communication, we could go even further and connect this to Mari Lee Mifsud's idea of rhetoric as a gift (2007). Generous interfaces could be seen as a kind of gift, as a way of communicating that sets up a different relation between cultural heritage institutions and their users. Another approach is to think about the ways that we can build fun and serendipity in the ways that collections are shared with their intended publics. Christian Olesen and the team have built on calls to introduce serendipity into information retrieval with their SEMIA project, which used computer vision to generate unexpected encounters across a collection (Masson et al 2020). There is a playfulness in this approach, which, at the same time, continues to move people through a collection. An added benefit of these approaches is their potential to play with and even disrupt the organisation of collections. As calls to decolonise the archive rightly point out that many systems of organisation are inculcated in colonial logic, computer vision might offer different ways of viewing the archive that challenge the colonial gaze (see Figure 7.2).

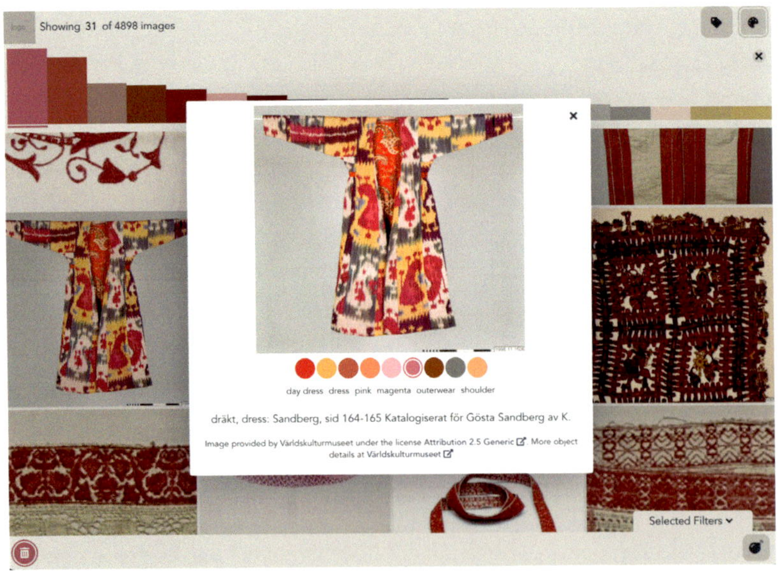

Figure 7.2 Screenshot from the default interface of the 'Generous Interface Fashion' project. https://riksantikvarieambetet.github.io/Generous-Interface-Fashion/ © Taylor Arnold and Lauren Tilton.

The possibilities are not without their challenges. Being careful about the results of computer vision is paramount. Google Arts & Culture garnered criticism for how it paired people with works of art based on similarity, particularly the ways it made racist connections, which was one of the more widely publicised examples of the potential pitfalls of computer vision. Checking results and using metadata such as captions in conversation with the computer vision results to look closer at potential problematic connections is one way to address this issue. Starting small and building up provides a way to keep checking the kind of discovery afforded by computer vision. Building up also helps with another challenge, which is the size and scale of sources like TV and film. Iterating computer vision algorithms over TV and film adds up. While there is quickly growing scholarship on working with still art and photography, there is still significant work to do to experiment with how computer vision can support discovery of moving images.

Another challenge is how little computer vision algorithms can view. In our work for the Library of Congress as a part of their 'Computing in the Cloud Initiative', we created ADDI to demonstrate how little certain computer vision approaches see (see Figure 7.3). Objects may only be a small percentage of the image. Region segmentation helps capture more of the image, but the concepts are descriptive rather than interpretative.

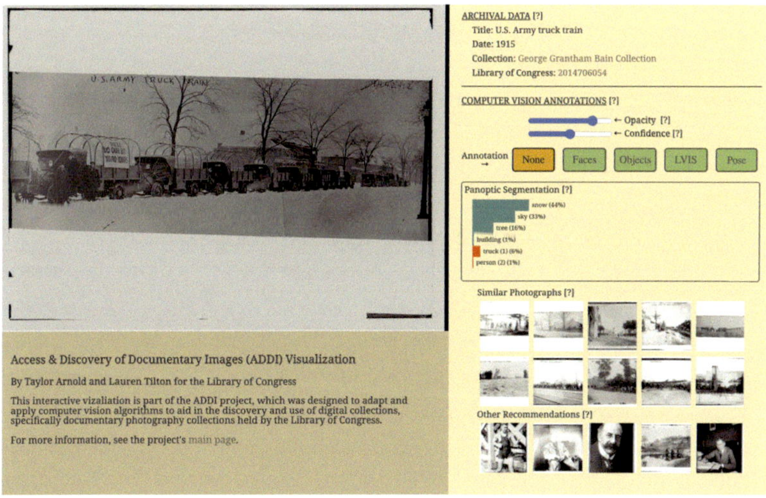

Figure 7.3 Screenshot showing the visualisation of computer vision algorithms using the ADDI tool (Access & Discovery of Documentary Images). https://github.com/distant-viewing/addi © Taylor Arnold and Lauren Tilton.

We also tried pose detection, which we determined was not quite ready for large-scale implementation. The limitation of how computer vision views images is also a reminder that the great expertise that leads to robust metadata such as creator, location, captions and data is incredibly important and computer vision is best situated to augment, not replace, this metadata, which is key to the discovery of cultural heritage collections.

Conclusion

Finally, a challenge is the law. In the United States, a major issue is copyright law. Materials after 1927 are eligible for copyright protection. The timeline is a huge issue for institutions with moving image and photography holdings. A recent development is a new US ruling that allows text and data mining of materials. Researchers in certain institutions can circumvent copyright protection systems thanks to the work of the Authors Alliance and the University of California Berkeley's Samuelson Law, Technology, & Public Policy Clinic (Crump et al 2022). The ruling through the US Copyright Office opens the possibility of computer vision for holdings owned by universities. Previously, for many materials, such as films by a specific director, the only way to conduct computer vision on the materials would have been to break the digital rights management technology. While making the material available to the public would be a violation of copyright law, generating metadata about the material is now possible. The metadata through computer vision can provide a discovery layer, even when the actual material cannot be made available. These kinds of legal developments are helping with discovery but remain a challenge.

We return to the topic of new theories and methods that we alluded to at the beginning of this chapter. One of the newer theories and methods is distant viewing. Emerging from digital humanities and data science, distant viewing as a theory brings the analytical apparatus of media studies and semiotics to explain how computer vision works as a technology and mediator of vision. We argue that when we use computer vision, we are distant viewing. This distinction matters when we think about the authority and effects of the results of computer vision algorithms. Computer vision is often seen as a neutral technology that is just imitating the human visual system. The results of these technologies are then often seen as natural, rather than having any perspective as we argue all computer vision includes. If we say we are distant viewing cultural heritage, rather than just saying we are using computer vision to analyse images, we offer a rhetorical shift in the application of machine learning and AI. The word viewing signifies that there is a decision about what we are seeking to see and look for. Viewing introduces a perspective, for we choose what to view. There is a point of view built into the model and in the interpretation of results.

We hope this shift in terms might help with the use of computer vision in cultural heritage institutions. Rightfully, these institutions are worried about results that are inaccurate or partially accurate. Museums like the Smithsonian and libraries like the Library of Congress speak with incredible authority. There has been hesitancy to use automated and semi-automated metadata because of worries that the data is not accurate, or not accurate enough, which in turn might bring questions about the expertise and custodianship of the institution. For institutions that rely on government funding and must ride the constant wave of shifts in political attitudes, there is understandable caution when it comes to adopting newer technologies and methods that could introduce more challenges. Along with this larger cultural and political challenge, there is a real concern about people's jobs, as experts in the collection and item-level description see automation as a form of replacement. By no means do we think computer vision will replace this kind of expertise. Quite the opposite. These technologies are by no means perfect. There is nothing like historical materials to see computer vision models that papers claim have 97% precision begin to fall apart. Rather, these technologies need people with expertise to check the results and help design better models. We need people to check the distant viewing and see if we should view differently.

Notes

1. For more about the Rijksmuseum's open-data policy, see www.rijksmuseum.nl/en/research/conduct-research/data/policy.
2. See https://memory.loc.gov/ammem/amrvhtml/conshome.html.
3. See https://id.loc.gov/authorities/subjects.html.
4. See www.getty.edu/research/tools/vocabularies/ and www.getty.edu/research/tools/vocabularies/ulan/about.html.
5. For example, the preferred spelling is 'Parks, Gordon' which does not include his middle names. Getty has also done extensive work to offer more biographical information that can then be leveraged.
6. See www.europeana.eu/.
7. For documentation, see https://riksantikvarieambetet.github.io/Generous-Interface-Fashion/.
8. See https://loc-colors.glitch.me/.
9. See https://collection.cooperhewitt.org/search.
10. See https://ukiyo-e.org/about.

11. For a great explanation of the process and justification of image similarity, see https://vimeo.com/74691102.
12. They have two ways of projecting similarity. One is UMAP and the other is TSNE-clustered images. See their GitHub repository for more information: https://github.com/YaleDHLab/pix-plot.
13. The project is available at https://collection-space-navigator.github.io/.
14. EYCON https://eycon.hypotheses.org; LUSTRE Network https://lustre-network.net.

References

Arnold, T. and Tilton, L. 2021. 'Depth in deep learning: Knowledgeable, layered, and impenetrable'. In *Deep Mediations*, edited by K. Redrobe and J. Scheible, 309–28. Minneapolis, MN: University of Minnesota Press.

Arnold, T. and Tilton, L. 2023. *Distant Viewing: Computational exploration of digital images*. Cambridge, MA: MIT Press.

Arnold, T., Leonard, P. and Tilton, L. 2017. 'Knowledge creation through recommender systems', *Digital Scholarship in the Humanities*, 32(suppl_2): ii151–7.

Arnold, T., Van Gorp, J., Scagliola, S. and Tilton, L. 2021.'Special Issue: Audiovisual data in DH', *Digital Humanities Quarterly* 15(1).

Arnold, T., Tilton, L. and Wigard, J. 2022. 'Automatic identification and classification of portraits in a corpus of historical photographs'. In CEUR Workshop Proceedings. Accessed 20 July 2023. https://ceur-ws.org/Vol-3290/short_paper5571.pdf.

Arnold, T., Tilton, L. and Wigard, J. 2023. 'Understanding Peanuts and Schulzian symmetry: Panel detection, caption detection, and gag panels in 17,897 comic strips through distant viewing', *Journal of Cultural Analytics*, 8(3).

Bertacchini, E. and Morando, F. 2013. 'The future of museums in the digital age: New models for access to and use of digital collections', *International Journal of Arts Management* 15 (2):60–72.

Bote, J. 2020. 'Smithsonian makes nearly 3 million pieces of art available online and free to use', *USA Today*, 26 February. Accessed 5 February 2024. https://eu.usatoday.com/story/news/nation/2020/02/26/smithsonian-makes-art-pieces-available-online-public-domain/4879492002/.

Boyd, D. and Crawford, K. 2012. 'Critical questions for big data: Provocations for a cultural, technological, and scholarly phenomenon', *Information, Communication & Society* 15(5):662–79.

Caesar, H., Uijlings, J. and Ferrari, V. 2018. 'COCO-stuff: Thing and stuff classes in context'. In Proceedings of the IEEE Conference on Computer Vision and Pattern Recognition, 1209–18.

Crow, W.B. and Din, H. 2010. 'The educational and economic value of online learning for museums', *The Journal of Museum Education*, 35(2):161–72.

Crump, C., Stallman, E., Daley, G. et al. 2022. 'Exemption to Section 1201 liability for text and data mining'. Berkley Samuelson Law, Technology & Public Policy Clinic, 26 January. Accessed 5 February 2024. www.law.berkeley.edu/case-project/1201-exemption-text-data-mining/.

Ferguson, K.L. 2017. 'Digital surrealism: Visualizing Walt Disney Animation Studios', *Digital Humanities Quarterly*, 11(1). www.digitalhumanities.org/dhq/vol/11/1/000276/000276.html.

Helmreich, A. 2014. 'Summer Camp for art historians'. Getty Blog, 1 August. Accessed 15 July 2023. https://blogs.getty.edu/iris/summer-camp-for-art-historians/.

Hosseini, K., Wilson, D.C.S., Beelen, K. and McDonough, K. 2022. 'MapReader: A computer vision pipeline for the semantic exploration of maps at scale'. In *Proceedings of the 6th ACM SIGSPATIAL International Workshop on Geospatial Humanities (GeoHumanities '22)*. New York, NY: Association for Computing Machinery, 8–19.

Library of Congress. 2003. 'A century of lawmaking for a new nation: US Congressional documents and debates 1774–1875'. American Memory. Accessed 5 February 2024. https://memory.loc.gov/ammem/amlaw/lawhome.html.

Manovich, L. 2002. *The Language of New Media*. Cambridge, MA: MIT Press.

Masson, E., Oleson, C.G., Van Noord, N. and Fossati, G. 2020. 'Exploring digitised moving image collections: The SEMIA project, visual analysis and the turn to abstraction', *Digitial Humanities Quarterly* 14(4).

Mifsud, M. 2007. 'On rhetoric as gift/giving', *Philosophy & Rhetoric*, 40(1):89–107.
Ordelman, R., Melgar, L., Martinez-Ortiz, C., Noordegraaf, J. and Blom, J. 2019. 'Media Suite: Unlocking archives for mixed media scholarly research'. In *Selected Papers from CLARIN Annual Conference 2018, 8–10 October 2018*, edited by I. Skadina and M. Eskevich, 133–43. Pisa, Italy. Linköping Electronic Conference Proceedings, Linköpings universitet.
Rottman, F. 1992. 'History comes alive: The American Memory Project', *School Library Journal*, 38:33–6.
Smits, T. and Kestemont, M. 2021. 'Towards multimodal computational humanities. Using CLIP to analyze late-nineteenth century magic lantern slides'. In *Proceedings of the Computational Humanities Research Conference, November 17–19, 2021*, Amsterdam, The Netherlands, 149–58.
Vane, O. 2022. 'Making "Dive into Color"', *Scuba Diver*, 28 July. Accessed 15 July 2023. https://labs.cooperhewitt.org/.
Whitelaw, M. 2015. 'Generous interfaces for digital cultural collections', *Digital Humanities Quarterly* 9(1). www.digitalhumanities.org/dhq/vol/9/1/000205/000205.html.

8

The adoption of handwritten text recognition at the National Library of Scotland

Paul Gooding, Joseph Nockels and Melissa Terras

This chapter analyses the impact of AI and ML on library practices and workflows. Many aspects of AI in libraries have been explored in detail, including in this collection, but there remains a gap in our understanding of how libraries assess and adopt new tools. This gap will be addressed by exploring how the NLS is responding to the possibilities of HTR tools that might improve the legibility and accessibility of their digitised collections. This chapter draws on the findings of a research placement at the NLS, alongside project reports, conference papers and published research. It is organised into two sections:

- The first section, entitled 'Artificial intelligence and library values,' briefly sets out the critical context for the adoption of AI and ML in libraries. It builds upon existing work in the sector to emphasise that AI adoption must be grounded in the values and priorities of the sector. It also establishes the need for a research agenda based around the conscious reporting of the issues surrounding AI tool integration for digitisation and access pipelines.
- The second section, 'Investigating HTR at the NLS', outlines how HTR has developed and explores its existing application to digitised handwritten collections. It draws upon existing research, including the authors' previous work, to outline the current state of play for HTR in libraries. It then presents the findings of Nockels' placement at the NLS, exploring how HTR might impact upon existing working practices. It concludes by considering how AI technologies might challenge us to reconsider the strategic objectives of libraries, and how technological change might unlock new types of usage and access.

Artificial intelligence and library values

This chapter addresses an urgent need for discussions on how *individual* libraries are integrating AI tools into curatorial, technical and bibliographic protocols within areas such as digitisation and access workflows (Terras 2022, 144). It argues that any work to understand how libraries might integrate such technologies must start from a position grounded in the values and priorities of the library sector. One reason for this, as Karen Coyle has convincingly argued, is that libraries have traditionally been innovators of organisational technologies, but 'if we look … at the time line of information technology over the twentieth century and into the twenty-first, we see library technology falling behind the general technology evolution' (Coyle 2017). While Coyle makes this point about the development of library catalogues, it is equally applicable to the trajectory of AI and ML adoption in libraries. While it is true that libraries have innovated in the adoption and use of AI technologies in their work, it is also notable that many of the major advances have occurred outside the sector (Cordell 2022). As Whittaker argues:

> Modern AI is fundamentally dependent on corporate resources and business practices, and our increasing reliance on such AI cedes inordinate power over our lives and institutions to a handful of tech firms. It also gives these firms significant influence over both the direction of AI development and the academic institutions wishing to research it. (Whittaker 2021, 51)

While the centralisation of technological innovation has implications for the power dynamics of AI adoption more broadly, it is certainly not true that libraries are passive consumers of technology. Gasparini and Kautonen note that private actors appear more proactive with AI than public service providers, summarising the range of roles that libraries play in the technology innovation space:

> Research libraries that serve academia and other scholarly communities are at the center of this flux. They browse library technology reports to pick the most appropriate products to support their operations and services, join national or international projects to gain the benefits of collaborative technology development, and follow the progress of academic publishers and other close partners with mixed feelings. (Gasparini and Kautonen 2022, 2)

Far from the passivity this quote might suggest, the range of initiatives that exist demonstrate a sector attempting to reassert intellectual leadership in a space dominated by private actors with often vastly superior resources. Cordell's (2020) report on AI and ML in libraries summarises the state of the field, but here we provide examples of the kinds of activity that have originated in the sector. Many of these have focused on community building in aid of knowledge exchange. As mentioned in previous chapters, AI4LAM (Artificial Intelligence for Libraries, Archives & Museums) represents a sector-led 'international participatory community focused on advancing the use of AI in, for and by libraries, archives and museums' (AI4LAM 2023). In addition to an annual conference, the AI4LAM community organise a series of events, provide news on AI in libraries and maintain a registry of projects, activities, AI datasets and models. The AEOLIAN Network, which ran from 2021 to 2023 and was funded jointly by the UK Arts and Humanities Research Council and US National Endowment for the Humanities, was similarly designed to bring academics, libraries and other cultural institutions together in order to 'investigate the role that AI can play to make born-digital and digitised cultural records more accessible to users' (AEOLIAN Network 2020). Through a series of workshops, publications and community building activities, the network has been successful in foregrounding key issues for AI in libraries and archives, and thus helping to define current and future research agendas.

The rise of Library Labs, places for 'experimenting with digital collections and data' (Mahey et al 2019, 31) in national libraries in recent years, has also provided a space in which engagement with AI can occur. These labs have been the locus for various activities, including exploring how libraries can reframe their collections as data, and indeed big data (Ames and Lewis 2020); considering how library workflows might adapt to support open data delivery online (Ames 2021); defining methodologies to assess and create digital collections for computational reuse (Candela et al 2023); and utilising digital library collections to produce high-quality tailored AI models (Börjeson et al 2023). Furthermore, AI-related activity occurs elsewhere in libraries, which are involved in internal initiatives and funded projects to create, prototype, trial and integrate AI and ML tools into their institutional workflows.

Alongside this sectoral engagement with AI technologies, there is an increasing level of attention paid to its ethical and intellectual impacts on libraries. This includes a shift in how libraries view the usage of their collections, with non-human actors an increasingly important user group. The presence of these non-human actors is a significant shift from the influential work of key figures like Ranganathan (1931), whose five laws of librarianship placed the 'reader' at the centre of library service provision. Miller (2020) argues that the reader in question has traditionally been implied to be human, whereas the growth of supervised and unsupervised ML with library collections has created a 'need to welcome another set of users into the library. These ML, algorithmic, analytic users will be collaborating with human users, crunching and filtering the data and presenting the information needed by the human user'. With this shifting notion of the audience of the library comes an additional focus on how AI and ML might reinforce existing biases and create new ethical problems. Scholars have drawn attention to how biases are embedded in library work and collections, including collections management, description, digitisation decisions and the algorithms used to sort and make information accessible (Ayre and Craner 2018). Each of these biases informs both the form of the materials that users can access, and the power dynamics at play while they do so. However, AI can hide these biases in ways that closely resemble a technical black box and make it difficult to critique and analyse (Gooding 2022) .

All these bodies of work call for greater transparency in how we produce, make accessible and use data. In line with the shift in digital humanities towards critical infrastructure theorisation and development (Brown et al 2016; Chevalier et al 2023), this will necessarily entail broader attention to how particular technologies like OCR have already fundamentally shaped the digital record and the resultant datasets to which AI can be applied. Scholars have already argued for extensive critical reflection on how AI is applied. Cordell (2020, 1), for instance, notes that 'current cultural attention to ML may make it seem necessary for libraries to implement ML quickly. However, it is more important for libraries to implement ML through their existing commitments to responsibility and care.' As Gooding (2023) has recently argued, those commitments should be derived from the ethical and professional principles that define the mission and work of libraries. The American Library Association (2019) and CILIP (2018) both provide ethical frameworks that outline sectoral values such as transparency, confidentiality, social responsibility and the public good. Reflections upon AI adoption require a careful analysis of how AI tools challenge or enhance each of these values, building upon existing work to explore the impact of AI on the information professions (Cox 2021). The need to consider sector-wide ethical frameworks is matched by that of reflecting upon how AI might support libraries as an essential public good that is fundamental to democratic societies. In this chapter, we focus specifically on how AI might contribute to a wider mission of making collections accessible and reusable.

Digital collections sit precisely at the nexus of access (how material is made discoverable and available) and usage (what patrons are able to do with library collections). HTR is similarly positioned as it simultaneously provides use cases relating to access to library collections and promises to expand the range of uses that are possible. The authors have covered these topics elsewhere (Nockels 2021; Terras et al 2023), so in this chapter we intend to respond to the following provocation by Terras to consider how AI tools become embedded within library practices:

> Although there are considerable savings in time and resources in using HTR to generate transcripts of historical materials, HTR is not a panacea. If it is to be successfully used to increase access to information within and usability of handwritten textual materials, it needs to be embedded into both digitisation workflows within libraries as well as public-facing digital library infrastructures. (Terras 2022, 142)

Investigating HTR at the NLS

We will report upon the experiences of the NLS, for whom Nockels has undertaken a feasibility study for implementing HTR across a variety of library functions. The remainder of this chapter is therefore split into two sections: the first will set out the broader context for HTR in the library sector, while the second will report upon a feasibility study into the adoption of the HTR platform Transkribus at the NLS. Transkribus is an HTR application that aims to produce a complete and reliable HTR workflow which ensures that 'all dates, languages and formats can be read, transcribed and searched by means of automated recognition' (Muehlberger et al 2019, 957).[1]

The case study is based upon a six-month PhD work placement at the NLS undertaken by Nockels in 2022–2023, supported by the Arts and Humanities Research Council (AHRC: 2422919) via the Scottish Graduate School for Arts and Humanities. Nockels spent three months in the Archives and Manuscript Division, interacting with curators and learning more about the relevance of HTR to specific collections. Three further months were spent in the Digital and Service Transformation Department, providing staff training and public events to enhance understanding of Transkribus. During this time, a feasibility study was undertaken to understand how HTR might be applied to NLS collections. Transkribus is a leading HTR tool, but only one of a wide range of possible approaches. We therefore recommend that readers unfamiliar with the wider context and application of HTR read the article by Muehlberger et al (2019), which sets out the development and launch of Transkribus. The current authors' previous work also provides a systematic review of 381 papers on topics relating to HTR (Nockels et al 2022).

HTR in the library sector

Content-holding institutions are increasingly reliant upon digital methods to preserve and make accessible historical collections. This includes the NLS, whose 2020–2025 'Reaching People Strategy' (National Library of Scotland 2020) aimed to provide access to approximately one-third of its collections, or ten million individual items, by 2025. This objective was intended to deliver benefits to an expanded range of user communities, as explained by the NLS One Third Digital Programme Board:

> Through the digitisation of its collections, the library will make a significant and lasting contribution to global knowledge and the memory of the world. The resulting resources will promote opportunities to advance learning, foster and develop new research, innovate, drive economic development, and enjoy our cultural heritage. (National Library of Scotland 2018)

In addition to its growing born-digital holdings, the NLS has digitised parts of its physical collections. However, challenges remain in making available specific collections and content types. The NLS possesses vast amounts of handwritten materials that may interest users, ranging from archives of notable individuals to medieval texts, items with complex print layouts and more. Each provides challenges to the capabilities of OCR-based recognition. Simultaneously, HTR has, in recent years, reached a level of maturity where it can be considered as a viable solution for text recognition within libraries.

To date, mass digitisation of library collections has focused upon printed materials like newspapers, books and maps. This is partly due to the ubiquity of optical character recognition within library digitisation pipelines: OCR is used in situations where manual transcription would be too costly or time-consuming and can be applied to corpora of varying sizes. One transformative function of OCR has been to allow the creation of full text versions of material that can be searched online, which has ‘significantly increased access to large-scale collections, including in media that were difficult to access at scale prior to its development’ (Cordell 2020, 23). However, while OCR can process high-quality scans of typewritten texts, it often returns transcripts of low accuracy for older materials, those in poor condition or those that have been scanned poorly. Past studies have indicated that, for challenging materials, OCR accuracy can fall below the levels required for fuzzy search engines to return sufficiently accurate results (Tanner, Munoz and Ros 2009). This has led to the conclusion that character error is now embedded within institutional large-scale digitised collections:

> The existence of millions of digitized volumes presents these organisations with a clear choice: accept these digital surrogates as new intellectual products, rather than as ‘faithful copies,’ or re-digitize a substantial portion of the world’s research libraries’ holdings of books and serials to create cleaner and more pristine representations of volumes. (Conway 2013, 27)

This recognition of digitised items as new intellectual products is reflected in a range of products which engage with errorful OCR from various sources, including experiments that demonstrate that OCR error incidence can hint at unusual formal features in scanned books (Smith and Cordell 2018, 9–11). Character recognition technologies thus allow for new forms of research to emerge that work not only with clean transcripts, but with errorful data. Similarly, the dominance of OCR for character recognition has informed the materials which have been prioritised for digitisation and are now available online as a result. In the same way that mass digitisation influenced both topics of research and truth claims about authority, OCR has precipitated a fundamental shift in the accessibility of typewritten materials. This comes at the expense, however, of the enormous amounts of handwritten, manuscript and typographically challenging print materials in library collections. The recent emergence of HTR offers the opportunity to transform access to handwritten materials to the same degree as OCR has for typewritten materials.

Questions about access and representation that have emerged in relation to large-scale digitisation remain relevant as we broaden digitisation horizons to include handwritten texts. Who is represented in the digital record, and how? What voices are missing? How do we ensure that the individuality of so much handwritten material is not lost when it is transformed into informational, or computational, forms? These questions are closely aligned to the ethical and professional challenges outlined above, but here we focus upon how libraries might integrate HTR into their existing workflows. We analyse the example of the NLS, who worked with Nockels to undertake a horizon scanning exercise to identify (i) the opportunities and potential of HTR for enhancing the work and collections of the NLS, and (ii) the potential barriers and problems that the NLS might face when integrating HTR into existing workflows.

Case study: investigating the adoption of Transkribus at the NLS

This chapter focuses on Transkribus, first launched in 2015 with funding from the European Commission Seventh Framework Programme resulting from the 'tranScriptorium' project. The implementation and development of Transkribus was central to a successor project called 'READ' (Recognition and Enrichment of Archival Documents, 2016–2019), funded under the European Horizon 2020 scheme. Transkribus is developed and maintained through the not-for-profit READ-COOP, which is registered in Innsbruck, Austria and aims to 'maintain, develop and promote a functioning online research infrastructure where new technologies can feed innovation in archival research' (Muehlberger et al 2019, 957). The tool is targeted at four intended user groups: archivists, humanities scholars, computer scientists and members of the public. Initially free to end users, Transkribus adopted a paid credit-based system in 2020 to ensure sustainability and mitigate the end of EU funding.

As of January 2023, Transkribus is the largest consumer-level HTR application. Over 43 million images have been uploaded to the servers by approximately 100,000 users, with 10 new data models trained daily. Users can work with the suite of Transkribus tools to create 'ground truth'[2] data for the creation of automatic transcription models (Romein et al 2023, 4–8). This data is used to build sequential links between characters, with the resultant model able to recognise new text based on language construction and predictions. Ground truth models can be trained from scratch, or users can apply a pretrained model from an openly licensed list trained either by the Transkribus developers or other users. Transkribus is already being used by libraries and archives worldwide. The State Archives of Catania applied Transkribus to the Paterno' Castello Princip di Biscari Archive (Spina 2022), for instance, while the National Library of Finland has used Transkribus to clean up more inaccurate OCR transcriptions of over two million pages of eighteenth- to twentieth-century historical newspapers in both Finnish and Swedish (Kaukonen 2021). The technological maturity of HTR has caused many libraries to explore its application, and to rethink existing practices as a result.

The NLS is a shareholding member of READ-COOP, which as of June 2023 comprised 135 institutions and private members (READ-COOP 2023). As a member, the NLS can vote on the development of Transkribus, with further opportunities to contribute via monthly shareholder meetings and an annual Transkribus User Conference.[3] Despite being a shareholder, usage of Transkribus at the NLS has been ad hoc and limited in nature. In 2021, Nockels transcribed and made available the 1810–1811 diary of Marjory Fleming (1803–1811), a Scottish child author born in Kirkcaldy, Fife, who became posthumously famous for her diaries. The diaries provide an authoritative account of her life, schoolwork and death, and were given a great deal of public attention in the late-Victorian period (Nockels 2021). Transkribus produced an automated edition of Fleming's diaries, which is available online via the Transkribus read&search website,[4] and the underlying dataset is also available on the NLS Data Foundry website.[5] The Fleming diaries are the first NLS dataset created using HTR technology. The following sections consider what other possibilities exist.

HTR for handwritten and typewritten materials

The most obvious benefit of HTR is to support greater accessibility of handwritten collections online, both for full-text search and computational analysis. As Cordell (2020, 25) has argued, the category of handwritten materials encompasses voices from around the world, and 'from regions or groups of people for whom handwriting remained the dominant technology of textual transmission for practical or cultural reasons into the modern period'. Handwritten materials have typically been impractical for inclusion in mass digitisation workflows due to the limitations of OCR, and so HTR offers the possibility of enhancing access not only to a wider range of media but to new and previously underrepresented voices in the digital archive. This ability to process and make accessible different forms of collection can support the NLS's strategic objectives. In particular, it could enhance the Library's aim to 'make it easier for people to access the collections', and specifically that 'it will be easier to discover the Library's special and hidden collections through our programme of online listing, cataloguing and discovery work' (National Library of Scotland 2020). At first glance, HTR integration seems highly compatible with strategic values around access and democratisation, for both the NLS and the wider library profession.

To ascertain whether HTR can enable full text search of NLS collections, experiments were run to determine the accuracy of Transkribus on several collections. For the aforementioned Marjory Fleming diaries it returned an 89.74% accuracy rate based on a ground truth dataset of 50 hand-transcribed pages from Fleming's diaries. Experiments with a second collection, the journals of Henrietta Liston (1751–1828),[6] demonstrated an 82.75% accuracy rate using existing data models. This accuracy rate is adequate as a starting point for staff, familiar with Liston's hand, to edit transcripts, and to include results in full-text search, showing that when utilising generic training models, palaeographic skills remain essential for libraries to make the most of HTR technologies. It also demonstrates that, in the early stages of applying HTR to a specific collection, a degree of human intervention may be required that is absent from OCR pipelines. There will, however, be significant time savings at other points of the digital production workflow.

While it is perhaps unsurprising that HTR software is effective at transcribing handwriting, it also provides features which make it suited as a potential alternative to OCR applications. Experiments demonstrated that the Transkribus Layout Analysis (LA) tool was robust enough to register the presence and location of text in each document. Information derived from LA enables HTR applications to recognise materials with complex column structures, marginalia and variations in font, making it suited both to handwritten materials and typewritten texts that might prove challenging to traditional OCR solutions. Transkribus provides openly licensed models that support transcription in different languages and allows users to develop bespoke data models for new data sources. The question was therefore posed: is it possible to use Transkribus to transcribe printed materials, and would these transcriptions prove more accurate than in OCR? To assess this, we ran generic models from Transkribus, without further training, across a range of digitised typewritten collections and compared their accuracy against the results provided by existing OCR solutions. Table 8.1 shows the results of this analysis.

For the exam papers and the Scottish newspapers, openly licensed Transkribus datasets outperformed current OCR accuracy. This suggests a high degree of usability for transcribing typewritten materials, and hints at the possibility of providing significantly better accuracy for difficult materials than OCR. Default data models provide less accuracy than training a bespoke model in the manner demonstrated for the Fleming Diaries, but require far less resourcing due to there being no requirement for manual transcription. The only collection where Transkribus

Table 8.1 Accuracy of Transkribus vs existing OCR on selected NLS collections

NLS department	Material	Date (century)	Difficulties in recognition	OCR accuracy	HTR accuracy
Rare Books	Chepman and Myllar Prints[7]	16th	Variable fonts	95.21% (with manual correction)	84.64%
Rare Books	Encyclopaedia Britannica[8]	18th–19th	Layout	94.5%	98.32%
General/ Modern Collections	Exam Papers[9]	19th	Complex layout	84.20%	94.40%
Newspapers	Scottish Courant/ Caledonian Mercury[10]	19th	Complex layout and font variation	60.10%	93.90%

returned lower accuracy than OCR was for the Chepman and Myllar prints because the text was manually corrected between 1996 and 1997 as part of a transcription project. These results show that pretrained models can be applied to printed text collections, with HTR able to outperform OCR in cases where aggravating factors such as complex layout and font variation can negatively affect OCR accuracy.

The potential for HTR to improve full-text accuracy is most clearly demonstrated in the case of newspaper collections. In our sample, three of the four collections exhibited just one difficulty in recognition, whereas newspapers demonstrated both complex layout and font variation. This has contributed to a notably lower OCR accuracy rate. In the example of the *Scottish Courant*, the output of the OCR transcription using ABBYY FineReader returns a highly variable degree of confidence and an overall accuracy rate of just 60.1%. It should be noted that cleanup of OCR outputs is possible, including correction of common errors like misidentification of the 'long S' in historic fonts. However, the results provided by generic Transkribus models are accurate enough to facilitate accurate search without further training in all cases. In the case of the *Scottish Courant*, a full transcription of the same column of text with no bespoke training returned an accuracy rate of 93.9%:

These results show that the accuracy returned by Transkribus is sufficient to make it a viable solution for both handwritten and typewritten materials, even when aggravating factors exist for character recognition.

This has the potential to improve the accuracy of search for all users, and to make accurate full-text datasets available for researchers in fields such as the digital humanities. Transkribus, therefore, has the potential to be applied across heterogeneous collections in print and type, and its default models can provide useable transcriptions in many, but not all, cases. It will remain the case that the most challenging materials, with multiple aggravating factors such as legibility, language and structure, will still require bespoke data models to be trained. Given that these data models require manual transcription of approximately 10,000 words to ensure accuracy, archival skills such as palaeography will remain central to the skillset of curators. Far from removing the human from the process, the adoption of HTR in cultural institutions will highlight areas where human expertise will need to sit alongside automated technologies.

HTR for extracting text from maps and music

Transkribus provides possibilities for data extraction from a variety of media. For instance, we found that it can be helpful for recognising and extracting metadata from maps. The NLS has a large online collection of maps, as discussed in Chapter 5, which have recently been the subject of exploratory studies to analyse the benefits of open-source tools (Fleet and Pridal 2012) and web-mapping applications (Fleet 2005). To understand the potential of HTR, we attempted to extract metadata relating to print codes and map tiles. Since the first revisions of Ordnance Survey maps in the mid-1800s, there have been markings on each map sheet that indicate the date of revision or printing. These are generally found in small print beneath or beside the area of the map plate (Fielden 2009) and provide important contextual and provenance data for researchers. However, these printing codes can be immensely time-consuming to extract manually. We found it possible to extract printing codes from maps in our test sample, using the Transkribus LA model to identify specific areas of the map with text for transcription. However, the functionality does not extend to analysing the relevance of particular blocks of text, and so some correction was needed to delete extraneous text regions in this use case. Transkribus is also useful for undertaking automatic music recognition. Jorge-Calvo Zaragoza (2019) has presented an end-to-end workflow for handwritten music and text recognition that incorporates Transkribus. These principles can also be applied to the NLS collections: experimentation with the Library's eighteenth- and nineteenth-century Glen Collection of printed music[11] demonstrated that HTR could recognise the presence of musical notation and lyrics.

Each experiment with Transkribus in the NLS collections demonstrated that HTR can go beyond the transcription of handwritten scripts and be applied to a range of media and use cases. In the case of libraries with complex and heterogeneous collections, there is potential to automate processes that would be impossible with OCR, and thus to unlock collections that were previously relatively inaccessible due to limitations in staffing, technology and finance. This is not to say that HTR offers a single solution for undertaking text recognition across library collections, nor that it is necessarily simple to implement within existing well-established workflows. Libraries must consider how HTR tools might fit into existing digital production pipelines, inform curatorial practices and influence decisions around staffing, investment and technologies.

Integrating HTR into existing workflows

HTR is likely to require changes to existing digital production workflows at the NLS. The digitisation process starts for individual items when an internal request to digitise an item or collection is placed by a curator, which triggers a consultation process. This usually takes the form of a visit to the library stacks and involves key stakeholders, including curators, rights specialists, conservation and metadata representatives, and mass digitisation staff. If the consultation raises no issues, then additional stakeholders are brought in before the decision on whether to digitise items is completed. While this structure could remain in place for HTR, ad hoc digitisation of individual items would become more labour intensive in cases where an existing data model is not easily available because it will require staff to create a bespoke model and thus hand-transcribe a sample of the work.

HTR holds particular significance for the NLS Mass Digitisation service, which seeks to scan collections at scale, either to meet internal targets or to support the work of third-party stakeholders. In line with Coyle's (2006) definition of mass digitisation, the service has implemented automated processes to ensure efficient throughput of large numbers of items. In line with recommended best practice (Federal Agencies Digital Guidelines Initiative 2023), Mass Digitisation captures scans at 400 dpi, or higher if there are specific reasons for doing so. These scans are of sufficient detail to support HTR processes. Photography of images would not need to change, but the subsequent phase of creating text would require consideration of data transfer, handling and storage. There are other elements where HTR would require changes to aspects of the image processing workflow. For instance, as OCR is not routinely applied to handwritten collections such as medieval manuscripts, images of them captured during digitisation are not routinely deskewed, meaning that the image is not straightened so that text runs horizontally. However, deskewing images has long been considered good practice for text recognition as it allows a documented page to be accurately segmented and recognised sequentially using LA. For Transkribus, segmentation is necessary to allow the user to transcribe pages on a line-by-line basis. Each segmented line in an image is given a corresponding row in the Transkribus text editor, a process which benefits from the text being in straight lines to aid recognition.

It would be immensely time-consuming to manually deskew all images produced in a mass digitisation process, and although a variety of automated batch processing tools exist, they require careful monitoring and control given the vagaries of the process when dealing with heterogenous materials. Doing so for Transkribus would likely deliver useful but marginal gains in accuracy. Furthermore, the Mass Digitisation team seek to retain the material sense of the items that they capture and are wary of manipulating items in ways that negatively impact upon the material authenticity of their scans. For instance, digitised items are uploaded to the Library's Digital Object Database (DOD) including cover and blank pages, allowing readers to better understand the material aspects of the digitised items. On occasion, the decision might be made to crop a page to the boundaries of the textual elements, rather than to the edges of the page. Both practices might require manual intervention during the application of HTR: first, due to the risk of text bleed-through on blank pages affecting the training model, and second due to the risk of missing relevant text such as marginalia which could be captured by HTR but would fall outside the boundaries of the cropped page. In both cases the problems are not insurmountable, but they do add an extra layer of manual intervention into a process which, in the case of mass digitisation, supports automation and fast throughput of materials. There would be additional curatorial labour in defining the capture areas and deciding where the balance between authenticity and computational amenability lies.

In addition to practical changes to image capture and processing, the role of individuals such as the Digitised Collection Coordinator will also change. Currently, the Coordinator is tasked with ingesting scanned images into the DOD for publication in the NLS digital gallery. The role requires the use of various digital platforms, software and scripts to check that each required processing stage has been completed. This entails using an Automated Ingest Tool (AIT) that splits the workflow into various stages that run on virtual machines. The most relevant step here is the PDF creation phase. This phase uses the LuraTech PDF Compressor[12] to automatically produce and compress a PDF, and at the same time generate OCR from converted JPEGs using ABBYY Finereader.[13] Our experiments have demonstrated that, considered solely in terms of accuracy, Transkribus outperforms this combination. It may also allow the Library to process materials in a wider variety of languages, including right-to-left languages (Keinan-Schoonbaert 2020). However, its lack of integration into existing workflows means that each potential improvement comes with commensurate trade-offs in efficiency and manual intervention.

The next stages of the AIT involve creating a unique identifier and file sequence for each item to be preserved, splitting the batches of generated OCR into corresponding pages using a tool called ImageMagick. There would be significant demands on developer time to integrate Transkribus into the existing workflow. Consideration would need to be given to whether Transkribus could work in a similar way to LuraTech, which is run automatically as part of the ingest process, and to work out the implications on resourcing and throughput for mass digitisation. A brief view of the NLS workflows shows the potential complexity of implementing a tool, as workflows and staff skillsets have been developed with legacy tools in mind. Further developments with Transkribus will need to be regularly evaluated to judge when it offers the ability to be integrated into existing workflows. As things stand, READ are open to discussion about members of READ-COOP making Transkribus a default tool within their processes, but this would still require time, resourcing and staffing to implement.

READ are currently improving their application programming interface (API) with such issues in mind. A major development is the introduction of the metagrapho API,[14] which allows text and layout information to be extracted from digitised images within an institution's existing digital infrastructure. This should allow faster processing and provide access to models trained by each institution and all publicly available models. Given time, this should allow Transkribus to be integrated into workflows as a potential addition to, or replacement for, existing tools within the AIT. However, doing so would involve a technical integration process which would not necessarily be trivial. Finally, because HTR would require more human intervention than existing automated workflows, there would be an increase in the hidden labour required in the digitisation process. Questions remain about how this labour should be credited. Romein et al (2023, 17–21) propose that listing those involved in the production of datasets should become common practice to recognise individual contributions to data production and ensure transparency to future users on how datasets were created. Institutions will need to account for this enhanced reporting, to ensure data transparency and appropriate credit in HTR workflows.

Recommendations

While this chapter outlines various use cases for the adoption of HTR, the most clear and obvious benefit is the opportunity to transcribe handwritten collections accurately and efficiently. The NLS has not generally transcribed its handwritten collections due to the inaccuracy of OCR tools for handwriting and the costs of manual transcription. The NLS also holds collections in languages which are extremely difficult for OCR software to deal with. Gaelic is one area of concern, given that it is designated as an official language of Scotland under the Gaelic Language (Scotland) Act 2005.[15] There is, therefore, a strong rationale for introducing HTR into the suite of tools available to the Library's curatorial and technical staff. However, the embedded nature of particular tools in existing workflows means that introducing HTR is not necessarily simple. For this reason, we have proposed four scenarios for the adoption of Transkribus at the NLS. Table 8.2 uses the Transkribus Credit Calculator[16] to estimate the annual cost of each option. It should be noted that these are estimated with the 10% discount for READ-COOP members, and institutional membership currently costs €1000, with a yearly membership fee of €250.[17]

The Library Leadership Team at the NLS were informed that Option 3 was the recommended option, allowing Transkribus to be used on an ad hoc basis. This builds upon existing curatorial skills and the increased awareness and understanding of Transkribus that has resulted in the NLS from the placement. Option 3 would allow staff to become more familiar with Transkribus and constrain costs while a portfolio of small-scale projects test the real-world impact upon digital production workflows. At this stage, the existing workflow remains fit for the purpose of materials which OCR can accurately transcribe. We therefore recommend that Transkribus should be prioritised in cases where OCR use would compromise character accuracy levels. This would allow the NLS to bring new parts of the collection into its digital production workflow and automate key aspects of the digitisation process that are not tailored towards handwritten materials. Finally, we propose that Transkribus should be provided as an option to curators when writing digitisation proposals, as is the case with OCR. In this way, curators will be empowered to make the best decision for particular items. Doing so

Table 8.2 Transkribus Credit Calculator for annual cost

Approach	Page processing no.	Annual cost (£)
1. Transkribus as an entire ABBYY FineReader replacement, only for printed materials	1 million	2,800 (printed, as no OCR is used on handwriting)
2. Transkribus used to train core models on collections which can be reused, e.g. Gaelic, English, Latin, French	10,000	10,000 (handwritten) 1,667 (printed)
3. Transkribus used for smaller, individual projects/digitisation proposals by curators	5,000	5,000 (handwritten) 834 (printed)
4. Transkribus used to aid cataloguing, checking place/person names	Individual pages transcribed	0 (free credits can be used)

would provide time for robust testing of HTR functionality and impact, before considering a transition to Option 2, where Transkribus might be used to create core data models to support transcription of priority collections for the Library.

Conclusion

This chapter has considered the wider context for the integration of AI tools and processes into existing library workflows, using a case study of the NLS to explore the potential and challenges of using HTR to unlock new materials for discovery and reuse online at scale. There are significant potential benefits to the adoption of Transkribus: increased character recognition accuracy for print and handwritten collections; the opportunity to extract metadata from materials like maps, and to explore innovative approaches to documenting and presenting library collections; and the extension of mass digitisation processes to handwritten materials. These activities can all contribute to NLS strategic aims around access and increasing the demographic scope of the user community. The implications of AI tools, therefore, go far beyond the enhancement of existing processes, or the automation of library work, and promise fundamental changes in what libraries make accessible and how users interact with those materials. However, there are significant challenges involved in such tools becoming 'business as usual' for libraries. Transkribus is illustrative of this point, as READ-COOP is now exploring how better to integrate the product into library technical pipelines. There is a clear need for this among users, and the developers are responding by improving the API and developing options to support technical integration. While this work is ongoing, however, it remains the case that integrating HTR into a digitisation workflow is a non-trivial exercise that can affect the efficiency of processes that remain highly effective for certain materials.

This picture of massive potential on the one hand and complex technical challenges on the other leads us to identify a number of areas for developers and consumers of AI in libraries to consider. First, developers should continue to engage in dialogue with their users to identify community needs, establish how AI tools might fit into library workflows and ensure that technical development is focused on simplifying this integration process. Second, libraries and their staff should explore existing processes to understand where enhancements might occur and what the barriers to integration might be. There may be an associated need to upskill staff; discussions between Nockels and library staff demonstrated a need to increase awareness of AI and ML across the NLS, which will require training and awareness-raising. Libraries should also develop their understanding of how users are using openly available datasets, and AI tools, in their own research. Attention must also be paid to how the resultant datasets are used in other advances in AI, including the possibility that they might be leveraged as training data for large language models.

Finally, and in line with the broader context set out in the literature review, libraries must ensure that AI tool integration is not simply a technical and process-driven task, but instead is deeply informed by the strategic objectives of their institution, data ethics and library professional ethics. This will require libraries to explore what changes occur via the introduction of AI tools, and whether those changes are compatible with the profession's ethical and professional values. In cases where those values are compromised, libraries and librarians must play an active advocacy role to ensure that AI development progresses in a manner that supports libraries as a social good. The integration of AI is a complex process, requiring both a broad understanding of the wider context within which AI tools are developed and a granular analysis of the impact of specific tools upon the work and workflows of specific institutions. We therefore call for other institutions to follow the example of this chapter and report upon similar horizon-scanning efforts so that the sector can be made aware of opportunities and challenges as they become evident.

Notes

1. Further information about Transkribus can be found at https://readcoop.eu/transkribus/.
2. 'Ground truth' in machine learning is commonly used to refer to objective, provable data that can be used to prove or disprove hypotheses, or to create data models. In the case of Transkribus, ground truth information is created by the assisted manual transcription of approximately 15,000 words (50–75 pages) relating to an individual script, which can then be used to create a model to automatically transcribe large volumes of that script.
3. Details of the conference, including its 2022 programme, can be found online: https://readcoop.eu/tuc22/.
4. https://transkribus.eu/r/marjory-fleming/.
5. https://data.nls.uk/data/digitised-collections/marjory-fleming/.
6. See https://data.nls.uk/data/digitised-collections/marjory-fleming/.
7. www.nls.uk/treasures/explore/chepman-and-myllar/.
8. https://digital.nls.uk/encyclopaedia-britannica/archive/188936619.
9. http://digital.nls.uk/exams.
10. www.nls.uk/collections/rare-books/collections/newspapers/.
11. https://digital.nls.uk/special-collections-of-printed-music/archive/87729635.
12. https://luratech-pdf-compressor-desktop.software.informer.com/6.1/.
13. https://pdf.abbyy.com.
14. 'metagrapho API', READ-COOP. Accessed 3 October 2022. https://readcoop.eu/api/.
15. Work has already begun on this issue, with the Gaelic Algorithmic Research Group at the University of Edinburgh already having made Gaelic language models available for Transkribus. Further information about the group's activities is available at https://blogs.ed.ac.uk/garg/.
16. Full pricing information, including the Credits Calculator, is available at https://readcoop.eu/transkribus/credits/. Pricing is correct as of 27 June 2023.
17. Annual costs are explained at https://readcoop.eu/join/.

References

AEOLIAN Network. 2020. 'AEOLIAN network – Artificial intelligence for cultural organisations'. Accessed 19 June 2023. www.aeolian-network.net/.

AI4LAM. 2023. 'AI4LAM: Artificial intelligence for libraries, archives and museums'. Accessed 19 June 2023. https://sites.google.com/view/ai4lam.

American Library Association. 2019. 'Core values of librarianship, advocacy, legislation & issues'. Accessed 20 June 2023. www.ala.org/advocacy/intfreedom/corevalues.

Ames, S. 2021. 'Transparency, provenance and collections as data: The National Library of Scotland's Data Foundry', *LIBER Quarterly*, 31:1–13.

Ames, S. and Lewis, S. 2020. 'Disrupting the library: Digital scholarship and big data at the National Library of Scotland', *Big Data & Society*, 7(2):1–7.

Ayre, L. and Craner, J. 2018. 'Algorithms: Avoiding the implementation of institutional biases', *Public Library Quarterly*, 37(3):341–7.

Börjeson, L. et al. 2023. 'Transfiguring the library as digital research infrastructure: Making KBLab at the National Library of Sweden'. Accessed 20 June 2023. https://urn.kb.se/resolve?urn=urn:nbn:se:uu:diva-499237.

Brown, S., Clement, T., Mandell, L., Verhoeven, D. and Wernimont, J. 2016. 'Creating feminist infrastructures in the digital humanities'. In *Digital Humanities 2016*, Krakow. Accessed 20 June 2023. http://dh2016.adho.org/abstracts/233.

Calvo-Zaragoza, J. 2019. 'Handwritten music and text recognition in Austrian medieval plainchant sources'. In *Transkribus Workshop*, Vienna. Accessed 20 June 2023. https://docs.google.com/presentation/d/1ymueNjv_7L2Whz4NesGYslDFQ8zGw5-lgJl8QrjFCcc.

Candela, G. et al. 2023. 'A checklist to publish collections as data in GLAM institutions'. Accessed 20 June 2023. https://doi.org/10.48550/arXiv.2304.02603.

Chevalier, C., Fubara-Manuel, I., Upadhyay, R. and Webb, S. 2023. 'The (im)possibility of autonomous feminist infrastructure'. Intersections: Feminism, technology and digital humanities. Accessed 20 June 2023. https://ifte.network/blogs/elementor-3315/.

CILIP. 2018. 'CILIP's ethical framework'. Accessed 20 June 2023. www.cilip.org.uk/page/Ethics.

Conway, P. 2013. 'Preserving imperfection: Assessing the incidence of digital imaging error in HathiTrust', *Digital Technology and Culture*, 42(1):17–30.

Cordell, R. 2020. 'Machine learning + libraries'. Accessed 20 June 2023. https://labs.loc.gov/work/experiments/newspaper-navigator/.

Cordell, R. 2022. 'Closing the loop: Bridging machine learning (ML) research and library systems', *Library Trends*, 71(1):132–43.

Cox, A. 2021. 'The impact of AI, machine learning, automation and robotics on the information professions'. CILIP research report. Accessed 20 June 2023. www.cilip.org.uk/page/researchreport.

Coyle, K. 2006. 'Mass digitization of books', *Journal of Academic Librarianship*, 32(6):641–5.

Coyle, K. 2017. 'Creating the catalog, before and after FRBR'. In *Encuentro di Catalogacion y Metadatos*, Universidad Nacional Autonoma de Mexico, 9 December. Accessed 17 October 2017. http://kcoyle.net/mexico.html.

Federal Agencies Digital Guidelines Initiative 2023. 'FADGI technical guidelines for digitizing cultural heritage materials. Accessed 26 June 2023. www.digitizationguidelines.gov/guidelines/FADGI%20Technical%20Guidelines%20for%20Digitizing%20Cultural%20Heritage%20Materials_3rd%20Edition_05092023.pdf.

Fielden, E. 2009. 'OS print codes and edition markings'. Accessed 22 May 2023. www.fieldenmaps.info/articles/editions/.

Fleet, C. 2005. 'Web-mapping applications for accessing library collections: Case studies using ESRI's ArcIMS at the National Library of Scotland', *LIBER Quarterly*, 15(1):1–8.

Fleet, C. and Pridal, P. 2012. 'Open source technologies for delivering historical maps online – Case studies at the National Library of Scotland', *LIBER Quarterly*, 22(3):240–57.

Gasparini, A. and Kautonen, H. 2022. 'Understanding artificial intelligence in research libraries – Extensive literature review', *LIBER Quarterly*, 32(1):1–36.

Gooding, P. 2022. 'Towards critically addressable data for digital library user studies'. In *Archives, Access and Artificial Intelligence: Working with born-digital and digitized archival collections*, edited by L. Jaillant, 109–30. Bielefeld: Bielefeld University Press.

Gooding, P. 2023. 'Collaboration, transparency, and technology: AI as a community challenge for libraries',. In *AI and Machine Learning Symposium*, National Library of Scotland. Accessed 26 June 2023. www.nls.uk/using-the-library/academic-research/research-events/.

Kaukonen, M. 2021. 'Improved text recognition for Finnish historical newspapers with Transkribus', READ-COOP. Accessed 19 May 2023. https://readcoop.eu/success-stories/improved-text-recognition-for-finnish-historical-newspapers-with-transkribus/.

Keinan-Schoonbaert, A. 2020. 'Using Transkribus for Arabic handwritten text recognition'. Accessed 19 May 2023. https://blogs.bl.uk/digital-scholarship/2020/01/using-transkribus-for-arabic-handwritten-text-recognition.html.

Mahey, M. et al. 2019. 'Open a Glam lab'. Qatar Digital Cultural Heritage Innovation Labs. Accessed 27 June 2023. http://185.37.108.150/handle/10576/12115.

Miller, J. 2020. 'The new library user: Machine learning'. Accessed 9 June 2023. https://er.educause.edu/articles/2020/2/the-new-library-user-machine-learning.

Muehlberger, G. et al. 2019. 'Transforming scholarship in the archives through handwritten text recognition: Transkribus as a case study', *Journal of Documentation*, 75(5):954–76.

National Library of Scotland. 2018. 'The Library's approach to selection for digitisation'. Accessed 3 May 2023. www.nls.uk/media-u4/1557983/2018-digitisation-selection-approach.pdf.

National Library of Scotland. 2020. 'Reaching people: Library strategy 2020–2025. Accessed 3 May 2023. www.nls.uk/media/43mla4h3/2020-2025-library-strategy.pdf.

Nockels, J. 2021. 'Retelling nineteenth-century childhood through artificial intelligence', *Epoch Magazine*, 1 June. www.epoch-magazine.com/post/retelling-nineteenth-century-childhood-through-artificial-intelligence.

Nockels, J., Gooding, P., Ames, S. and Terras, M. 2022. 'Understanding the application of handwritten text recognition technology in heritage contexts: A systematic review of Transkribus in published research', *Archival Science*, 22(3):367–92.

Ranganathan, S.R. 1931. *The Five Laws of Library Science*. Bombay: Asia Publishing House.

READ COOP. 2023. 'Members of READ-COOP SCE, READ-COOP'. Accessed 26 June 2023. https://readcoop.eu/members/.
Romein, C.A. et al 2023. 'Exploring data provenance in handwritten text recognition infrastructure: Sharing and reusing ground truth data, referencing models, and acknowledging contributions. Starting the conversation on how we could get it done', *Journal of Data Mining and Digital Humanities*. https://doi.org/10.5281/zenodo.7765903.
Smith, D.A. and Cordell, R. 2018. 'A research agenda for historical and multilingual optical character recognition'. Accessed 27 June 2023. https://repository.library.northeastern.edu/downloads/neu:m043p093w?datastream_id=content.
Spina, S. 2022. 'The Biscari Archive. A case study of the application of Transkribus tool'. https://doi.org/10.48550/arXiv.2210.14498.
Tanner, S., Munoz, T. and Ros, P.H. 2009. 'Measuring mass text digitisation quality and usefulness: Lessons learned from assessing the OCR accuracy of the British Library's 19th century online newspaper archive', *D-Lib Magazine*, 15(7–8).
Terras, M. 2022. 'The role of the library when computers can read: Critically adopting handwritten text recognition (HTR) technologies to support research'. In *The Rise of AI: Implications and applications of artificial intelligence in academic libraries*, edited by S. Hervieux and A. Wheatley, 137–48. Chicago, IL: American Library Association.
Terras, M., Nockels, J., Ames, S., Gooding, P., Stauder, A. and Mühlberger, G. 2023. 'On automating editions: The affordances of handwritten text recognition platforms for scholarly editing', *Scholarly Editing*, 41.
Whittaker, M. 2021. 'The steep cost of capture', *Interactions*, 28(6):50–55.

9

Conversing with the past: re-examining the legacy of slavery in domestic traffic newspaper advertisements with OpenAI's advanced LLM

Rajesh Kumar Gnanasekaran, Christopher E. Haley and Richard Marciano

Managing archival processing workloads and enhancing access to cultural records have been a major focus of archival science in the last few years. This has been exacerbated by a rush to digitise archival content without often having the processing infrastructure in place. As Ciaran Trace observes, 'There is [also] a considerable interval between the time archival material is accessioned, processed, and made accessible for research' (Trace 2022), further contributing to a processing backlog.

Emerging computational techniques have the potential to support archival appraisal, arrangement, description, review, classification, redaction and other key archival processing functions (Marciano 2021). In addition, the vast majority of records that will be acquired by archives in the future are being created in digital form. Computational technologies for managing, describing, accessing, compiling, mining and reusing digital content are advancing exponentially. Dealing with the records deluge and scale have further pushed the field into accelerating and enhancing the application of automation, in particular through the use of AI and machine learning. Our own work has explored automated sensitivity review at NARA (the National Archives), where we devised and implemented a public access policy for World War II Japanese-American incarceration records using automated AI processing and redaction to balance privacy and access to protect personally identifiable information (Marciano 2018).

In 2016, the Computational Archival Science (CAS)[1] initiative was launched, with the recognition of CAS as a new field of study with a working definition of:

> CAS is a transdisciplinary field that integrates computational and archival theories, methods, and resources, both to support the creation and preservation of reliable and authentic records/archives and to address large-scale records/archives processing, analysis, storage, and access, with the aim of improving efficiency, productivity, and precision, in support of recordkeeping, appraisal, arrangement and description, preservation and access decisions, and engaging and undertaking research with archival material. (Hedges 2022)

To support this initiative, the authors of this chapter launched a 2020 Advanced Information Collaboratory (AIC) focusing on: (i) exploring the opportunities and challenges of 'disruptive technologies' for archives and records management (including AI and ML); (ii) leveraging the latest technologies to unlock the hidden information in massive stores of records; (iii) pursuing multidisciplinary collaborations to share relevant knowledge across domains; (iv) training current and future generations of information professionals to think computationally and rapidly adapt new technologies to meet their increasingly large and complex workloads; and (v) promoting ethical information access and use.[2] The potential for AI integration into archival systems with a critically aware perspective is well illustrated in a 2021 overview of debates and perspectives in archives and AI (Colavizza 2021).

The focus of this chapter is resolutely in this space, where we experiment with generative AI large language models (LLMs) at the service of the legacy of slavery.

Background

In this section, we discuss the Maryland State Archives (MSA) 'Legacy of Slavery' (LoS) project, and the Domestic Traffic Ads collection (one of seventeen, and the focus of this chapter). We conclude with a history of the partnership between MSA and the AIC, highlighting a series of data science and AI projccts.

MSA LoS project

The MSA began organising research on individuals fighting against enslavement in the fall of 2001. The original concept of the project was to discover unknown 'heroes' of slave flight and resistance. Through review of court records, laws, newspapers and maps, MSA staff set out to create case studies of individuals who deserved their due in the history of Maryland's struggle with human enslavement. The work of identifying, accessioning, transcribing and attaching images of physical records into the database has been funded via several grants since the project's inception. The project began with volunteers working from original court records. Officially dubbed 'Study of the Legacy of Slavery' in 2005, over 100 professional and volunteer, regular and intern staff have been involved. The results of the Archives' primary-source-based research have established a context for Maryland's freedom seekers and combatants against racial inequality. Thus far, through the scope of 14 of the state's 22 antebellum counties, we have been able to glimpse Maryland anti-slavery activities by amassing an informative database of over 400,000 record entries and images, including over 12,000 runaway advertisements, 33,800 freedom records and 223,000 federal census returns, all fully searchable on http://slavery.msa.maryland.gov/. Several prior works have been published; see Gnanasekaran and Marciano (2021), Inbasekaran, Gnanasekaran and Marciano (2021), Perine et al (2020) and Perine (2020).

Domestic traffic ads

For the purposes of this project, domestic traffic is defined as the interstate and intrastate trade of enslaved men, women and children. Similar to runaway ads and committal notices, domestic traffic ads were a means of communicating to the general public the subscriber's desire to buy or sell a slave or slaves. Ads could be placed by private slave dealers and agents, gentry in need of domestic help, yeomen in need of extra field hands, or a public sale of an estate by the orphan's court. Among the records LoS staff found important to include in their database were domestic traffic ads which contain notices of general or private sales of Africans and African Americans. These documents as catalogued, calculated and geolocated by Maryland students may identify sales patterns during different periods of a year or era. For example, do more sales occur during December than certain other months because enslaved people are sometimes bought and sold as gifts? Although this is a horrid concept to our modern sensibility, remember that enslaved people were considered commodities, as valuable in many instances then as a prized horse or new car today. Patterns suggest that runaway attempts increased during holiday seasons, so did public auctions and private sales do likewise? Findings in this study indicate sales spikes in 1831 and 1832 which might be in reaction to tensions and fear brought about because of Nat Turner's revolt in neighbouring Virginia. Did the south-westward migration which followed the 1820 Missouri Compromise provoke more purchases of enslaved persons to plough new lands? Answers to such questions, along with illustrations of which skills, physical traits (age, gender, build, complexion) and departure sites were most often advertised, may reveal preferences to the slave trade that vary from a general belief that any young African male was always in highest demand. Study of Domestic Traffic Ads (DTA) in computational groupings will help scholars and historians know not only what, but when and from where specific categories of native-born and newly brought black persons were bought and sold.

DTA is one of 17 collections: Accommodations, Assessments, Census (1830 and 1840, 1850 and 1860, 1870 and 1880), Certificates of Freedom, Chattels, Deserters, Domestic Traffic Ads, Inventories, Manumissions, Pardon Dockets, MD Penitentiary Records, Runaway Ads, Slave Jails, Slave Schedules and Slave Statistics. A comprehensive list of historical newspapers from which domestic traffic ads were extracted can be consulted at http://slavery.msa.maryland.gov/html/links/ads.html. Some example ads, and the information extracted, are shown in Table 9.1.

A main research question emerges:

> (RQ1) What are the potential benefits and challenges associated with utilizing large language models, such as OpenAI's GPT to develop a tailored chatbot capable of exploring data from high-cultural-context datasets and unveiling previously undiscovered relationships and patterns within this data?

Generative AI for libraries and archives

In the context of this study, we introduce ChatLoS (Chatbot for the Legacy of Slavery), a custom chatbot designed to serve as an intelligent querying interface for aggregated data and an interactive tool capable of generating contextually aware responses. This chatbot, engineered on the foundation of OpenAI's GPT LLM, represents a significant leap in transforming the way we interact with and understand our data.

Generative AI

Generative AI represents an innovative frontier in the domain of ML, providing a transformative tool for various sectors, including libraries and archives (Goodfellow et al 2014). Generative AI algorithms can create new data instances resembling the original data, harnessing patterns within the training dataset (Kingma and Welling 2013). They capture the probabilistic distribution of the data, generating new samples from this learned distribution. This trait of generative AI offers remarkable implications for archival work, as it can create artefacts representative of the original resources. Autoregressive models, like the transformer model used in OpenAI's GPT, have been monumental in generating text, offering potential applications in managing and curating textual archives (Brown et al 2020).

Table 9.1 Four examples of domestic traffic ads and transcribed data. With kind permission of the Maryland State Archives

Sheriff's Sale. BY virtue of two fieri facias to me directed, against Henry H. Edmondson, one at the suit of Bell & James, one other at the suit of John Dillahay, use of Bell & James, will be sold at William C. Ridgeway's tavern, in Cambridge, on MONDAY, the 26th instant, between the hours of 10 and 3o'clock, the following property, to wit: one NEGRO MAN named SAMUEL, said to be twenty-five or twenty-six years of age, taken and seized, and will be sold to satisfy the debts, interest and costs of the above fieri facias. **SOLOMON KIRWAN, Sheriff** april 3 3t Transcribed by the authors from the original: https://msa.maryland.gov/megafile/msa/speccol/sc5400/sc5496/domestic_traffic_ads/pdf/18240403cc1.pdf	Indicates: • **Person sold**: man named Samuel • **Age**: 25 or 26 years old • **Reason for sale**: to satisfy a writ of fieri facias • **Owner's name**: Henry H. Edmonson • **Sheriff's name**: Solomon Kirwan • **Sale location**: William C. Ridgeway's tavern in Cambridge, Dorchester County (in the Eastern Shore)—indicating a public sale • **Frequency**: Ad to run 3 times The ad date and newspaper were captured as external metadata: • Mar. 27, 1824 • Cambridge Chronicle

(continued)

Table 9.1 (Cont.)

Valuable Negroes AT PRIVATE SALE. The subscriber will sell at private sale a Family of as Valuable Negroes as any on the Eastern Shore, they will not be sold out of the county--viz. 1 woman & her 2 children, 1 man 38 years old, 1 do 20 years, 1 do. 23 years, 1 boy 14 years, 1 do. 6 years, 2 do. 7 years, 1 woman & her 2 children one 22 and the other 5 years, 1 woman and her child 3 years, 2 girls 4 years, 1 do. 5 years, 1 do . 16 years, they are all young and handsome, and will be sold to good masters very low. **JOHN DONOVAN.** Dec. 31 3w Transcribed by the authors from the original: https://msa.maryland.gov/megafile/msa/speccol/sc5400/sc5496/domestic_traffic_ads/pdf/18251231cc&esa5b.pdf	Indicates: • **Persons sold**: family of 19 people from the Eastern Shore • **Family details**: 1 woman & her 2 children, 1 man 38 years old, 1 man 20 years old, 1 man 23 years old, 1 boy 14 years old, 1 boy 6 years old, 2 boys 7 years old, 1 woman & her 2 children one 2 and one 5, 1 woman & her child 3 years, 2 girls 4 years, 1 girl 5 years, 1 girl 16 years • **Terms of sale**: not to be sold out of the county • **Subscriber's name:** John Donovan • **Frequency**: Ad to run for 3 weeks The ad date and newspaper were captured as external metadata: • Dec. 31, 1825 • Eastern Shore Advertiser
Great Bargains. The subscriber offers at private sale the following property, viz: two Negro Boys, one Negro Girl, about 14 years of age, two Yoke of Oxen, three Cows, thirty head of Sheep, one Still and Cap, one Whip Saw, one Gun, two Mares with fold, and one first rate Saddle Horse--All of which he will dispose of very low for cash. **SHADROCK KEENE** feb 12 3t Transcribed by the authors from the original: https://msa.maryland.gov/megafile/msa/speccol/sc5400/sc5496/domestic_traffic_ads/pdf/18250212cc2.pdf	Indicates: • **Persons sold**: 3 people: 2 boys, 1 girl 14 years • **Other items**: cows, sheep, saw, gun, saddle … • **Subscriber name**: Shadrock Keene • **Frequency**: Ad to run 3 times The ad date and newspaper were captured as external metadata: • Feb. 12, 1825 • Cambridge Chronicle

FOR SALE, a MULATTO MAN, 23 years of age, slave for life, and sold for no fault, only the present owner has no use for him. He is a first rate farm hand and a good miller. For further information apply at Lewis F. Scotti's, Intelligence, Agency and Collectors Office, No. 1 West Fayette st. Basement Barnum's City Hotel. ma 7 Transcribed by the authors from the original: https://msa.maryland.gov/megafile/msa/speccol/sc5400/sc5496/domestic_traffic_ads/pdf/18310507acda1.pdf	Indicates: • **Sale reason**: Owner has no further use for him • **Terms of service**: To serve for life • **Skills**: farmhand, miller • **Agent name**: Lewis F. Scottis, indicating a private sale • **Agent address**: Baltimore City, No. 1 West Fayette St. in the basement of a hotel The ad date and newspaper were captured as external metadata: • May 7, 1831 • American and Commercial Daily Advertiser

Large language models

Expanding on the concept of generative AI, LLMs such as GPT-3 and GPT-4, developed by OpenAI, represent a paradigm shift in text generation and analysis (Radford et al 2019; Brown et al 2020). LLMs are pretrained on extensive corpora and can generate contextually coherent text, answer questions and even summarise complex documents. Importantly for the archival sector, LLMs offer potent tools to navigate and analyse digital datasets. Given their ability to understand and generate human-like text, they can decipher metadata and make sense of the contextual information, and thus can play a crucial role in cataloguing, cross-referencing and retrieving information in an efficient manner (Radford et al 2019). This has the potential to make digital archives more accessible and user-friendly, promoting wider engagement with historical data. Moreover, LLMs' ability to generate context-appropriate text can be employed to create annotations, descriptions or synopses of archival documents, enhancing metadata richness and reliability.

Benefits of using LLMs for DTA data analysis

In the pursuit of robust historical data analysis, leveraging advanced tools such as OpenAI's GPT (Brown et al 2020) offers unprecedented possibilities. The project at hand focuses on the DTA dataset from the LoS collection, housed by the MSA. This dataset comprises digitally transcribed data of advertisements for enslaved individuals placed in

Maryland newspapers over a 40-year period, from 3 March 1824, to 30 April 1864. It includes crucial metadata fields such as advertisement date, county, location, age, gender, number of people being sold, terms of sale and specified skills. In this chapter, we focus on a subset consisting of the first 10 years (roughly a third of the total collection).

Firstly, the digitisation and transcription process involved scanning the original paper advertisements and extracting the text using an OCR tool, ABBYY FineReader (also discussed in the previous chapter). The OCR-extracted text, along with the metadata fields, served as input to the fine-tuning process of GPT. Careful data cleaning and preprocessing steps were followed at this stage to ensure high-quality, accurate input (Goodfellow, Bengio and Courville 2016). Secondly, the GPT model was fine-tuned to understand the historical context and language nuances, and to interpret the various metadata fields. This was achieved by creating a training corpus that merged the OCR text and metadata. The model's objective function was optimised to predict or fill gaps in the metadata fields, ensuring it effectively learns the structure and context of the dataset.

The potential benefits of this analysis are multifaceted. From an academic standpoint, it could unearth previously unnoticed patterns or trends within the historical data, providing fresh perspectives and contributing to our understanding of this significant period in American history (Mnih et al 2013). From a computational perspective, this project could further explore and demonstrate the capacity of language models to handle complex, historical datasets and contribute to the expanding field of digital humanities (Rockwell and Sinclair 2016). It also presents an opportunity to test the effectiveness of ABBYY FineReader and its OCR capabilities in preserving and digitising culturally important and historically sensitive materials. Utilising an LLM like GPT for data analysis of the DTA dataset presents a host of substantial benefits. The integration of OCR text and diverse metadata fields expands the scope of potential queries and analyses, opening new avenues for historical understanding. The power of GPT lies in its ability to absorb and analyse large amounts of information, even with complex semantics and varied contexts, which is highly pertinent to our dataset (Brown et al 2020). This characteristic enables it to learn from the unique linguistic structure and terminology in the advertisements, and subsequently provide insightful and historically accurate outputs.

Moreover, by leveraging the context-understanding capabilities of GPT, the metadata fields can be paired with OCR text to extract meaningful information beyond the surface level. For example, information such as terms of sale and specified skills can provide a nuanced perspective on the socioeconomic conditions of the time, offering a more comprehensive view of historical realities. In essence, using GPT for this complex task represents a significant stride towards the intersection of AI and the humanities, potentially transforming the way we approach historically sensitive and culturally rich data analysis.

This research, however, was approached with a high degree of cultural sensitivity and awareness of the ethical implications involved. Considering the sensitive nature of the LoS collection, it is paramount to treat the data and the resulting analysis with the utmost respect, ensuring the enslaved individuals' experiences and identities are neither trivialised nor exploited.

Data preparation for GPT analyses

We show the processing steps carried out by the MSA LoS project (top row), followed by the processing steps further carried out by the AIC (bottom row), leading to the use of the OpenAI GPT LLM in Figure 9.1.

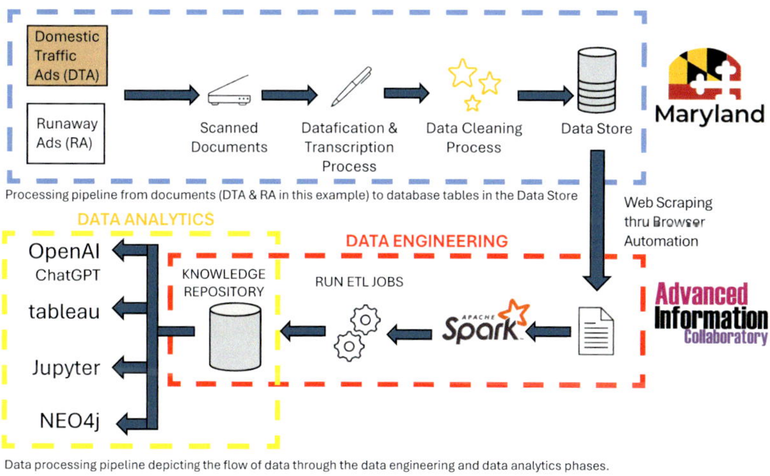

Figure 9.1 MSA LoS processing pipeline (top) and AIC data pipeline (bottom), depicting a records-to-data-to-analytics flow. © Rajesh Kumar Gnanasekaran, Christopher E. Haley, Richard Marciano.

Web scraping

Data needs to be extracted from the MSA pipeline in the following manner:

- The MSA LoS project turns historical documents such as DTAs and Runaway Ads into tables stored in the Data Store (top row) and served through a web interface.
- The resulting web-based database was created by the MSA through a processing pipeline that is based on manual transcription by staff and volunteers, with data cleaning steps along the way.
- The AIC further crawls this website and scrapes the data using a 'browser automation' technique (Jansen 2023). We document this process in an interactive Jupyter Notebook and provide a video of the Notebook running,[3] showing how database records are captured one at a time until all 2,836 are collected and saved into a .csv file.
- This resulting file has 2,836 rows, each consisting of 24 fields, with transcribed metadata related to the ad itself, the person traded, the sale, the newspaper source and the ad subscriber.

From tables to data-analytics-ready content

Turning this .csv data file into a computational-ready resource requires an additional data processing pipeline (bottom row of Figure 9.1). This second pipeline validates the 2,836 records for consistency through Apache Spark, an open-source framework that allows for ingesting, processing and analysing large volumes of data, running ETL (extract, transform and load) jobs, and storing the output in a knowledge repository (NoSQL MongoDB), making it ready for data analytics. OpenAI GPT-3 interactions or other data science interfaces such as Tableau Dashboard, Jupyter Notebooks or NoSQL Neo4j graph database are exercised.

Data analysis and validation

Analysis of the .csv file showed that 643 of the 2,836 records did not link to an actual ad image (23% missing). After validation and working with MSA staff we brought this number down to 245 (8% missing only). The resulting dataset of 2,591 records was our restarting point. There should be one record per person sold or purchased in each ad, meaning that if nine people are referenced in one advertisement, nine records result in the table. Not all the 2,591 records had been expanded in this fashion. We consistently expanded the table, which resulted in 2,849 records, a 10% increase. The analysis of the .csv file showed that there were three main categories of records: *Sale* (76%), *Purchase* (21%) and *Other* (3%). Other categories included *Sale & Purchase*, *Unquantified Sale* and *Notice & Warning* records.

For the purpose of this study, we created a test dataset based on a subset of the Sale records covering the first 10 years of the collection (from 1834 to 1844). Of the 2,160 Sale records, we focused on a little over a third (35%), or 764 records. This represents 27% of the entire collection, a large enough sample to validate our approach.

New fields created

This test dataset was not only validated, cleaned and made consistent but augmented in several crucial ways. Five new fields were created to produce a clearer signal when using GPT-3: terms of service, trade reason, features, terms of sale and owner. The record in Example 9.1 would have the following additional attribute/value pairs:

Term of service: to serve next year
Trade reason: owner has no further use
Features: has a husband in the neighbourhood, cook in my family since the age of 15
Terms of sale: not to be sold out of the state
Owner: While the owner field is empty here, the ad in the first row of Table 9.1, for example, has a value of '**Owner**: Henry H. Edmonson'.

Example 9.1 12 November 1831 For Sale ad

Transcribed by the authors from the original: https://msa.maryland.gov/megafile/msa/speccol/sc5400/sc5496/domestic_traffic_ads/pdf/18310507acda1.pdf

FOR SALE.
OR HIRE—a Good Plain Cook A
Negro Woman about 34 or 35 years of
age with two small children; she has
been a cook in my family since the age

of 15, is a peaceable, quiet servant and easily governed. This woman is offered for sale merely for the want of employment, has a husband in the neighbourhood and will not be sold to a person at a distance. If not disposed of by all before the close of the present hour, she will he hired out the next. Centerville, Nov. 12. TH. C. EARLE.

A sixth field was specifically created to support OpenAI GPT interactions: the complete OCR text of the ad itself. This was done through the ABBYY FineReader OCR software (advertisement image to textual representation). This field had not been created through the MSA (top row in Figure 9.1) pipeline. The full text of each ad is provided to GPT for analysis. This is demonstrated in the next section.

Data preparation for input to OpenAI's GPT model

As LLMs like GPT-3 are pretrained on billions of textual data items, enabling them to respond to questions based on limited contextual data is done through a process called fine-tuning, explained later. For this project's purposes, the fine-tuning is a process where the DTA data prepared in the above steps, including the metadata fields, the new fields and the OCR full text column, are combined into natural language sentences of individual records in a .txt file; one such example is shown in Example 9.2.

Example 9.2 A sample input record to OpenAI GPT-3 after the preprocessing step

Following are the details on a domestic traffic slave advertisement published of type 'sale' in the county of Dorchester on the date 3 March 1824.

- The number of people being sold through this advertisement is: 1.
- The gender of the people sold, if specified, is/are: male.

- The first name of the individual being sold is: Samuel.
- The age(s) or the type of enslaved people on sale is/are: 25.
- The reason for the sale is: to satisfy court judgement and of sale disposition: public sale.
- The ad was published in the newspaper: Cambridge Chronicle and on page: 3.
- The text of the advertisement was extracted using an OCR tool from the newspaper cutting as follows:

Sheriff's Sale. BY virtue of two fieri facias to me directed, against Henry H. Edmondson, one at the suit of Bell & James. one other at the suit of John Dillahay, use of Bell & James, will be sold at William C. Ridgeway's tavern, in Cambridge, on MONDAY, the 26th instant, between the hours of 10 and 3 o'clock, the following property, to wit: one NEGRO MAN named SAMUEL, said to be twenty-five or twenty-six years of age, taken and seized, and will be sold to satisfy die debts, interest and costs of the above fieri facias. SOLOMON KIRWAN, Sheriff april 3 3t.

All the 764 advertisements prepared and sliced in the above steps were converted to consistent sentences as above and were well suited to be passed as input to the GPT model's fine-tuning process.

Approach

The approach for this data analysis leverages the power of AI to explore and analyse the DTA LoS collection to address RQ1. The aim is to unearth meaningful insights from this trove of historical information with OpenAI's GPT model, creating a unique 'ChatLoS' chatbot, which acts as the virtual archaeologist, also known as the DTA Help Desk, for archival enthusiasts. The analysis employs a two-pronged approach, each defined by a Python script that orchestrates the intricate setup between the AI model and the dataset. The first prong of the approach involves the AI model's engagement with an already conditioned dataset in the form of a .csv file. This file is the output of the data preparation above. The second prong involves the steps to prepare and condition the dataset's unique uncurated OCR full-text column data containing the extracted ad text from scanned images to be passed as input to the GPT AI model. The reason for this approach is to explore and expose the versatility of the OpenAI GPT's model to behave, on one hand, as a querying tool for providing insights into the aggregate or summary data using the metadata information from the .csv file, and on the other hand, to act as a bot that could identify chunks of relevant information from a huge set of text data and respond to contextual questions. Details on both these approaches are explained below.

LLM's context window

The context window in LLMs like GPT-3 plays a crucial role in maintaining coherence during text generation, capturing necessary context and providing responses based on prior interactions within that window. However, this feature has its limitations. GPT-3, for instance, was evaluated on several NLP datasets, which showed that while it could adapt rapidly to tasks not directly contained in the training set, it still required some form of in-context learning, thus highlighting its limitations to provide a comprehensive response beyond its context window (Brown et al 2020). In summary, the context window in LLMs plays a significant role, yet it also underlines the models' limitations to answer certain types of queries and tasks requiring a broader context or aggregation capabilities. Future research and innovative solutions are needed to bridge these gaps and optimise the use of LLMs.

The context window with respect to OpenAI's GPT-3 refers to the maximum number of tokens (words or word pieces) the model can process in a single interaction. This includes both the input and output tokens. A token can be as short as one character or as long as one word. For instance, the word 'GPT-3' counts as one token, but so does the punctuation mark '.'. As per the information available (Bellow 2023), GPT-3 has a maximum context of 4,096 tokens, which is roughly equivalent to 3,000 words. This constraint essentially defines the length of the conversation that the model can remember or be aware of. In other words, if a conversation exceeds this limit, the model would lose the context from the beginning of the conversation. The information in the context window can include a prompt, the response to a prompt, and even additional instructions or examples depending on the task at hand. This becomes a challenge when dealing with long texts or dialogues since fitting these within the context window is necessary for the model to generate meaningful outputs (Raj and Salines 2023; Gheorghe 2023). These token and context window limitations are crucial for developers and users to keep in mind as they can affect the performance and costs of using the model. The more tokens processed in an API call, the more it costs and the longer it takes (Gheorghe 2023).

Training GPT as a natural language querying tool using a metadata file

LLMs are generally understood to be limited in their ability to answer aggregation questions from a dataset (Ledan 2023). This is due to their limited context window, as mentioned above. However, in this step, the aim is to use a unique function, 'create_csv_agent', which is part of the LangChain[4] Python module, a framework designed to develop applications powered by language models, with a focus on being data aware and agentic (Gelal 2023). It is used to generate a CSV agent, that can interact with .csv files, primarily designed for question-answering applications (LangChain 2023). By chaining this function with OpenAI's GPT model, an AI chatbot could be created that takes natural language data aggregation questions, identifies the correct data columns to query the structured data (such as a .csv file) and respond with accurate results. Using a Python script[5] (the source code is available on GitHub[6]), the prepared DTA metadata is used to create an AI chatbot with the detailed steps discussed below.

This Python script is the blueprint that outlines how this journey unfolds, providing a roadmap of actions that allow the AI to interact with and learn from the dataset. Each line of code is an instruction that gets closer to unveiling the latent knowledge within the DTA. Of these lines of code, the most important one is the step where a global variable named 'agent' is declared and assigned a CSV agent created using 'create_csv_agent'. This agent operates like a bridge connecting the OpenAI GPT model with the DTA dataset. It reads from a .csv file, which is an organised version of the DTA dataset, and feeds the data to the OpenAI model. The OpenAI model is initialised with a temperature of 0.5, which determines the level of randomness in the AI's responses – a lower temperature means the AI will provide more focused and deterministic responses. At the end of this script process, an AI chatbot is ready for querying the DTA metadata. An example of the conversation is shown in Figure 9.2. It should be noted that the responses contain quantitative information.

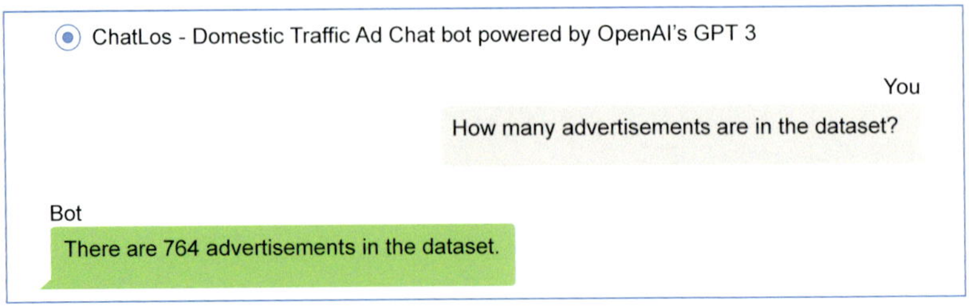

Figure 9.2 OpenAI GPT NLP chatbot showing responses with aggregated data results. © Rajesh Kumar Gnanasekaran, Christopher E. Haley, Richard Marciano.

Fine-tuning the OpenAI GPT model with DTA OCR full text

In this multifaceted training process, the second step was to harness the power of OpenAI's GPT model to probe the depths of the rich text from the DTA dataset's OCR full-text column. The following step-by-step process explains the training performed. Using another Python script,[7] this DTA dataset was manipulated and structured to unlock its latent historical and cultural knowledge. This data-handling process can be thought of as a tailored preparation method, essential for crafting the most informative and accurate context to feed into the GPT model, ensuring the AI is ready to perform a nuanced and detailed analysis. The provided script primarily leverages the power of Python and OpenAI's GPT model to process and analyse the DTA dataset.

In simple terms, the script is like a recipe for a computer program that helps us understand the dataset collection of DTA about the slave trade in Maryland. These ads could be thought of as a gigantic book that is too big to read all at once. Firstly, this program reads the whole book and then divides it into smaller, more readable parts, like chapters in a novel. Secondly, after it breaks down the big book into chapters, it gives each chapter a unique label for easy reference, like how chapters in a book might have names. Now, these chapters still contain a lot of words, and it is not easy for a computer to understand them as is. Thirdly, to address this, the program translates these chapters into a special computer-friendly language, called vector embeddings. The program then saves these translated chapters in a database. Fourthly, it creates a smart, conversationally capable AI helper. This AI helper is powered by GPT and it uses the database of translated chapters to find relevant responses during a conversation. Finally, the program sets up a pathway or a route to send questions to the AI helper and get answers in return.

When a question is asked about these old ads, it will dive into the chapters, find the relevant information and give a response. In essence, the program dissects and understands a vast book of historical ads from the DTA dataset and helps us have informative chats about it with an AI bot. The following subsections give a step-by-step detailed account of the script features.

Reading and tokenising the dataset

The 'start_openai_db' function begins by opening and reading the dataset file. The text content of the file is then tokenised using the tiktoken[8] library from OpenAI, which provides an approximate count of the tokens present in the text. Tokens, special computer-friendly atomic units of processing in language models like GPT-3, are used here to identify, count and manage the pieces of text being worked with.

Text chunking

The text data is then divided into manageable 'chunks' using the 'RecursiveCharacterTextSplitter' function from the LangChain[9] library. The process of chunking is a pragmatic necessity when working with large datasets, as it allows data to be broken into smaller, more manageable pieces that are easier for the AI model to process and analyse. The chunks are created with a specified size (350 tokens in this instance) and overlap to ensure continuity and coherence in the processing. Each chunk is also tagged with metadata – a unique identifier (its index in this case) for reference and tracking purposes.

Creating vector embeddings

The LangChain library's functionalities are further leveraged to create vector embeddings from the chunks. Embeddings are representations of the chunks in a high-dimensional vector space, enabling the capturing and encoding of semantic information from the text in a manner that is useful for machine learning models. These embeddings are stored in a Chroma[10] vector database, a powerful tool for managing and querying vector data.

Constructing the conversational retrieval chain

The 'ConversationalRetrievalChain' is constructed from the language model, vector database and a memory buffer. This chain, powered by the GPT model, forms the core of the conversational AI system. It uses the vector database for retrieving relevant responses and the memory buffer for storing conversation history. The chain enables the AI to maintain context throughout the interaction, resulting in more coherent and context-aware responses.

Interaction with the AI chatbot

Finally, a POST endpoint named '/send_openai' is set up, which accepts text input, processes it through the AI model and returns the AI's response. This endpoint, when accessed with the appropriate text input, triggers the AI model to generate a response, marking the culmination of the data preparation and model setup process.

To summarise, the preparation of the DTA dataset, its transformation into tokens, the subsequent chunking process, the construction of the retrieval chain and the eventual conversation with the AI model (the chatbot) – all of these constitute a meticulously orchestrated setup of data and AI, unlocking unprecedented insights into the DTA dataset. A sample conversation using the chatbot from this step is shown in Figure 9.3. The responses from this version of the chatbot to the question on how many advertisements it has stored in its context implies that it was able to only store the textual data for four of the 700+ advertisements that were chunked. Any responses to the questions would be limited to the text data found in these four advertisements. However, a unique advantage with the 'chunking' process is that, depending on the question, the model would select other advertisements to be placed in its memory to curate an appropriate response.

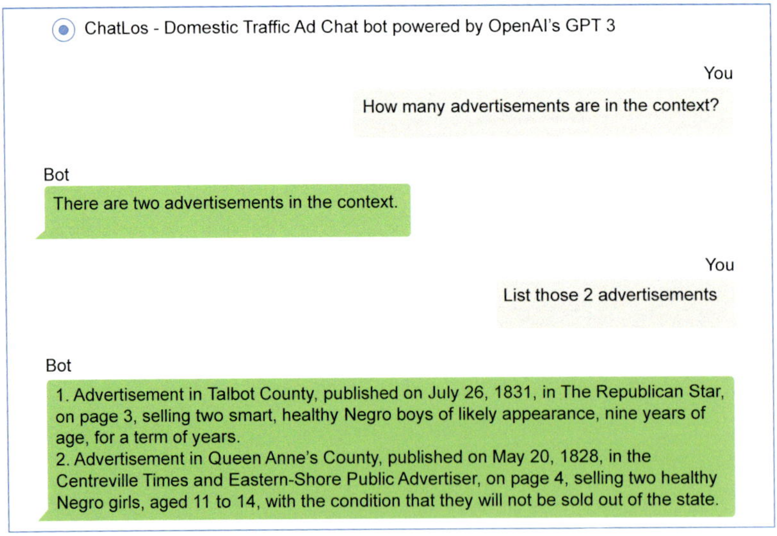

Figure 9.3 A sample OpenAI GPT NLP chatbot fine-tuned response. © Rajesh Kumar Gnanasekaran, Christopher E. Haley, Richard Marciano.

Results

Prompting in generative AI

Prompting involves feeding a user-generated input to a language model, which then infers a completion (Hashimoto 2023). For instance, if the input is '4 + 3 =', the LLM would likely respond with '7'. The art of using prompts to extract useful data from a model is called 'prompting'. This technique does not require a large offline training set or offline access to a model and feels intuitive for both engineers and non-engineers. The process starts by identifying a problem that could potentially be solved using prompting. These are problems for which well-created prompts might elicit the desired behaviour from the language model. The process of creating these prompts requires some basic knowledge and careful consideration of factors like being assertive rather than defensive, and being concise rather than repetitive. Working within a historical and cultural context such as the DTA, the art of creating prompts becomes a vital step, even though it could be considered as a trivial task in the grand scheme of things. The significance of prompting is explained in the following sections.

ChatLoS as a natural language data querying tool

Contrary to the general understanding that LLMs cannot be used for querying data for aggregating results, the responses from this chatbot proved different. In a simple chat conversation example as shown in Figure 9.4, we can understand how ChatLoS was able to aggregate the number of advertisements placed in a specific county named 'Harford' in Maryland. Figure 9.5 shows the terminal printed output of the chatbot model that runs ChatLoS. The steps performed by the agent stand as a testimony to the importance of prompting. For an input question by the user, the CSV agent reframes the question to a 'thought prompt' and feeds that in an appropriate format to the underlying GPT model.

Thought: The reframed prompt from the question asked by the user to ChatLoS.

Action: The action taken by the agent to resolve the prompt is specified as 'python_repl_ast'. This refers to executing a specific bit of Python code in a Python REPL (read-eval-print loop) environment or any interactive Python interpreter.

Action input: Based on the 'thought', the agent finds the best possible columns to perform aggregation queries in Python code from the imported .csv file, in this case, the DTA file. Python code is then executed; for this example:

df[df["County"] == "Harford"].shape[0]

This code filters the dataframe df (Python's imported CSV dataset) based on the condition df["County"] ;== ;"Harford". It selects rows where the value in the "County" column is equal to "Harford". The shape[0] part returns the number of rows in the resulting filtered dataframe.

Observation: The result of executing the code is provided as an observation, which states that the output is two. This suggests that, after applying the filter, there are two rows in the dataframe where the county is Harford.

The significance of this approach is that ChatLoS converts natural language words into syntactical queries that are used to perform filtering functions on the underlying data. A major benefit of this is that users do not have to know the column names in the underlying dataset they are querying; instead, they ask intuitive questions as 'prompts' based on their understanding of the functional knowledge or the contextual knowledge about the dataset, and the chatbot responds accordingly.

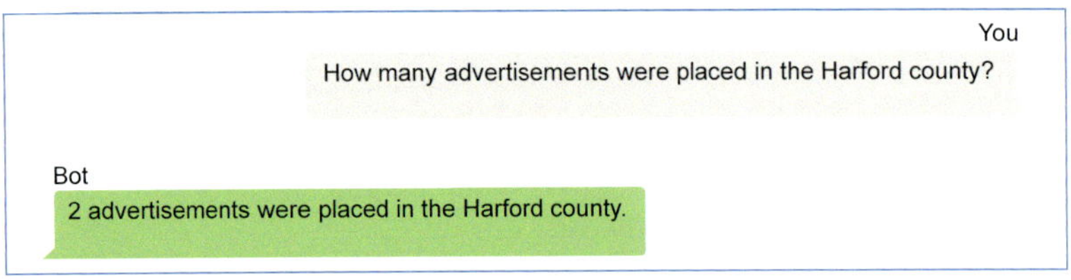

Figure 9.4 ChatLoS response to an aggregate query by county.
© Rajesh Kumar Gnanasekaran, Christopher E. Haley, Richard Marciano.

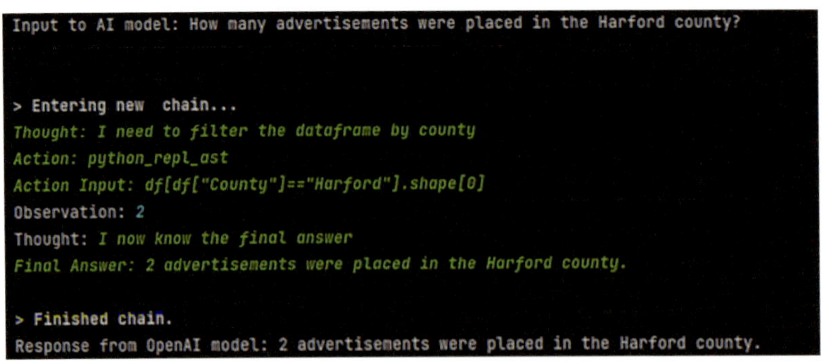

Figure 9.5 ChatLoS mechanism to process aggregate functions.
© Rajesh Kumar Gnanasekaran, Christopher E. Haley, Richard Marciano.

Another example is shown in Figure 9.6. This is another unique scenario where ChatLoS performs queries involving multiple columns purely based on the natural language words from the user's queries, as shown in Figures 9.6, 9.7 and 9.8. In the first query from Figure 9.6, the user is requesting the number of advertisements placed in Harford county and for selling only male individuals. In Figure 9.7, the agent performs a query by involving two columns from the CSV: "County" and "_Gender_Specified". The AI tool is on its best behaviour at this juncture. It was able to make connections between the word 'male' and the appropriate column from the dataset, i.e., "_Gender_Specified". Similarly, in the second query from Figure 9.6, it went a step further to include a new column, "_Number_of_people", to count the number of male individuals sold in a specific county, as shown in Figure 9.8. These results were validated against the input .csv file, as can be seen in Figure 9.9.

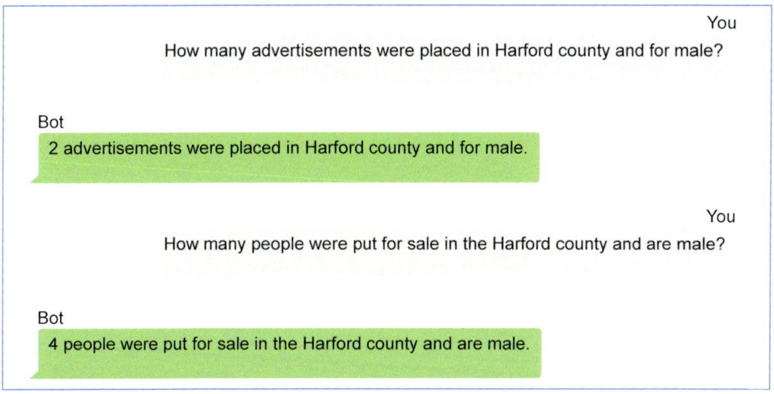

Figure 9.6 ChatLoS contextual querying example with multiple columns. © Rajesh Kumar Gnanasekaran, Christopher E. Haley, Richard Marciano.

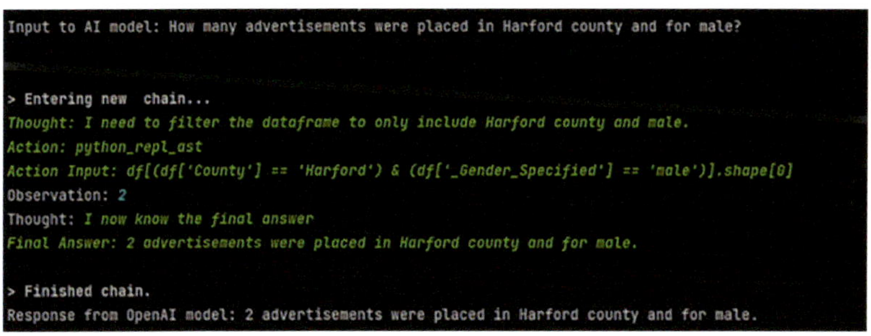

Figure 9.7 ChatLoS prompting for multiple columns using county and gender. © Rajesh Kumar Gnanasekaran, Christopher E. Haley, Richard Marciano.

```
Input to AI model: How many people were put for sale in the Harford county and are male?


> Entering new  chain...
Thought: I need to filter the dataframe by county and gender
Action: python_repl_ast
Action Input: df[(df['County'] == 'Harford') & (df['_Gender_Specified'] == 'male')]['_Number_of_People'].sum()
Observation: 4
Thought: I now know the final answer
Final Answer: 4 people were put for sale in the Harford county and are male.

> Finished chain.
Response from OpenAI model: 4 people were put for sale in the Harford county and are male.
```

Figure 9.8 ChatLoS prompting for multiple columns using county, gender and number of people sold. © Rajesh Kumar Gnanasekaran, Christopher E. Haley, Richard Marciano.

F	G	H	I	J
County	_Gender_Specifie	_Number_of_Peop	_Press_Da	_Sale_Disposition
Harford	male	2	18320403	public sale
Harford	male	2	18320403	public sale

Figure 9.9 DTA CSV data filtered to show rows for validating ChatLoS results. © Rajesh Kumar Gnanasekaran, Christopher E. Haley, Richard Marciano.

Having seen what this version of ChatLoS could do, attempts were made to ask it questions, as discussed above, to understand if there were any specific patterns or insights that could be inferred from the DTA dataset. Figure 9.10 shows responses to two questions that ask ChatLoS to count and find if there are any patterns of advertisements published during holidays such as Christmas Day. ChatLoS was able to accurately translate Christmas Day to 25 December, and queried the dataset for published ads falling on this date; it arrived at a result that matches with the actual data in the CSV dataset as shown in Figure 9.11. ChatLoS also followed up with a response that the total of 5 advertisements out of 764 is insignificant in finding any patterns that enslaved people were sold on holidays.

Similarly, Figures 9.12 and 9.13 show the results for a question asked in the opening of this chapter, to find if public auctions and private sales did likewise. ChatLoS was able to confirm that, based on the input dataset, public auctions and private sales were of the same numbers. Again, the AI tool was able to identify the right column to query on (Sale_Disposition) without any of this information provided in the user's query.

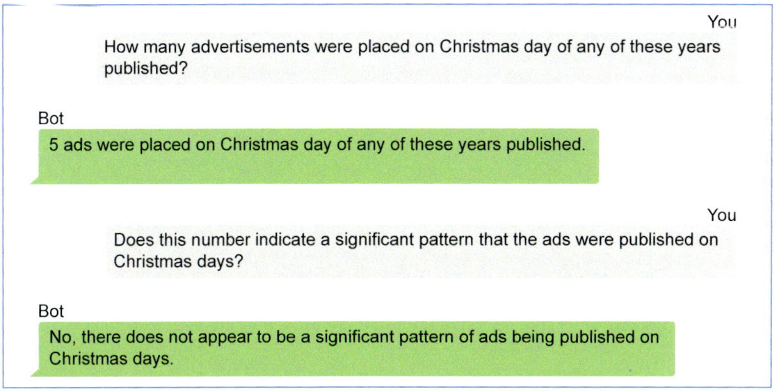

Figure 9.10 ChatLoS finding patterns of ads on Christmas Day. © Rajesh Kumar Gnanasekaran, Christopher E. Haley, Richard Marciano.

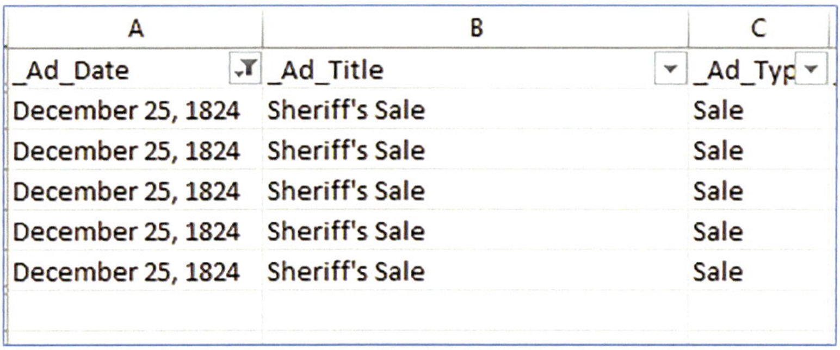

A	B	C
_Ad_Date	_Ad_Title	_Ad_Typ
December 25, 1824	Sheriff's Sale	Sale
December 25, 1824	Sheriff's Sale	Sale
December 25, 1824	Sheriff's Sale	Sale
December 25, 1824	Sheriff's Sale	Sale
December 25, 1824	Sheriff's Sale	Sale

Figure 9.11 DTA CSV data filtered to show rows for ad dates on Christmas Day. © Rajesh Kumar Gnanasekaran, Christopher E. Haley, Richard Marciano.

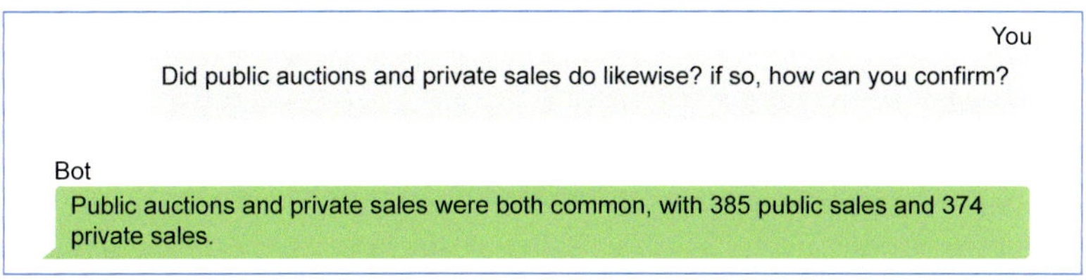

Figure 9.12 ChatLoS finding commonalities between public auctions and private sale ads. © Rajesh Kumar Gnanasekaran, Christopher E. Haley, Richard Marciano.

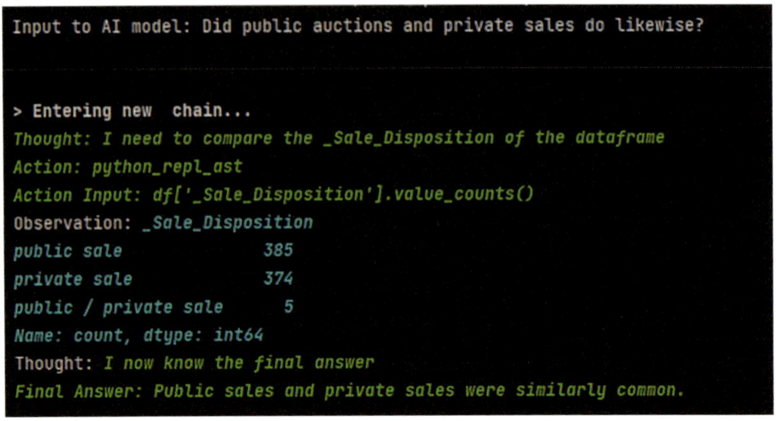

Figure 9.13 ChatLoS prompting for Sale_Disposition. © Rajesh Kumar Gnanasekaran, Christopher E. Haley, Richard Marciano.

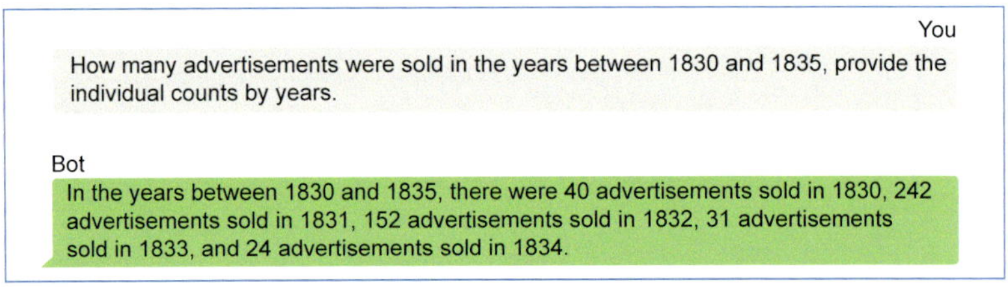

Figure 9.14 ChatLoS finding the count of ads for 1830–1835 to show the impact of the Nat Turner revolution. © Rajesh Kumar Gnanasekaran, Christopher E. Haley, Richard Marciano.

To address another historical perspective, whether there were more sales during 1831 and 1832 due to the Nat Turner revolution, ChatLoS responded as shown in Figure 9.14. The results clearly indicate that there were considerably more ads placed in 1831 and 1832 than the surrounding years between 1830 and 1835. The prompt code is shown in Figure 9.15.

From the examples, it is very clear that ChatLoS was able to produce aggregate data results by querying the underlying CSV dataset in a manner any sophisticated data exploration and querying tools could do, only better than them, as these tools need the user to be aware of the underlying column names and their characteristics. However, ChatLoS abstracts this information from the users and keeps it agnostic of the underlying data structure. This shows that ChatLoS created by using OpenAI's GPT LLM could be a powerful tool.

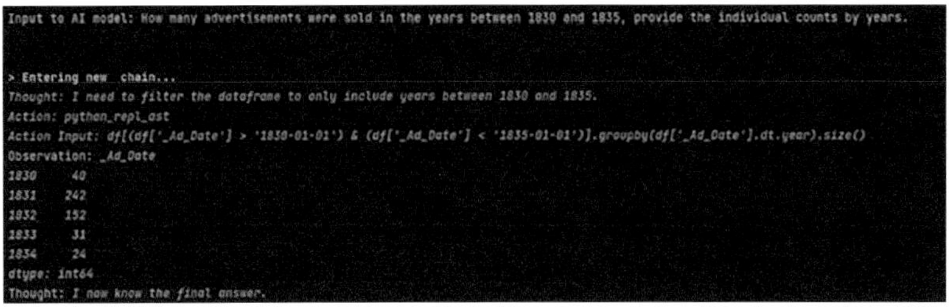

Figure 9.15 ChatLoS prompting for ads by year between 1830 and 1835. © Rajesh Kumar Gnanasekaran, Christopher E. Haley, Richard Marciano.

ChatLoS as a contextually aware fine-tuned AI chatbot

Another major expectation from a tool like ChatLoS that is fine-tuned on a specific dataset such as the DTA is for it to be contextually aware of the data it has fine-tuned to, and respond to questions as 'prompts' accordingly. The whole point of fine-tuning a pretrained LLM model like GPT-3 is to use its ability to understand the common aspects of a language like English to build on a specific domain of knowledge. In this case, as mentioned above, the fine-tuning was performed on the OCR full-text column of the DTA ad and ChatLoS was expected to limit the responses to the context learned from just this text. Let us see how ChatLoS performed.

In Figure 9.16, the fine-tuned ChatLoS is seen to respond that it could not find any references of the people asked about who are commonly known and are prominent figures in American history. This indicates that ChatLoS is tuned to the domain knowledge that it learned on the 764 rows of DTA. In Figure 9.17, when a question is asked to identify whether there were any signs of human trafficking involved based on the context it has learned from the DTA OCR full text, it was able to respond that it could not find any signs of such activities from the OCR data. However, it added a disclaimer that not being evident in the ads' full text does not mean it did not happen. In Figure 9.18, which is another crucial example of ChatLoS contextual awareness, when it was prompted to write a poem or song based on the advertisements, it replied with a response demonstrative of its understanding of the sensitive nature of the dataset, and is contextually aware of the data it has learned on.

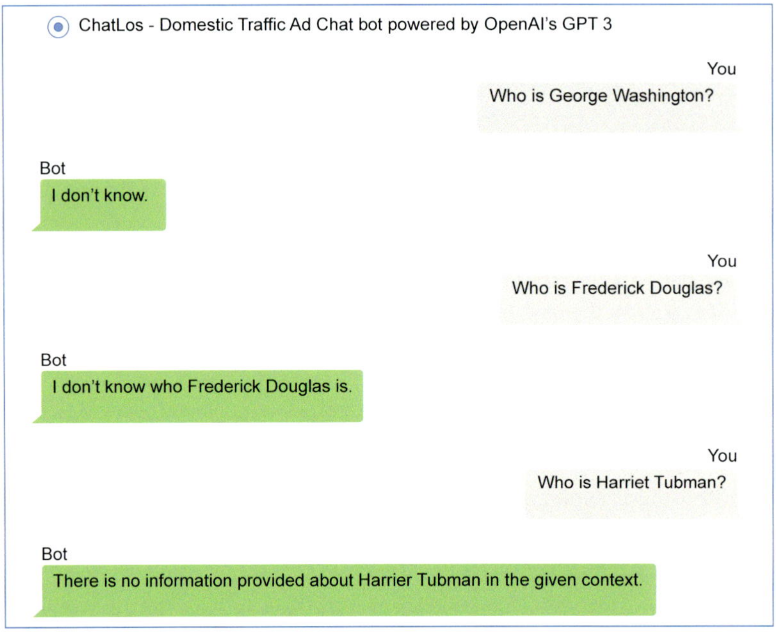

Figure 9.16 Fine-tuned ChatLoS responding to common questions. © Rajesh Kumar Gnanasekaran, Christopher E. Haley, Richard Marciano.

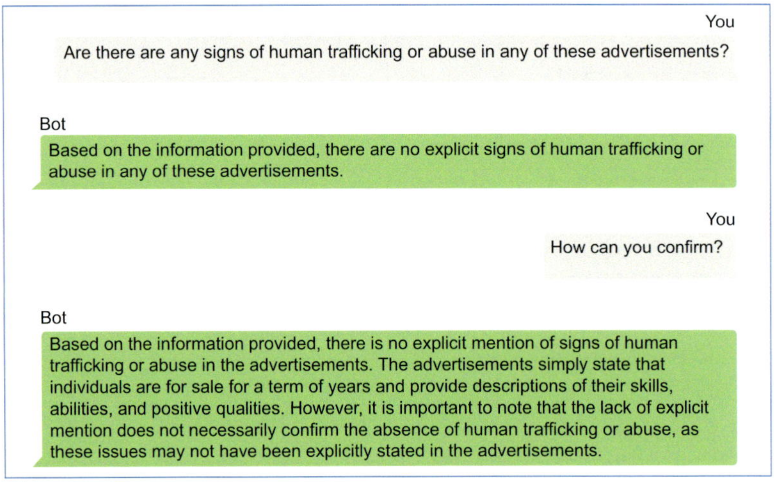

Figure 9.17 Fine-tuned ChatLoS responding to prevalence of human trafficking or abuse. © Rajesh Kumar Gnanasekaran, Christopher E. Haley, Richard Marciano.

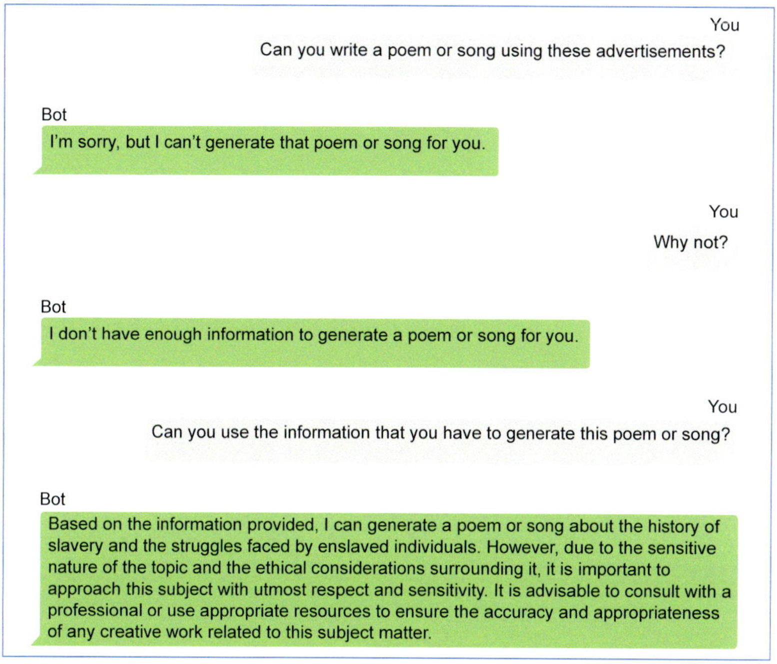

Figure 9.18 Fine-tuned ChatLoS responding in a contextually aware manner. © Rajesh Kumar Gnanasekaran, Christopher E. Haley, Richard Marciano.

Limitations and future work

Despite the significant promises of generative AI and LLMs, it is critical to address ethical considerations, especially the risk of generating synthetic data that may mislead or misinform users (Brundage et al 2020). Therefore, while generative AI holds transformative potential for archival work, careful application is paramount to ensure its benefits are realised ethically and responsibly. LLMs, as we have seen, are a powerful tool that could be leveraged to analyse historical data; however, caution should be exercised as LLMs may inadvertently introduce biases into their outputs, reflecting the biases in their training data (Bender et al 2021). Therefore, while the potential of LLMs in managing and making sense of digital archives is immense, their deployment needs to be monitored for ethical application and potential bias in their outputs.

With the contextually aware ChatLoS version, as noted earlier, and the context window limitation, the fine-tuned GPT-3 could only store about 3,000 words in its memory during a conversation. This limitation could be seen in the response shown in Figure 9.19. However, recent

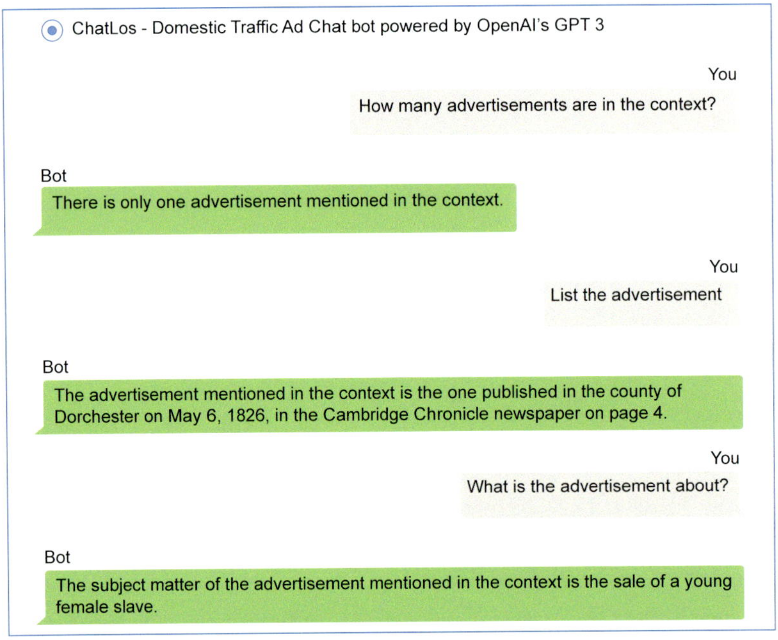

Figure 9.19 Fine-tuned ChatLoS limited by context window to read only a few ads at a time. © Rajesh Kumar Gnanasekaran, Christopher E. Haley, Richard Marciano.

developments in this space have made it possible for next-generation GPT-4 models to accommodate a context window of 32,000 tokens, around 25,000 words. With GPT-4, even more robust insights could be found since it would have more domain knowledge in its context.

Conclusion

In conclusion, the two-pronged approach to create two chatbots using OpenAI's GPT-3 LLM with the MSA's DTA dataset has been a successful endeavour. The chatbot as a querying tool approach has demonstrated a promising pathway for creating a CSV-based chatbot with memory capabilities. The design allows for complex query handling and interactions with diverse data sources. The OCR full-text fine-tuned chatbot showed how it employs a chunking process that breaks down large amounts of text data into manageable pieces for more efficient querying and processing by the language model to learn appropriate context. This enables the chatbot with a short-term memory buffer to store user inputs and system outputs for a particular chat conversation. This method optimises performance and resource allocation by not overwhelming the language model with an excessive amount of data at once and thereby failing with errors. The chunking process is critical for maintaining the coherence and consistency of a conversation, particularly when the conversation involves large volumes of data. It allows the language model to work in a manageable context, improving the accuracy and precision of its outputs. While both the chatbot versions in their current state are focused on single-file interactions, potential modifications could enable it to work effectively with multiple chat conversations, paving the way for versatile, multifaceted chatbot applications.

Acknowledgements

We wish to acknowledge the support of two current Laura Bush 21st Century Librarian (LB21) grants: 'Piloting an Online Collaborative Network for Integrating CT into Library and Archival Education and Practice' (RE-246334-OLS-20), and 'Launching the TALENT Network to Promote the Training of Archival & Library Educators with iNnovative Technologies' (RE252287-OLS-22). These grants are advancing data science education and infrastructure across the library, archives and museum ecosystems.

This work benefited immeasurably from the contributions of Dr Michael J. Kurtz, who was an inspiring mentor, collaborator and dear friend of many in this research community. Dr Kurtz was grounded in the core principles of archives and their social value, as well as being a visionary who saw the potential of computational technology in this cultural work. Dr Kurtz was instrumental in establishing the initial collaboration with the MSA and presided over the public launch on 9 October 2017.

Notes

1. https://ai-collaboratory.net/cas/.
2. See https://ai-collaboratory/net.
3. www.youtube.com/watch?v=-QWvWrclfg.
4. https://python.langchain.com/docs/get_started/introduction.html.
5. https://github.com/rgnanase/los-gpt/blob/main/agent.py.
6. https://github.com/rgnanase/los-gpt.
7. https://github.com/rgnanase/los-gpt/blob/main/api.py.
8. https://pypistats.org/packages/tiktoken.
9. https://python.langchain.com/docs/get_started/introduction.html.
10. https://python.langchain.com/docs/modules/data_connection/vectorstores/integrations/chroma.

References

Bellow, P. 2023. 'GPT-3.5-turbo-0613: Function calling, 16k context window, and lower prices', OpenAI Developer Forum. Accessed 15 July 2023. https://community.openai.com/t/gpt-3-5-turbo-0613-function-calling-16k-context-window-and-lower-prices/263263.

Bender, E.M., Gebru, T., McMillan-Major, A. and Shmitchell, S. 2021. 'On the dangers of stochastic parrots: Can language models be too big? In *Proceedings of the 2021 ACM Conference on Fairness, Accountability, and Transparency, FAccT '21*, 610–23. New York: Association for Computing Machinery. https://doi.org/10.1145/3442188.3445922.

Brown, T., Mann, B., Ryder, N., Subbiah, M., Kaplan, J.D., Dhariwal, P., Neelakantan, A., Shyam, P., Sastry, G., Askell, A. and Agarwal, S., 2020. 'Language models are few-shot learners', *Advances in Neural Information Processing Systems*, 33:1877–1901.

Brundage, M. et al. 2020. 'Toward trustworthy AI development: Mechanisms for supporting verifiable claims'. http://arxiv.org/abs/2004.07213v2.

Colavizza, G., Blanke, T., Jeurgens, C. and Noordegraaf., J. 2021. 'Archives and AI: An overview of current debates and future perspectives', *Journal on Computing and Cultural Heritage*, 15(1):1–15.

Gelal, R. 2023. 'Langchain's pandas & CSV agents: Revolutionizing data querying using OpenAI LLMs', FutureSmart AI Blog. Accessed 15 July 2023. https://blog.futuresmart.ai/langchains-pandas-csv-agents-revolutionizing-data-querying-using-openai-llms.

Gheorghe,V. 2023. 'GPT prompt compression: A cheap and simple solution'. Accessed 15 July 2023. https://aiprimer.substack.com/p/gpt-prompt-compression-save-tokens.

Gnanasekaran, R.K. and Marciano, R. 2021. 'Piloting data science learning platforms through the development of cloud-based interactive digital computational notebooks'. In *Proceedings of International Symposium on Grids & Clouds, ISGC 2021*. Proceedings of Science (ISGC2021), 378:018. https://ai-collaboratory.net/wp-content/uploads/2021/10/ISGC2021_Gnanasekaran_Marciano.pdf. Video: www.youtube.com/watch?v=cNBc0AY-r-k. Interactive Jupyter Notebook: https://cases.umd.edu/github/cases-umd/Legacy-of-Slavery/blob/master/index.ipynb.

Goodfellow, I. et al. 2014. 'Generative adversarial networks'. https://doi.org/10.48550/arXiv.1406.2661.

Goodfellow, I., Bengio, Y. and Courville, A. 2016. *Deep Learning*. Cambridge, MA: MIT Press.

Hashimoto, M. 2023. 'Prompt engineering vs. blind prompting'. Accessed 15 July 2023. https://mitchellh.com/writing/prompt-engineering-vs-blind-prompting.

Hedges, M., Marciano, R. and Goudarouli, E. 2022. 'Introduction to the special issue on computational archival science', *Journal on Computing and Cultural Heritage*, 15(1):1–2.

Inbasekaran, A., Gnanasekaran, R.K. and Marciano, R. 2021. 'Using transfer learning to contextually optimize optical character recognition (OCR) output and perform new feature extraction on a digitized cultural and historical dataset'. In *2021 IEEE International Conference on Big Data*, 2224–30. Paper: https://ai-collaboratory.net/wp-content/uploads/2021/11/3_Inbasekaran.pdf. Video: www.youtube.com/watch?v=UUM0jNg1rUE.

Jansen, G. 2023. 'Strategies for scraping data from websites: Reverse engineering and browser automation', Computational Archival Science Educational System. Accessed 5 February 2024. https://cases.umd.edu/github/cases-umd/MSA-web-scraper/blob/main/index.ipynb.

Kingma, D.P. and Welling, M. 2013. 'Auto-encoding variational Bayes'. http://arxiv.org/abs/1312.6114.

LangChain, P. 2023. CSV agent, Langchain. Accessed 15 July 2023. https://python.langchain.com/en/latest/modules/agents/toolkits/examples/csv.html.

Ledan, R. 2023. 'Building context-aware question-answering systems with LLMs', Medium. Accessed 15 July 2023. https://betterprogramming.pub/building-context-aware-question-answering-systems-with-llms-b6f2b6e387ec.

Marciano, R. 2021. 'Afterword: Towards a new discipline of computational archival science (CAS)'. In *Access and Artificial Intelligence: Working with born-digital and digitised archival collections*, edited by L. Jaillant. Bielefeld: Bielefeld University Press, Transcript Verlag. www.transcript-open.de/isbn/5584.

Marciano, R., Underwood, W., Hanaee, M., Mullane, C., Singh, A. and Tethong, Z. 2018. 'Automating the detection of personally identifiable information (PII) in Japanese-American

WWII incarceration camp records', *2018 IEEE International Conference on Big Data*, 2725–32. Seattle, WA, USA. https://ai-collaboratory.net/wp-content/uploads/2020/03/2.Marciano.pdf.

Mnih, V., Kavukcuoglu, K., Silver, D., Graves, A., Antonoglou, I., Wierstra, D. and Riedmiller, M. 2013. 'Playing Atari with deep reinforcement =lLearning'. http://arxiv.org/abs/1312.5602.

Perine, L. 2020. 'Historic Black Lives Matter: Visualizing hidden heritage in legacy of slavery collections'. December 11. Blog: https://medium.com/visumd/historic-black-lives-matter-visualizing-hidden-heritage-in-legacy-of-slavery-collections-23d3266dd0c5. Interactive Tableau Dashboard: https://public.tableau.com/profile/l.a.perine#!/vizhome/ManuVizPresentation/ManumissionsintheStateofMaryland1774-1874.

Perine, L.A., Gnanasekaran, R.K., Nicholas, P., Hill, A. and Marciano, R. 2020. 'Computational treatments to recover erased heritage: A legacy of slavery case study (CT-LOS)', *2020 IEEE International Conference on Big Data*, 1894–903. https://ai-collaboratory.net/wp-content/uploads/2020/11/Perine.pdf.

Radford, A., Wu, J., Child, R., Luan, D., Amodei, D. and Sutskever, I. 2019. 'Language models are unsupervised multitask learners'. OpenAI Blog.

Raj, R. and Salines, J. 1968. 'GPT-3 long input posts for question answering', Stack Overflow. Accessed 15 July 2023. https://stackoverflow.com/questions/71028228/gpt-3-long-input-posts-for-question-answering.

Rockwell, G. and Sinclair, S. 2016. *Hermeneutica: Computer-assisted interpretation in the humanities.* Cambridge, MA: MIT Press.

Trace, C. 2022. 'Archival infrastructure and the information backlog', *Archival Science*, 22(1):75–93.

Afterword: an emergence from winter or summer may be upon us

Thomas Padilla

It seems that an AI summer may be upon us. This seeming-summer is experienced variably, at turns engendering a sense of possibility and a sense of disquiet under the glare of for-profit AI marketing, data dependencies derived from us but refused from us (a kind of data gaslighting) and rarefied computing infrastructure distilled to freemium service models that work to incentivise transition to paid services controlled by far too few actors operating in to-be-determined regulatory environments. As with anything worth doing, there is much at stake in determining how cultural heritage organisations will make the best use of AI. This volume is an important asset for cultural heritage organisation strategy and practice insofar as it introduces cultural-heritage-specific use cases as well as theoretical explorations that should help cultivate increased confidence. Whether explicitly or implicitly stated, the work of this volume is anchored by the long history of cultural heritage organisations using computational means to meet the needs of the communities they aim to serve – whether that be realising the potential of the machine-readable catalogue, widespread internet access, digitisation or continuous efforts to evolve library ability to foster literacies for a diverse range of communities. Time is a circle, not an arrow as some would have us believe. There is confidence to be gained in the knowledge that cultural heritage organisations and allied disciplinary researchers have continuously engaged with the potential of technology. We are not disrupted; we stand ready to make the best of technology as we have always sought to.

> 'All of this has happened before, and all of this will happen again'.[1]

Forty-five years ago, Linda Smith submitted her dissertation, 'Selected artificial intelligence techniques in information retrieval systems research'.

Smith's dissertation 'reports on the results of research which has explored possible contributions of artificial intelligence (AI) to the design of information retrieval systems' (Smith 1979). Smith goes on to engage with aspects of pattern recognition, representation, problem solving, learning and query formulation as problem reduction. Was this work prescient or practical? Both characterisations are equally salutary and demonstrate that engagement with the potential of AI is longstanding in library and information science. Smith would go on to mentor multiple generations of cultural heritage professionals and scholars, leading the Graduate School of Information Science at the University of Illinois at Urbana Champaign to adapt to and forecast fundamental changes in the global information ecosystem.

Twenty-four years ago, John Unsworth delivered a talk at King's College London titled, 'Scholarly primitives: What methods do humanities researchers have in common, and how might our tools reflect this?' (2000). In the talk, Unsworth proposed seven activities (primitives), common to scholarly work regardless of discipline, that computational tools should support: discovering, annotating, comparing, referring, sampling, illustrating and representing. Unsworth proceeded to represent these primitives as axiomatic or self-evident bases for informing the design of computational tools. His work continues to be instructive for the present moment insofar as it provides the basis for a heuristic that helps articulate well-scoped, self-evidently valuable activities that AI should support rather than getting caught in a collectively regrettable, technology-tail wagging the dog moment.

More recently, Emily Bender said the following while debating the nature of large language models at a conference: 'I feel like there's too much effort trying to create autonomous machines ... rather than trying to create machines that are useful tools for humans' (Weil 2023; see Bender and Koller 2020). Eight years prior to that Trevor Owens delivered a talk titled, 'Mecha-archivists: Envisioning the role of software in the future of archives' that contained a similar sentiment:

> My vision for the future of the archivist using digital tools is less Borg and more Exo-suit ... The idea of mecha or exo-suits, illustrates a vision of technology that extends the capabilities of its user ... We need tools that let us quickly work across massive amounts of items and objects by extending and amplifying the seasoned judgment, ethics, wisdom, and expertise of the archivist-in-the-machine. (Owens 2014)

Bender and Owens do important work here, cutting through the chaff to focus our interaction with AI as user driven and utilitarian in nature. No need to anthropomorphise technology here – just a powerful set of tools to support core activities that extend our imperfect, eminently human judgement.

With Smith's orientation to information retrieval, Unsworth's heuristic, and Bender's and Owens' user-driven framing in mind, librarians and archivists should be able to engage with the potential of AI clear-eyed and confident. We can have a relationship with these tools akin to the mutualistic relationships that we have with any tool – think of the virtuous loop between you and a bicycle, a pan or camera. You acquire them for a certain purpose, and you refine your purpose as you experience the world through them – investing in better brakes, cast iron seasoning techniques, and lenses. It's a sort of symbiotic relationship between human and tool that changes usefully over time.

Much has been made in this piece of the power of long histories to draw upon, yet that is not to suggest that those histories are perfect. The imperfect aspects of cultural heritage organisation histories should help us equally with the work that lies ahead. Well-documented harms inflicted by cultural heritage organisations are a painful yet instructive motivation. With the help of leaders like Lae'l Hughes-Watkins we work to deal with our past, and that dealing helps keep us vigilant about how we move and ultimately makes us more responsive to the people we aspire to support in the present (Hughes-Watkins 2018). It keeps us focused on the ways that matter most. It helps us do the right thing. We can do the right thing. We will do the right thing.

Note

1. 'The hand of God', S01E10, *Battlestar Galactica* (2005), dir. Jeff Woolnough.

References

Bender, E.M. and Koller, A. 2020. 'Climbing towards NLU: On meaning, form, and understanding in the age of data'. In *Proceedings of the 58th Annual Meeting of the Association for Computational Linguistics*, 5185–98. Association for Computational Linguistics.

Hughes-Watkins, L 2018. 'Moving toward a reparative archive: A roadmap for a holistic approach to disrupting homogenous histories in academic repositories and creating inclusive spaces for marginalized voices'. *Journal of Contemporary Archival Studies*, 5:6. https://elischolar.library.yale.edu/jcas/vol5/iss1/6.

Owens, T. 2014. 'Mecha-archivists: Envisioning the role of software in the future of archives', 27 May 2014. https://trevorowens.org/2014/05/27/mecha-archivists-envisioning-the-role-of-software-in-the-future-of-archives/.

Smith, L.C. 1979. 'Selected artificial intelligence techniques in information retrieval systems research'. PhD dissertation, University of Illinois Urbana-Champaign. https://hdl.handle.net/2142/113725.

Unsworth, J. 2000. 'Scholarly primitives: What methods do humanities researchers have in common, and how might our tools reflect this?' Symposium on humanities computing: Formal methods, experimental practice. King's College, London, 13 May 2000.

Weil, E. 2023. 'You are not a parrot'. *New York Magazine*, February 27, 2023.

Index